FROM THE MAKER OF THE TEST

The Official SAT Subject Test Study Guide

World History

The College Board
New York, N.Y.

About the College Board

The College Board is a mission-driven not-for-profit organization that connects students to college success and opportunity. Founded in 1900, the College Board was created to expand access to higher education. Today, the membership association is made up of over 6,000 of the world's leading educational institutions and is dedicated to promoting excellence and equity in education. Each year, the College Board helps more than seven million students prepare for a successful transition to college through programs and services in college readiness and college success—including the SAT® and the Advanced Placement Program®. The organization also serves the education community through research and advocacy on behalf of students, educators, and schools.

For further information, visit collegeboard.org

Copies of this book are available from your bookseller or may be ordered from College Board Publications at store.collegeboard.org or by calling 800-323-7155.

Editorial inquiries concerning this book should be addressed to the College Board, SAT Program, 250 Vesey Street, New York, New York 10281.

ISBN 13: 978-1-4573-0933-5

Printed in the United States of America

3 4 5 6 7 8 9   23 22 21 20 19 18

Distributed by Macmillan

Contents

1 About SAT Subject Tests

1 The Benefits of SAT Subject Tests

2 Who Should Consider Subject Tests?

2 Who Requires the SAT Subject Tests?

3 Subject Tests Offered

3 Who Develops the Tests

4 Deciding to Take an SAT Subject Test

4 Which Tests Should You Take?

5 When to Take the Tests

5 How to Register for the Tests

6 Student Search Service®

7 Keep the Tests in Perspective

7 Fee Waivers

7 Score Choice™

8 About collegeboard.org

8 How to Do Your Best on the SAT Subject Tests

8 Get Ready

10 The Day Before the Test

12 On Test Day

12 Making an Educated Guess

15 After the Tests

17 World History

17 Purpose

17 Format

17 Content

18 Topics Covered

18 How to Prepare

18 Sample Questions

28 World History – Practice Test 1

52 How to Score the SAT Subject Test in World History

53 Answers to Practice Test 1 for World History

55 Finding Your Scaled Score

58 Answer Explanations for Practice Test 1

74 World History – Practice Test 2

98 How to Score the SAT Subject Test in World History

99 Answers to Practice Test 2 for World History

101 Finding Your Scaled Score

104 Answer Explanations for Practice Test 2

120 World History – Practice Test 3

139 How to Score the SAT Subject Test in World History

140 Answers to Practice Test 3 for World History

142 Finding Your Scaled Score

145 Answer Explanations for Practice Test 3

165 World History – Practice Test 4

183 How to Score the SAT Subject Test in World History

184 Answers to Practice Test 4 for World History

186 Finding Your Scaled Score

189 Answer Explanations for Practice Test 4

213 SAT Subject Test Answer Sheets

The SAT Subject Tests

About SAT Subject Tests

SAT Subject Tests™ are a valuable way to help you show colleges a more complete picture of your academic background and interests. Each year, nearly one million Subject Tests are taken by students throughout the country and around the world to gain admission to the leading colleges and universities in the U.S.

SAT Subject Tests are one-hour exams that give you the opportunity to demonstrate knowledge and showcase achievement in specific subjects. They provide a fair and reliable measure of your achievement in high school—information that can help enhance your college admission portfolio. The World History Subject Test is a great way to highlight your understanding, skills, and strengths in history.

This book provides information and guidance to help you study for and familiarize yourself with the World History Subject Test. It contains actual, previously administered tests and official answer sheets that will help you get comfortable with the tests' format, so you feel better prepared on test day.

The Benefits of SAT Subject Tests

SAT Subject Tests let you put your best foot forward, allowing you to focus on subjects that you know well and enjoy. They can help you differentiate yourself in a competitive admission environment by providing additional information about your skills and knowledge of particular subjects. Many colleges also use Subject Tests for course placement and selection; some schools allow you to place out of introductory courses by taking certain Subject Tests.

Subject Tests are flexible and can be tailored to your strengths and areas of interest. These are the **only** national admission tests where **you** choose the tests that best showcase your achievements and interests. You select the Subject Test(s) and can take up to three tests in one sitting. With the exception of listening tests, you can even decide to change the subject or number of tests you want to take on the day of the test. This flexibility can help you be more relaxed on test day.

REMEMBER

Subject Tests are a valuable way to help you show colleges a more complete picture of your academic achievements.

Who Should Consider Subject Tests?

Anyone can take an SAT Subject Test to highlight their knowledge of a specific subject. SAT Subject Tests may be especially beneficial for certain students:

- Students applying to colleges that require or recommend Subject Tests—be aware that some schools have additional Subject Test requirements for certain students, majors, or programs of study

- Students who wish to demonstrate strength in specific subject areas

- Students who wish to demonstrate knowledge obtained outside a traditional classroom environment (e.g., summer enrichment, distance learning, weekend study, etc.)

- Students looking to place out of certain classes in college

- Students enrolled in dual-enrollment programs

- Homeschooled students or students taking courses online

- Students who feel that their course grade may not be a true reflection of their knowledge of the subject matter

Who Requires the SAT Subject Tests?

Most college websites and catalogs include information about admission requirements, including which Subject Tests are needed or recommended for admission. Schools have varying policies regarding Subject Tests, but they generally fall into one or more of the following categories:

- Required for admission

- Recommended for admission

- Required or recommended for certain majors or programs of study (e.g., engineering, honors, etc.)

- Required or recommended for certain groups of students (e.g., homeschooled students)

- Required, recommended, or accepted for course placement

- Accepted for course credit

- Accepted as an alternative to fulfill certain college admission requirements

- Accepted as an alternative to fulfill certain high school subject competencies

- Accepted and considered, especially if Subject Tests improve or enhance a student's application

In addition, the College Board provides a number of resources where you can search for information about Subject Test requirements at specific colleges.

- Visit the websites of the colleges and universities that interest you.

- Visit College Search at www.collegeboard.org.

- Purchase a copy of *The College Board College Handbook*.

Some colleges require specific tests, such as mathematics or science, so it's important to make sure you understand the policies prior to choosing which Subject Test(s) to take. If you have questions or concerns about admission policies, contact college admission officers at individual schools. They are usually pleased to meet with students interested in their schools.

Subject Tests Offered

SAT Subject Tests measure how well you know a particular subject area and your ability to apply that knowledge. SAT Subject Tests aren't connected to specific textbooks or teaching methods. The content of each test evolves to reflect the latest trends in what is taught in typical high school courses in the corresponding subject.

The tests fall into five general subject areas:

English	History	Mathematics	Science	Languages	
				Reading Only	**with Listening**
Literature	United States History	Mathematics Level 1	Biology E/M	French	Chinese
	World History	Mathematics Level 2	Chemistry	German	French
			Physics	Italian	German
				Latin	Japanese
				Modern Hebrew	Korean
				Spanish	Spanish

Who Develops the Tests

The SAT Subject Tests are part of the SAT® Program of the College Board, a not-for-profit membership association of over 6,000 schools, colleges, universities, and other educational associations. Every year, the College Board serves seven million students and their parents, 24,000 high schools, and 3,800 colleges through major programs and services in college readiness, college admission, guidance, assessment, financial aid, and enrollment.

Each subject has its own test development committee, typically composed of teachers and college professors appointed for the different Subject Tests. The test questions are written and reviewed by each Subject Test Committee, under the guidance of professional test developers. The tests are rigorously developed, highly reliable assessments of knowledge and skills taught in high school classrooms.

Deciding to Take an SAT Subject Test

Which Tests Should You Take?

The SAT Subject Tests that you take should be based on your interests and academic strengths. The tests are a great way to indicate interest in specific majors or programs of study (e.g., engineering, pre-med, cultural studies).

You should also consider whether the colleges that you're interested in require or recommend Subject Tests. Some colleges will grant an exemption from or credit for a freshman course requirement if a student does well on a particular SAT Subject Test. Below are some things for you to consider as you decide which test(s) to take.

Think through your strengths and interests

- List the subjects in which you do well and that truly interest you.

- Think through what you might like to study in college.

- Consider whether your current admission credentials (high school grades, SAT scores, etc.) highlight your strengths.

Consider the colleges that you're interested in

- Make a list of the colleges you're considering.

- Take some time to look into what these colleges require or what may help you stand out in the admission process.

- Use College Search to look up colleges' test requirements.

- If the colleges you're interested in require or recommend SAT Subject Tests, find out how many tests are required or recommended and in which subjects.

Take a look at your current and recent course load

- Have you completed the required coursework? The best time to take SAT Subject Tests is at the end of the course, when the material is still fresh in your mind.

- Check the recommended preparation guidelines for the Subject Tests that interest you to see if you've completed the recommended coursework.

- Try your hand at some SAT Subject Test practice questions on collegeboard.org or in this book.

Don't forget, regardless of admission requirements, you can enhance your college portfolio by taking Subject Tests in subject areas that you know very well.

If you're still unsure about which SAT Subject Tests to take, talk to your teacher or counselor about your specific situation. You can also find more information about SAT Subject Tests on collegeboard.org.

When to Take the Tests

We generally recommend that you take Subject Tests after you complete the relevant course work, prior to your senior year of high school, if possible. This way, you will already have your Subject Test credentials complete, allowing you to focus on your college applications in the fall of your senior year. If you are able to, take the World History Subject Test right after your course ends, when the content is still fresh in your mind.

Since not all Subject Tests are offered on every test date, be sure to check when the Subject Tests that you're interested in are offered and plan accordingly.

You should also balance this with college application deadlines. If you're interested in applying early decision or early action to any college, many colleges advise that you take the SAT Subject Tests by October or November of your senior year. For regular decision applications, some colleges will accept SAT Subject Test scores through the December administration. Use College Search to look up policies for specific colleges.

This book suggests ways you can prepare for the SAT Subject Tests in World History. Before taking a test in a subject you haven't studied recently, ask your teacher for advice about the best time to take the test. Then review the course material thoroughly over several weeks.

How to Register for the Tests

There are several ways to register for the SAT Subject Tests.

- Visit the College Board's website at collegeboard.org. Most students choose to register for Subject Tests on the College Boar website.

- Register by telephone (for a fee) if you have registered previously for the SAT or an SAT Subject Test. Call, toll free from anywhere in the United States, 866-756-7346. From outside the United States, call 212-713-7789.

- If you do not have access to the internet, find registration forms in *The Paper Registration Guide for the SAT and SAT Subject Tests*. You can find the booklet in a guidance office at any high school or by writing to:

  The College Board
  SAT Program
  P.O. Box 025505
  Miami, FL 33102

When you register for the SAT Subject Tests, you will have to indicate the specific Subject Tests you plan to take on the test date you select. You may take one, two, or three tests on any given test date; your testing fee will vary accordingly. Except for the Language Tests with Listening, you may change your mind on the day of the test and instead select from any of the other Subject Tests offered that day.

Student Search Service

The Student Search Service® helps colleges find prospective students. If you take the PSAT/NMSQT®, the SAT, an SAT Subject Test, or any AP® Exam, you can be included in this free service.

Here's how it works: During SAT or SAT Subject Test registration, indicate that you want to be part of the Student Search. Your name is put in a database along with other information such as your address, high school grade point average, date of birth, grade level, high school, email address, intended college major, and extracurricular activities.

Colleges and scholarship programs then use the Student Search to help them locate and recruit students with characteristics that might be a good match with their schools.

Here are some points to keep in mind about the Student Search Service:

- Being part of Student Search is voluntary. You may take the test even if you don't join Student Search.

- Colleges participating in Student Search do not receive your exam scores. Colleges can ask for the names of students within certain score ranges, but your exact score is not reported.

- Being contacted by a college doesn't mean you have been admitted. You can be admitted only after you apply. The Student Search Service is simply a way for colleges to reach prospective students.

- Student Search Service will share your contact information only with approved colleges and scholarship programs that are recruiting students like you. Your name will never be sold to a private company or mailing list.

Keep the Tests in Perspective

Colleges that require Subject Test scores do so because the scores are useful in making admission or placement decisions. Schools that don't have specific Subject Test policies generally review Subject Test scores during the application process because the scores can give a fuller picture of your academic achievement. The Subject Tests are a particularly helpful tool for admission and placement programs because the tests aren't tied to specific textbooks, grading procedures, or instruction methods but are still tied to curricula. The tests provide level ground on which colleges can compare your scores with those of students who come from schools and backgrounds that may be far different from yours.

It's important to remember that test scores are just one of several factors that colleges consider in the admission process. Admission officers also look at your high school grades, letters of recommendation, extracurricular activities, essays, and other criteria. Try to keep this in mind when you're preparing for and taking Subject Tests.

Fee Waivers

Students who face financial barriers to taking the SAT Subject Tests can be granted College Board fee waivers through schools and authorized community-based organizations to cover the cost of testing. Seniors who use a fee waiver to take the SAT will automatically receive four college application fee waivers to use in applying to colleges and universities that accept the waivers. You can learn about eligibility and other benefits offered to help you in the college application process at sat.org/fee-waivers.

Score Choice

In March 2009, the College Board introduced Score Choice™, a feature that gives you the option to choose the scores you send to colleges by test date for the SAT and by individual test for the SAT Subject Tests—at no additional cost. Designed to reduce your test day stress, Score Choice gives you an opportunity to show colleges the scores you feel best represent your abilities. Score Choice is optional, so if you don't actively choose to use it, all of your scores will be sent automatically with your score report. Since most colleges only consider your best scores, you should still feel comfortable reporting scores from all of your tests.

REMEMBER

Score Choice gives you an opportunity to show colleges the scores you feel best represent your abilities.

About collegeboard.org

The College Board website collegeboard.org is a comprehensive tool that can help you be prepared, connected, and informed throughout the college planning and admission process. In addition to registering for the SAT and SAT Subject Tests, you can find information about other tests and services, browse the College Board Store (where you can order *The College Board College Handbook*, *The Official Study Guide for all SAT Subject Tests* and other guides specific to mathematics, science and history), and send emails with your questions and concerns. You can also find free practice questions for each of the 20 SAT Subject Tests. These are an excellent supplement to this Study Guide and can help you be even more prepared on test day.

Once you create a free online account, you can print your SAT admission ticket, see your scores, and send them to schools.

More college planning resources The College Board offers free, comprehensive resources at Big Future™ to help you with your college planing. Visit **bigfuture.org** to put together a step-by-step plan for the entire process, from finding the right college, exploring majors and careers, and calculating costs, to applying for scholarships and financial aid.

How to Do Your Best on the SAT Subject Tests

Get Ready

Give yourself several weeks before the tests to read the course materials and the suggestions in this book. The rules for the SAT Subject Tests may be different than the rules for most of the tests you've taken in high school. You're probably used to answering questions in order, spending more time answering the hard questions and, in the hopes of getting at least partial credit, showing all your work.

When you take the SAT Subject Tests, it's OK to move around within the test section and to answer questions in any order you wish. Keep in mind that the questions go from easier to harder. You receive one point for each question answered correctly. For each question that you try but answer incorrectly, a fraction of a point is subtracted from the total number of correct answers. No points are added or subtracted for unanswered questions. If your final raw score includes a fraction, the score is rounded to the nearest whole number.

Avoid Surprises

Know what to expect. Become familiar with the test and test day procedures. You'll boost your confidence and feel a lot more relaxed.

- **Know how the tests are set up.** All SAT Subject Tests are one-hour multiple-choice tests. The first page of each Subject Test includes a background questionnaire. You will be asked to fill it out before taking the test. The information is for statistical purposes only. It will not influence your test score. Your answers to the questionnaire will assist us in developing future versions of the test. You can see a sample of the background questionnaire at the start of each test in the book.

- **Learn the test directions.** The directions for answering the questions in this book are the same as those on the actual test. If you become familiar with the directions now, you'll leave yourself more time to answer the questions when you take the test.

- **Study the sample questions.** The more familiar you are with the question formats, the more comfortable you'll feel when you see similar questions on the actual test.

- **Get to know the answer sheet.** At the back of this book, you'll find a set of sample answer sheets. The appearance of the answer sheets in this book may differ from the answer sheets you see on test day.

- **Understand how the tests are scored.** You get one point for each right answer and lose a fraction of a point for each wrong answer. You neither gain nor lose points for omitting an answer. Hard questions count the same amount as easier questions.

A Practice Test Can Help

Find out where your strengths lie and which areas you need to work on. Do a run-through of a Subject Test under conditions that are close to what they will be on test day.

- **Set aside an hour so you can take the test without interruption.** You will be given one hour to take each SAT Subject Test.

- **Prepare a desk or table that has no books or papers on it.** No books, including dictionaries, are allowed in the test room.

- **Read the instructions that precede the practice test.** On test day, you will be asked to do this before you answer the questions.

- **Remove and fill in an answer sheet from the back of this book.** You can use one answer sheet for up to three Subject Tests.

- **Use a clock or kitchen timer to time yourself.** This will help you to pace yourself and to get used to taking a test in 60 minutes.

The Day Before the Test

It's natural to be nervous. A bit of a nervous edge can keep you sharp and focused. Below are a few suggestions to help you be more relaxed as the test approaches.

Do a brief review on the day before the test. Look through the sample questions, answer explanations and test directions in this book or on the College Board website. Keep the review brief; cramming the night before the test is unlikely to help your performance and might even make you more anxious.

The night before test day, prepare everything you need to take with you. You will need:

- Your admission ticket.
- An acceptable photo ID. (see page 11)
- Two No. 2 pencils with soft erasers. (Do not bring pens or mechanical pencils.)
- A watch without an audible alarm.
- A snack.

Know the route to the test center and any instructions for finding the entrance.

Check the time your admission ticket specifies for arrival. Arrive a little early to give yourself time to settle in.

Get a good night's sleep.

REMEMBER

You are in control.
Come prepared.
Pace yourself.
Guess wisely.

Acceptable Photo IDs

- Driver's license (with your photo)

- State-issued ID

- Valid passport

- School ID card

- Student ID form that has been prepared by your school on school stationery and includes a recognizable photo and the school seal, which overlaps the photo (go to www.collegeboard.org for more information)

The most up-to-date information about acceptable photo IDs can be found on collegeboard.org.

REMINDER   **What I Need on Test Day**

Make a copy of this box and post it somewhere noticeable.

I Need   **I Have**

Appropriate photo ID

Admission ticket

Two No. 2 pencils with clean soft erasers

Watch (without an audible alarm)

Snack

Bottled water

Directions to the test center

Instructions for finding the entrance on weekends

I am leaving the house at _____ a.m.

Be on time or you can't take the test.

On Test Day

You have good reason to feel confident. You're thoroughly prepared. You're familiar with what this day will bring. You are in control.

Keep in Mind

You must be on time or you can't take the test. Leave yourself plenty of time for mishaps and emergencies.

Think positively. If you are worrying about not doing well, then your mind isn't on the test. Be as positive as possible.

Stay focused. Think only about the question in front of you. Letting your mind wander will cost you time.

Concentrate on your own test. The first thing some students do when they get stuck on a question is to look around to see how everyone else is doing. What they usually see is that others seem busy filling in their answer sheets. Instead of being concerned that you are not doing as well as everyone else, keep in mind that everyone works at a different pace. Your neighbors may not be working on the question that puzzled you. They may not even be taking the same test. Thinking about what others are doing distracts you from working on your own test.

Making an Educated Guess

Educated guesses are helpful when it comes to taking tests with multiple-choice questions; however, making guesses is not a good idea. To correct for random guessing, a fraction of a point is subtracted for each incorrect answer. That means random guessing—guessing with no idea of an answer that might be correct—could lower your score. The best approach is to eliminate all the choices that you know are wrong. Make an educated guess from the remaining choices. If you can't eliminate any choices, move on.

REMEMBER

All correct answers are worth one point, regardless of the question's difficulty level.

Cell phone use is prohibited in the test center or testing room. If your cell phone is on, your scores will be canceled.

10 Tips
FOR TAKING THE TEST

1. **Read carefully.** Consider all the choices in each question. Avoid careless mistakes that will cause you to lose points.

2. **Answer the easy questions first.** Work on less time-consuming questions before moving on to the more difficult ones.

3. **Eliminate choices that you know are wrong.** Cross them out in your test book so that you can clearly see which choices are left.

4. **Make educated guesses or skip the question.** If you have eliminated the choices that you know are wrong, guessing is your best strategy. However, if you cannot eliminate any of the answer choices, it is best to skip the question.

5. **Keep your answer sheet neat.** The answer sheet is scored by a machine, which can't tell the difference between an answer and a doodle. If the machine mistakenly reads two answers for one question, it will consider the question unanswered.

6. **Use your test booklet as scrap paper.** Use it to make notes or write down ideas. No one else will look at what you write.

7. **Check off questions as you work on them.** This will save time and help you to know which questions you've skipped.

8. **Check your answer sheet regularly.** Make sure you are in the right place. Check the number of the question and the number on the answer sheet every few questions. This is especially important when you skip a question. Losing your place on the answer sheet will cost you time and even points.

9. **Work at an even, steady pace and keep moving.** Each question on the test takes a certain amount of time to read and answer. Good test-takers develop a sense of timing to help them complete the test. Your goal is to spend time on the questions that you are most likely to answer correctly.

10. **Keep track of time.** During the hour that each Subject Test takes, check your progress occasionally so that you know how much of the test you have completed and how much time is left. Leave a few minutes for review toward the end of the testing period.

If you erase all your answers to a Subject Test, that's the same as a request to cancel the test. All Subject Tests taken with the erased test will also be canceled.

REMEMBER

Check your answer sheet. Make sure your answers are dark and completely filled in. Erase completely.

7 Ways
TO PACE YOURSELF

1. Set up a schedule. Know when you should be one-quarter of the way through and halfway through. Every now and then, check your progress against your schedule.

2. Begin to work as soon as the testing time begins. Reading the instructions and getting to know the test directions in this book ahead of time will allow you to do that.

3. Work at an even, steady pace. After you answer the questions you are sure of, move on to those for which you'll need more time.

4. Skip questions you can't answer. You might have time to return to them. Remember to mark them in your test booklet, so you'll be able to find them later.

5. As you work on a question, cross out the answers you can eliminate in your test book.

6. Go back to the questions you skipped. If you can, eliminate some of the answer choices, then make an educated guess.

7. Leave time in the last few minutes to check your answers to avoid mistakes.

After the Tests

Most, but not all, scores will be reported online several weeks after the test date. A few days later, a full score report will be available to you online. You can request a paper score report too, which arrives later. Your score report will also be mailed to your high school and to the colleges, universities and scholarship programs that you indicated when you registered or on the correction form attached to your admission ticket. The score report includes your scores, percentiles and interpretive information.

What's Your Score?

Scores are available for free at www.collegeboard.org several weeks after each SAT is given. You can also get your scores—for a fee—by telephone. Call customer service at 866-756-7346 in the United States. From outside the United States, call 212-713-7789.

Some scores may take longer to report. If your score report is not available online when expected, check back the following week. If you have requested a paper score report and you have not received it by eight weeks after the test date (by five weeks for online reports), contact customer service by phone at 866-756-7346 or by e-mail at sat@info.collegeboard.org.

Should You Take the Tests Again?

Before you decide whether or not to retest, you need to evaluate your scores. The best way to evaluate how you really did on a Subject Test is to compare your scores to the admission or placement requirements, or average scores, of the colleges to which you are applying. You may decide that with additional work you could do better taking the test again.

? Contacting the College Board

If you have comments or questions about the tests, please write to us at the College Board SAT Program, P.O. Box 025505, Miami, FL 33102, or e-mail us at sat@info.collegeboard.org.

World History

Purpose

The Subject Test in World History measures your understanding of the development of major world cultures and your use of historical techniques, including the application and weighing of evidence and the ability to interpret and generalize. The test covers all historical fields:

- political and diplomatic
- intellectual and cultural
- social and economic

Format

This one-hour test consists of 95 multiple-choice questions. Many of the questions are global in nature, dealing with issues and trends that have significance throughout the modern world.

The chart on the following page shows you what chronological and geographical materials are covered on the test and the approximate percentages of questions covering that content.

Content

The questions test your:

- familiarity with terms commonly used in the social sciences
- understanding of cause-and-effect relationships
- knowledge of the history and geography necessary for understanding major historical developments
- grasp of concepts essential to historical analysis
- capacity to interpret artistic materials
- ability to assess quotations from speeches, documents, and other published materials
- ability to use historical knowledge in interpreting data based on maps, graphs, and charts

Topics Covered

Topics	Approximate Percentage of Test
Chronological Material Covered	
Prehistory and Civilizations to 500 Common Era (C.E.)*	25
500–1500 C.E.	20
1500–1900 C.E.	25
Post-1900 C.E.	20
Cross-chronological	10
Geographical Material Covered	
Global or Comparative	25
Europe	25
Africa	10
Southwest Asia	10
South and Southeast Asia	10
East Asia	10
Americas	10

* The SAT Subject Test in World History uses the chronological designations B.C.E. (before common era) and C.E. (common era). These labels correspond to B.C. (before Christ) and A.D. (anno Domini), which are used in some world history textbooks.

How to Prepare

You can prepare academically for the test by taking a one-year comprehensive course in world or global history at the college-preparatory level and through independent reading of materials on historic topics. Because secondary school programs differ, the SAT Subject Test in World History is not tied to any one textbook or particular course of study. Familiarize yourself with the directions in advance. The directions in this book are identical to those that appear on the test.

Score

The total score is reported on the 200-to-800 scale.

Sample Questions

All questions on the Subject Test in World History are multiple choice, requiring you to choose the best response from five choices. The following sample questions illustrate the types of questions on the test, their range of difficulty, and the abilities they measure. Questions may be presented as separate items or in sets based on quotations, maps, pictures, graphs, or tables.

Directions: Each of the questions or incomplete statements below is followed by five suggested answers or completions. Select the one that is best in each case and then fill in the corresponding circle on the answer sheet.

1

The strongest evidence that the peoples of the Paleolithic Age believed in an afterlife is found in their

A) weapons and tools

B) ceremonial human sacrifices

C) cave paintings

D) stone sculptures

E) burial practices

Choice (E) is the correct answer to question 1. Evidence related to Paleolithic burial practices strongly suggests that peoples of the Paleolithic Age (2.5 million to 10,000 B.C.E.) believed in an afterlife. Paleolithic people were often buried with useful items indicating preparation for an afterlife. The other choices are incorrect. Paleolithic weapons and tools (A) provide information about how these people hunted and lived, but tell us little or nothing concerning their belief in an afterlife. There is not much evidence of human sacrifice (B) by Paleolithic peoples. The few surviving cave paintings from this era (C) reveal little about religious beliefs, focusing mostly on animals. Paleolithic stone sculptures (D) may suggest some religious belief, but they do not provide strong evidence of belief in an afterlife.

2

Which of the following adults had full citizenship in Athens in the fifth century B.C.E.?

A) All who spoke Greek

B) All freeborn men and women

C) Only adults of noble birth

D) Only land-owning free men and women

E) All free men of Athenian parentage

Choice (E) is the correct answer to question 2. All free men of Athenian parentage possessed full citizenship in Athens in the fifth century B.C.E. The other choices are incorrect. A majority of the population, including slaves, women, and resident aliens (choices A and B), was excluded from full citizenship. However, there were no property requirements for citizenship (D), and a citizen did not have to be of noble birth (C), as long as both his parents were Athenians.

3

The Chinese concept of the Mandate of Heaven included all of the following EXCEPT:

A) The people will naturally rebel against a government that does not follow the "way of heaven."

B) A ruler has a responsibility to be benevolent toward the people.

C) Natural disasters are a sign of heaven's displeasure with a country's rulers.

D) Heaven would bless the authority of a just ruler.

E) A legitimate ruler must be of noble birth.

Choice (E) is the correct answer to question 3. Choices (A), (B), (C), and (D) are all consistent with the concept of the Mandate of Heaven. Rulers of the Chinese Zhou dynasty in the eleventh century B.C.E. originated the concept to justify their overthrow of the previous dynasty. The concept states that heaven would bless a king who ruled justly (D), but would pass the Mandate to someone else if the king began to misuse his power. The Mandate of Heaven claimed that because the ruler's authority is granted by heaven, he had a responsibility to be benevolent toward the people (B). If the ruler abused the Mandate and strayed from the "way of heaven," natural disasters could be expected (C), and a revolution would be acceptable (A). Because the Mandate was based solely on the ruler's fair use of his power, a legitimate ruler did not necessarily have to be of noble birth; in fact, some of the most powerful Chinese dynasties were established and ruled by people of modest birth.

4

The ancient trade route known as the Silk Road facilitated the exchange of goods between

A) Japan and Portugal

B) Japan and Korea

C) China and the Roman Empire

D) China and Japan

E) China and Southeast Asia

Choice (C) is the correct answer to question 4. The ancient trade route known as the Silk Road facilitated the exchange of goods between China and the Roman Empire. This 4,000-mile trade route across central Asia connected China and Europe. Caravans traveled back and forth on the Silk Road, carrying silk from China and gold, silver, and other products from the Roman Empire. The other choices are incorrect. The Silk Road originated in China, not Japan (choices A and B), and went westward into Europe, not toward Japan (D) or Southeast Asia (E).

5

Filial piety and veneration of ancestors are central to the teachings of

A) Buddha

B) Confucius

C) Hammurabi

D) Krishna

E) Zoroaster

Choice (B) is the correct answer to question 5. Filial piety and veneration of ancestors are central to the teachings of Confucius. Chinese philosopher Confucius (circa 551–479 B.C.E.), whose teachings became the basis of Confucianism, stressed the importance of maintaining proper relationships within society, especially within families. According to Confucius, children should respect and obey their parents and elder family members ("filial piety"), while the elder members should love and nurture the younger members. Veneration for one's ancestors, those elder members who have died, follows from this principle. The other choices are incorrect. While the teachings of Buddha (A), Hammurabi (C), Krishna (D), and Zoroaster (E) may have touched on the importance of family relationships, the elements of filial piety and veneration of ancestors were central only to the teachings of Confucius.

6

In the thirteenth and fourteenth centuries, an important economic link between Europe and Africa was the export of

A) cotton from East Africa to Europe

B) gold from West Africa to Europe

C) grain from Europe to Egypt

D) timber from Europe to West Africa

E) grain from Europe to East Africa

Choice (B) is the correct answer to question 6. During the thirteenth and fourteenth centuries, the main export from Africa to Europe was gold. In the thirteenth century, the Mali Empire in West Africa took control of the lucrative trans-Saharan trade of gold and salt, sending gold north across the Sahara Desert to the Mediterranean Sea and Europe, and bringing salt and other goods south of the Sahara. As the Europeans had yet to discover the riches of the Americas, most gold circulating in Europe came from Africa. The other choices are incorrect since none of them describes a major pattern of trade between Europe and Africa.

7

The emergence of which of the following is most closely identified with the practice of manorialism?

A) Cities

B) Capitalism

C) The three-field system

D) Overseas expansion

E) Long-distance trade

Choice (C) is the correct answer to question 7. The European medieval social and economic system of manorialism is closely linked to the three-field system. Manorialism was the system in which the European countryside was divided into manors that were each controlled by a lord. The peasants on many of these manors used the three-field system of crop rotation. In the three-field system, the land was divided into thirds: one-third for fall crops, one-third for spring crops, and one-third left fallow or unused. The crops were then rotated each year, allowing the soil's nutrients time to regenerate and increasing agricultural productivity. The other choices are incorrect. Manorialism was a system of land use in the European countryside, not cities (A). Manorialism was an economic system that preceded the rise of capitalism throughout Europe (B). Manorialism is generally associated with locally self-sufficient economies and did not do much to generate overseas expansion (D) or long-distance trade (E).

8

Which of the following can be found as part of the original design of Gothic but not of Romanesque cathedrals?

A) Rounded arches

B) Flying buttresses

C) Windows

D) Transepts

E) Wooden pews

Choice (B) is the correct answer to question 8. Flying buttresses are found in Gothic cathedrals, not in Romanesque cathedrals. Flying buttresses are half arches on the outside of Gothic cathedrals that help hold up the weight of the buildings' stone ceilings. These external buttresses, by supporting part of the weight of the buildings' ceilings, lessen the need for thick walls, thus they make possible the large stained glass windows typical of Gothic cathedrals. The other choices are incorrect. Rounded arches (A) are typically found in Romanesque, not Gothic cathedrals. Windows (C), transepts (D), and wooden pews (E) are found in both types of cathedrals.

9

Most Africans taken to the Americas as slaves lost their freedom when they were

A) taken as prisoners in raids and wars among African states

B) captured by roving bands of European slave raiders

C) forced into indentured servitude by their relatives

D) taken captive resisting European infiltration

E) captured by Asian slave traders

Choice (A) is the correct answer to question 9. Most Africans taken to the Americas as slaves originally lost their freedom when they were taken as prisoners in raids and wars among African states. The practice of enslaving prisoners of war was common in Africa before colonization by Europeans. European slave traders gave African groups an opportunity to exchange their prisoners of war for manufactured goods and firearms at European slave-trading posts on the African coast. Occasionally, raids among African nations were undertaken for the sole purpose of capturing prisoners to be sold as slaves bound for America. The other choices are incorrect. Europeans rarely infiltrated (D) or raided (B) the African continent themselves in search of slaves. Africans were not generally offered the opportunity of indentured servitude in America (C). The African slaves bound for America were acquired by European, not Asian, slave traders (E).

10

By the seventeenth century, Spain's American colonies were governed by

A) papal nuncios

B) elected assemblies

C) private trading companies

D) a hierarchy of bureaucratic officials

E) native leaders under Spanish supervision

Choice (D) is the correct answer to question 10. By the seventeenth century, Spain's American colonies, known collectively as New Spain, were governed by a hierarchy of bureaucratic officials. The Spanish empire in the Americas was divided into regions called viceroyalties, each of which was governed by an appointed viceroy and his staff. The other choices are incorrect. The regions were governed by appointed officials from Spain or of Spanish descent, not native leaders (E), elected assemblies (B), or private trading companies (C). Although Catholicism was strictly enforced and used as a justification for exploitation of the colonies, church ambassadors known as papal nuncios (A) did not govern the colonies.

11

Which of the following statements is characteristic of Social Darwinist thinking?

A) Nature is not a useful model for human social organization.

B) Charity and government help for the poor only encourage the unfit to survive.

C) Society has an obligation to support writers and artists.

D) All persons have a natural right to existence by virtue of their shared humanity.

E) Laissez-faire economic policies are ruinous in the long run.

Choice (B) is the correct answer to question 11. Social Darwinism is a social theory that applies the idea of natural selection from Charles Darwin's theory of evolution to the development of human societies. In Darwin's writings, "survival of the fittest" describes how some organisms develop mutations that make them fitter for survival than others. These organisms survive while others die out. Similarly, according to Social Darwinism, some members of society, typically the rich, possess characteristics that cause them to "naturally" succeed and survive, while others, typically the poor, do not. According to the Social Darwinists, since the poor in society are inherently unfit to survive, it is improper to provide them charity and other assistance. The other choices are incorrect. Social Darwinism claims that human societies share the same organization as nature (A). Although Social Darwinism does not necessarily imply that writers and artists are unfit for survival, it would not hold society obliged to support any of its members (C). According to Social Darwinism, nobody has a natural "right" to exist (D). The principles of laissez-faire economics, which state that government should not restrict the natural competition of businesses, are generally in line with Social Darwinism and would not be considered ruinous (E).

12

"THE ANGEL IN 'THE HOUSE'": OR, THE RESULT
OF FEMALE SUFFRAGE

The intent of the 1884 cartoon above was to

A) attack women as too politically uninformed to be granted suffrage

B) argue that women's suffrage would lead to a female majority in Parliament

C) appeal for women's suffrage in order to raise the moral tone of parliamentary debate

D) suggest that a political role for women is contrary to the virtues of femininity

E) suggest that women would make just as effective legislators as men

Choice (D) is the correct answer to question 12. This 1884 cartoon is intended to suggest that a political role for women is contrary to the virtues of femininity. By the late ninteenth century, social movements in Great Britain calling for the right to vote and increased political involvement of women were becoming stronger. These movements, however, were met with opposition from those who felt women had specific abilities or virtues that were contrary to the tasks of politics. The caption of the cartoon is a play on words of the title of a popular mid-nineteenth century poem, "The Angel in the House," by Coventry Patmore, which argued that women had a moral role to play but one that should be confined to the domestic sphere. The cartoon suggests that women would be out of place in the political activity of the "House," or Parliament. The other choices are incorrect. The cartoon does not address the issue of women's knowledge of politics (A). Nothing in the cartoon suggests that women might achieve a political majority (B). The cartoon does not suggest that women would raise the moral tone of Parliament (C). The disarray of the domestic objects surrounding the woman in the cartoon does not suggest effectiveness (E).

13

"Imperialism is capitalism in that stage of development in which the dominance of monopolies and finance capital has established itself; in which the export of capital has acquired pronounced importance; in which the division of the world among the international trusts has begun; in which the division of all territories of the globe among the great capitalist powers has been completed."

The definition of imperialism above was written by

A) Max Weber

B) Mary Wollstonecraft

C) Benito Mussolini

D) Arnold Toynbee

E) V. I. Lenin

Choice (E) is the correct answer to question 13. This definition of imperialism was written by V. I. Lenin and published in his 1917 pamphlet entitled "Imperialism, the Highest Stage of Capitalism." Lenin (1870–1924) helped lead the Russian Communist Revolution and eventually became the first premier of the Soviet Union. He published this pamphlet as part of his effort to educate revolutionaries and organize the Russian workers. By 1917, industrialization was increasingly allowing a few large companies to control the majority of production. Lenin thought that this concentration of power in capitalist economies, in which a few wealthy company owners would, in effect, control the lives of millions of workers, was a form of imperialism and must be resisted. The other choices are incorrect; none of the other people mentioned addressed capitalism and imperialism in this way.

14

Which of the following was an important component of India's foreign policy under Indira Gandhi?

A) The maintenance of a formal alliance with Great Britain

B) The formation of a military alliance with China

C) Support for United States policy in Southeast Asia

D) The maintenance of friendly relations with the Soviet Union

E) Advocacy of an armed invasion of Afghanistan

Choice (D) is the correct answer to question 14. Maintaining friendly relations with the Soviet Union was an important component of India's foreign policy under Indira Gandhi, who served as prime minister from 1966 to 1977 and from 1980 to 1984. Under Gandhi's leadership, India signed the Treaty of Peace, Friendship, and Cooperation with the Soviet Union in 1971. The support from the Soviet Union helped India defeat Pakistan in December 1971, and helped deter aggressive behavior by China

towards India. The other choices are incorrect. Under Indira Gandhi, India was not formally aligned with Great Britain (A) or militarily aligned with China (B). The partnership with the Soviets clearly signaled a worsening of relations with the United States (C). Although the Soviet Union invaded Afghanistan during this time, India was not officially involved (E).

15

Which of the following led to one of the major crises of the Cold War era?

A) The sinking of the *Lusitania*

B) The Italian invasion of Ethiopia

C) Gandhi's civil disobedience campaign

D) The sentencing of Nelson Mandela to life imprisonment

E) The installation of missiles with nuclear warheads in Cuba

Choice (E) is the correct answer to question 15. The installation of Russian nuclear missiles in Cuba led to one of the major crises of the Cold War. The Cold War refers to the geopolitical struggle between the United States and the Soviet Union that started at the end of World War II and ended with the collapse of the Soviet Union in 1991. The closest the United States and the Soviet Union came to actual war was in 1962, when the Soviet Union installed nuclear missiles in Cuba capable of hitting Washington, D.C., within twenty minutes from launch. President John F. Kennedy learned about the missile sites and announced a naval "quarantine" around Cuba to block the Soviets from reaching Cuba. Eventually the Soviet Union agreed to remove the missiles and the United States ended the quarantine and removed nuclear missiles they had installed in Turkey. The other choices are incorrect. The sinking of the *Lusitania* (A), the Italian invasion of Ethiopia (B), and Gandhi's civil disobedience campaign in India (C), all occurred before the Cold War. The sentencing of South African activist Nelson Mandela to life imprisonment (D) did not create a major crisis during the Cold War.

World History – Practice Test 1

Practice Helps

The test that follows is an actual, previously administered SAT Subject Test in World History. To get an idea of what it's like to take this test, practice under conditions that are much like those of an actual test administration.

- Set aside an hour when you can take the test uninterrupted.

- Sit at a desk or table with no other books or papers. Dictionaries, other books, or notes are not allowed in the test room.

- Tear out an answer sheet from the back of this book and fill it in just as you would on the day of the test. One answer sheet can be used for up to three Subject Tests.

- Read the instructions that precede the practice test. During the actual administration, you will be asked to read them before answering test questions.

- Use a clock or kitchen timer to time yourself.

- After you finish the practice test, read the sections "How to Score the SAT Subject Test in World History" and "How Did You Do on the Subject Test in World History?"

- The appearance of the answer sheet in this book may differ from the answer sheet you see on test day.

WORLD HISTORY TEST

The top portion of the page of the answer sheet that you will use to take the World History Test must be filled in exactly as illustrated below. When your supervisor tells you to fill in the circle next to the name of the test you are about to take, mark your answer sheet as shown.

○ Literature	○ Mathematics Level 1	○ German	○ Chinese Listening	○ Japanese Listening
○ Biology E	○ Mathematics Level 2	○ Italian	○ French Listening	○ Korean Listening
○ Biology M	○ U.S. History	○ Latin	○ German Listening	○ Spanish Listening
○ Chemistry	● World History	○ Modern Hebrew		
○ Physics	○ French	○ Spanish	Background Questions: ①②③④⑤⑥⑦⑧⑨	

After filling in the circle next to the name of the test you are taking, locate the Background Questions box on your answer sheet (as shown above). This is where you will answer the following Background Questions on your answer sheet.

BACKGROUND QUESTIONS

Please answer the two questions below by filling in the appropriate circle in the Background Questions box on your answer sheet. The information you provide is for statistical purposes only and will not affect your test score.

Question I

How many semesters of world history, world cultures, or European history have you taken from grade 9 to the present? (If you are taking a course this semester, count it as a full semester.) Fill in only one circle of circles 1-4.

- One semester or less   —Fill in circle 1.
- Two semesters   —Fill in circle 2.
- Three semesters   —Fill in circle 3.
- Four or more semesters   —Fill in circle 4.

Question II

For the courses in world history, world cultures, or European history you have taken, which of the following geographical areas did you study? Fill in all of the circles that apply.

- Africa   —Fill in circle 5.
- Asia   —Fill in circle 6.
- Europe   —Fill in circle 7.
- Latin America   —Fill in circle 8.
- Middle East   —Fill in circle 9.

When the supervisor gives the signal, turn the page and begin the World History Test. There are 100 numbered circles on the answer sheet and 95 questions in the World History Test. Therefore, use only circles 1 to 95 for recording your answers.

WORLD HISTORY TEST

Directions: Each of the questions or incomplete statements below is followed by five suggested answers or completions. Select the one that is best in each case and then fill in the corresponding circle on the answer sheet.

Note: The World History Test uses the chronological designations B.C.E. (before common era) and C.E. (common era). These labels correspond to B.C. (before Christ) and A.D. (anno Domini), which are used in some world history textbooks.

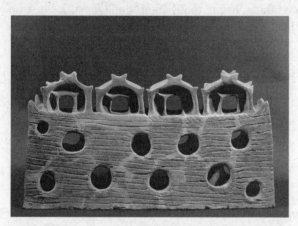

Erich Lessing / Art Resource, NY

1. The clay model above was made in eastern Europe circa 4,000 B.C.E. and shows a village with places for storing grain underground. The model is most likely associated with which of the following periods?

   (A) Paleolithic
   (B) Neolithic
   (C) Iron Age
   (D) Classical Greek
   (E) Hellenistic

2. Which of the following is true of civilizations in pre-Columbian America as compared to civilizations in Eurasia?

   (A) They were subject to more epidemic disease.
   (B) They were less dominated by religion.
   (C) They had higher levels of literacy.
   (D) They had fewer domesticated animals.
   (E) They were more technologically advanced.

3. Which of the following ruled the areas known as Akkad and Sumer and established a dynasty that lasted nearly two centuries?

   (A) Sargon the Great
   (B) Cyrus the Great
   (C) Hatshepsut
   (D) Alexander the Great
   (E) Asoka

4. Copper and tin, the main components of bronze, are rarely found together in nature, and bronze objects are often made using a casting process. The presence of a large number of bronze objects at an archaeological site, combined with a lack of used casts and crucibles, would therefore most likely indicate that

   (A) the site had a strong tradition of producing bronze locally
   (B) the bronze objects found at the site were smelted from bronze acquired through the raiding of neighboring regions
   (C) there were especially rich copper mines near the site
   (D) the site was part of a wider trade network
   (E) the site was an important religious center

5. Which of the following best explains why early civilizations tended to develop along major river systems?

   (A) Bricks made of river mud provided a cheap building material.
   (B) Forts built along rivers were easy to defend.
   (C) Rivers were often considered sacred by people living in arid regions.
   (D) Rivers provided water for crop irrigation.
   (E) The ability to travel along rivers facilitated trade and made it easier to forge alliances.

GO ON TO THE NEXT PAGE

Questions 6-7 refer to the following passage.

Nunnu was an official in the province of Arzawa, but he did not bring silver and gold [to the king]. What silver and gold he collected, he brought to his own house. King Hattusili sent for Nunnu and ordered another man, Sarmassu, to take his place. But before the replacement had departed for his post, the king commanded that he and Nunnu be led to a mountain, where they were tied together like oxen. . . . Sarmassu called out to the king: "My Lord, I have not yet gone to Arzawa!" The King replied: "Go now, for this was a lesson for you!"

Hittite chronicle, commissioned by King Hattusili I, Asia Minor, circa 1600 B.C.E.

6. The inclusion in the chronicle of the story of Nunnu and Sarmassu quoted above was most likely intended to

   (A) record an important change in the method of recruiting Hittite officials
   (B) highlight the importance of the province of Arzawa to the economy of Hattusili's kingdom
   (C) portray Hattusili as a stern but just ruler who was determined to root out abuses of power by his officials
   (D) criticize Hattusili for administering harsh and arbitrary punishments
   (E) illustrate the Hittite belief in the inevitability of divine retribution

7. Which of the following conclusions about the Hittite Kingdom is best supported by the passage above?

   (A) Corruption among government officials was not a major concern for the rulers.
   (B) The system of criminal law was based on a uniform written code.
   (C) The economy was based on taxing agricultural products.
   (D) The king presided over a centralized government.
   (E) The political system was dominated by a hereditary aristocracy.

8. "All is changed by the flood—it is a healing-balm for all mankind.

   River, establisher of justice! Mankind desires you, supplicating you to answer their prayers— you answer them by [sending] the flood! Men offer [you] the first fruits of grain; all the gods adore you!"

   The hymn quoted above best reflects the relationship between people and their environment in which of the following ancient civilizations?

   (A) Minoan
   (B) Assyrian
   (C) Egyptian
   (D) Harappan
   (E) Maya

9. In which of the following ancient Greek city-states did women typically have the greatest amount of economic independence and the highest social status?

   (A) Athens
   (B) Sparta
   (C) Corinth
   (D) Thebes
   (E) Argos

10. "Life is suffering; suffering is caused by man's desires" is a statement that can be found in

   (A) Plato's *Republic*
   (B) the Qur'an
   (C) the Four Noble Truths of the Buddha
   (D) the *Epic of Gilgamesh*
   (E) *Beowulf*

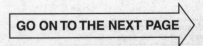

11. Which of the following belief systems that appeared during the late (Eastern) Zhou period has had the most lasting influence on East Asian civilizations?

    (A) Jainism
    (B) Confucianism
    (C) Hinduism
    (D) Mohism
    (E) Legalism

12. The Egyptian Book of the Dead was significant because it

    (A) contained a list of dead ancestors for continued worship
    (B) provided instructions to ensure a safe journey to the afterlife
    (C) offered detailed directions for the construction of pyramids
    (D) contained ritual procedures intended to gain earthly rewards from the gods
    (E) established the credibility of the divine kingship of the pharaohs

GO ON TO THE NEXT PAGE

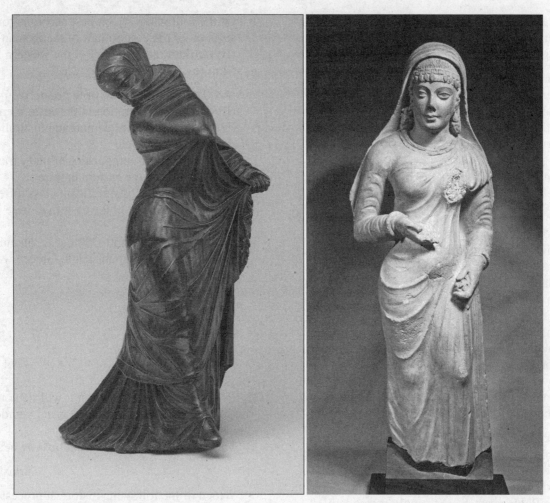

© The Metropolitan Museum of Art / Art Resource, NY   © Barney Burstein / CORBIS # BE006396

13. The photo on the left shows a sculpture created circa 250–150 B.C.E. in Alexandria, Egypt; the photo on the right shows a sculpture created circa 150–200 C.E. in Gandhara, Indus River valley. The style similarities in the two statues are attributable to which of the following historical events?

(A) The Roman emperor Justinian's reconquest of the Italian Peninsula
(B) The spread of Buddhism during Ashoka's reign in India
(C) The Tang dynasty's expansion into central Asia
(D) Alexander the Great's conquest of parts of south Asia
(E) The increased use of silk clothing in the first few centuries C.E.

GO ON TO THE NEXT PAGE

14. In the earliest cities of Mesopotamia, Egypt, and the Indus Valley, which of the following pairs of groups generally had the most power?

(A) Kings and priests
(B) Merchants and priests
(C) Warriors and merchants
(D) Artists and kings
(E) Farmers and priests

15. The term "foraging" refers to a mode of subsistence in which humans survive by

(A) staying in one place and living off domesticated plants and animals
(B) moving from place to place and living off their herds of domesticated animals
(C) gathering foodstuffs and other needed materials from the environment
(D) living off trade goods acquired from migrating peoples
(E) practicing slash-and-burn agriculture in the forests

16. Which of the following was true of the Polynesian migrations in the Pacific Ocean?

(A) The Polynesians' ancestors originally came from the Americas.
(B) The Polynesians brought crops and domesticated animals to Pacific islands.
(C) The Polynesians were the only premodern human group to have migrated across an ocean.
(D) The Polynesian migrations to all major Pacific island groups occurred within a period of a few decades.
(E) The Polynesian migrations were centrally planned by a single state authority.

17. Of the following, which best accounts for the survival of the eastern half of the Roman Empire (Byzantium) after the fall of the western Roman Empire in the fifth century C.E.?

(A) The greater wealth of the eastern empire
(B) Religious toleration in the eastern empire
(C) The existence of democratic institutions in Constantinople
(D) A system of compulsory military training and service in the eastern empire
(E) The absence of significant class differences and conflicts in the eastern empire

18. In the period circa 550–300 B.C.E., an empire stretching from Afghanistan to Greece was built by the

(A) Assyrians
(B) Han Chinese
(C) Persians
(D) Romans
(E) Hittites

19. Do not cultivate a vineyard, it will tie you down.
Do not cultivate grain, it will grind you down.
Lead the camel, herd the sheep.
Then maybe one day you will be crowned.

Turkish proverb

Which of the following historical processes best explains the existence of the worldview expressed in the proverb above?

(A) The disruption of Byzantine agriculture caused by the Crusades of the eleventh to thirteenth centuries
(B) The political instability of the Ottoman Empire after the sixteenth century
(C) The spread of Islam from Arabia in the wake of the Muslim conquests of the seventh and eighth centuries
(D) The large-scale migration of nomadic Turkic groups to Asia Minor after the eleventh century
(E) The reforms of Mustafa Kemal Atatürk in the late 1920s

GO ON TO THE NEXT PAGE

20. The "counsels of perfection"—chastity, poverty, and obedience—are most closely associated with which of the following aspects of Christianity?

   (A) The selling of indulgences
   (B) Confession
   (C) Infant baptism
   (D) Caesaropapism
   (E) Monasticism

21. As the Mongols swept over much of central Eurasia in the thirteenth century, which of the following areas escaped the Mongol conquest?

   (A) Japan and western Europe
   (B) India and the Middle East
   (C) Egypt and China
   (D) Russia and North Africa
   (E) Southeast Asia and Persia

22. A follower of the Sufi tradition in Islam is most likely to emphasize which of the following?

   (A) Strict adherence to a literal interpretation of the Qur'an
   (B) A mystical approach to religious devotion and ritual
   (C) Religious conversion among members of non-Muslim societies
   (D) Traditional education in Islamic law
   (E) The unknowability of God

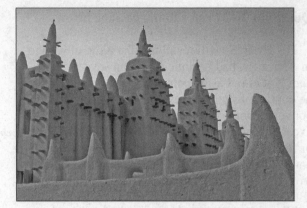

© Wolfgang Kaehler / CORBIS # WK001664

23. The architectural style represented in the photograph above originated in

   (A) the Indus River valley
   (B) Japan
   (C) North America
   (D) West Africa
   (E) western Europe

24. By 1500 C.E., Buddhism in central Asia had been largely supplanted by

   (A) Confucianism
   (B) Islam
   (C) Judaism
   (D) Catholicism
   (E) Orthodox Christianity

25. The political history of both Japan and western Europe between 600 C.E. and 1450 C.E. suggests

   (A) the continued vulnerability of settled agricultural societies to nomadic attacks
   (B) the difficulty of forming durable centralized states
   (C) the unifying role of monotheistic religions
   (D) the importance of transoceanic trade for economic and political development
   (E) the inability of premodern states to rule over ethnically diverse populations

GO ON TO THE NEXT PAGE

Questions 26-27 refer to the passage below.

His Holiness will recall that the King of Kongo in Africa . . . had become Christian several years ago. Not only has he persevered in his faith, but he continuously preaches to his vassals and has converted some of them. . . . Given the king's excellent intentions, if His Holiness were to find three or four priests to send to the Kongo . . . the country could easily be converted. From what I have heard from the king's ambassadors here in Portugal, the [European] priests currently in the Kongo are more likely to observe the religion of gluttony and pleasure than that of Christ. It would therefore be a good idea to send people who would turn them onto the right path. . . . I also think it would be necessary to allow these newly-sent priests to marry—the country's climate is very hot, so people are less masters of themselves there and less likely to remain chaste.

> Marco della Rovere, papal envoy to Portugal, letter to the Vatican, 1534 C.E.

26. Which of the following conclusions about the Kingdom of Kongo in the mid-sixteenth century is best supported by the passage?

(A) It was the dominant power in sub-Saharan Africa

(B) Its climate posed a significant obstacle to its political unification

(C) It was a key player in the trans-Atlantic slave trade

(D) Its rulers were the target of proselytizing efforts by both European Christian and West African Muslim missionaries

(E) Its rulers' conversion to Christianity had not been followed by the conversion of the majority of its population

27. Della Rovere's proposal that priests sent to the Kingdom of Kongo be allowed to marry most strongly supports the conclusion that the Catholic Church hierarchy

(A) was engaged in a concerted effort to abolish clerical celibacy

(B) saw missionary activity in Africa as a counterweight to the loss of Catholic influence in northern Europe due to the Reformation

(C) was willing to consider modifying established practices to suit local conditions

(D) was unwilling to impose discipline upon its inept and corrupt lower clergy

(E) had given rulers of individual Catholic countries, such as the kings of Spain and Portugal, a free hand in designing missionary policy in Africa

---

28. One of the most important actions of the Roman Emperor Constantine was his

(A) defeat of a powerful Muslim attack on Constantinople

(B) encouragement of more democratic forms of local government within the Roman Empire

(C) reconquest of the Eastern Empire from the Persians

(D) establishment of Christianity as the most favored religion within the Roman Empire

(E) peaceful resolution of the Iconoclastic Controversy

GO ON TO THE NEXT PAGE ▶

29. "The Hindus are unlike other peoples, because in other peoples various groups mingle with each other, whereas the Hindus ever since the time of Adam (upon whom be peace!) have practiced the following custom: namely, the members of a particular trade will not associate with any groups outside that trade. Thus grocers will give their daughters only to grocers, butchers to butchers, bakers to bakers, and soldiers to soldiers."

                    Persian treatise, eleventh century C.E.

The differences between Hindus and other peoples noted in the account above are mostly attributable to which of the following?

(A) The absence of slavery and other forms of forced labor in Hindu society
(B) The practice of arranged marriages among south Asian Muslims
(C) The determination among Hindus not to reveal the true nature of their social system to foreigners
(D) Muslim attitudes toward practitioners of polytheistic religions
(E) The social implications of Hinduism's caste system

30. "We order and command, that under no consideration can any ship go from the provinces of Peru, Panama, Guatemala, New Spain, or any other part of our Western Indies, to China to trade or traffic, or for any other purpose; nor can any ship go to the Philippines, except from New Spain, in accordance with the laws, under penalty of the confiscation of the ship. . . . We prohibit any merchandise being taken from New Spain to the provinces of Peru and Panama, that shall have been taken there from the Philippines, even if the duties should be paid according to the rules and ordinances; for it is our purpose that no goods shipped from China and the Philippines be consumed in the said provinces of Peru and Panama."

                              Spanish royal edict, 1593

The law quoted above is an example of

(A) feudalism
(B) manorialism
(C) mercantilism
(D) laissez-faire capitalism
(E) socialism

31. "We owe boundless gratitude to the compassion of Almighty God, since in our time He has deigned to wrest the Church in Asia from the hands of the infidels and to open Jerusalem to Christian [Crusader] soldiers. . . . However, we ought to follow that Divine grace and effectively aid our brethren who have remained in those districts. Urge, therefore, all the soldiers of your regions to strive for forgiveness of their sins by hastening to our Mother Church in the East. . . . Moreover, we decree that those be held in disgrace who left the siege of Antioch [conquered by the Crusaders in 1098] before the city fell; . . . let them remain in excommunication, unless they affirm that they will return [to the East]."

                    Pope Paschal II,
                    letter to the clergy of France, 1099

Which of the following can be inferred about the First Crusade from the excerpt above and your knowledge of world history?

(A) The Crusaders routinely massacred the Muslim inhabitants of the cities they conquered.
(B) The Crusaders believed that Antioch was not an important strategic target.
(C) The Crusaders' numbers were insufficient to hold the territories they had conquered.
(D) The Crusaders' provisions and reinforcement came mostly from France.
(E) The Crusaders were mostly motivated by the possibility of acquiring material wealth for themselves.

32. All of the following are true of both the Aztec (Mexica) and the Inca Empires EXCEPT:

(A) Their cities featured monumental stone buildings.
(B) Their rulers played important roles in religious ceremonies.
(C) They were much larger in area than the largest Eurasian empires at the time.
(D) They collapsed as a result of the Spanish conquest of the Americas.
(E) They were created and consolidated through a series of wars of conquest against neighboring peoples.

33. In Tsarist Russia, Moscow was often called the "Third Rome" as an expression of Russia's religious and cultural links to Rome and

(A) Antioch
(B) Jerusalem
(C) Athens
(D) Carthage
(E) Constantinople

34. At the time of their first contacts with Europeans in the seventeenth and eighteenth centuries C.E., most indigenous Australians lived in

(A) highly urbanized societies based on long-distance inland trade
(B) a unified empire that stretched across the continent
(C) complex hunter-gatherer societies that did not use metal tools
(D) densely populated rural societies based on intensive agriculture and animal husbandry
(E) seafaring merchant communities

35. Even though French kings in the sixteenth century were Roman Catholic, they aided the rebellions of German Lutherans because

(A) they wished to weaken the power of the Holy Roman Empire
(B) Lutherans were the key to defending Europe against the Ottoman Empire
(C) the French royal family was related by marriage to several German Lutheran families
(D) most of the French people were converting to Lutheranism
(E) the German states were France's most important trading partners

36. The medieval Roman Catholic Church most objected to the activities of which of the following groups?

(A) Nobles
(B) Artisans
(C) Warriors
(D) Small farmers
(E) Moneylenders

37. In 1850 the largest part of Brazil's population consisted of

(A) Africans and their descendants who had been brought by the slave trade
(B) Portuguese and their descendants who had come as colonists
(C) indigenous peoples whose numbers had rebounded
(D) East Indians newly arrived as indentured laborers
(E) Spanish-speaking immigrants from neighboring countries

38. Which of the following was the most important factor in Britain's Industrial Revolution?

(A) The ready availability of coal as an energy source
(B) A long period of peace that allowed Britain to concentrate on economic growth
(C) Mass education programs that created a more skilled workforce
(D) Cooperation with other countries in technical and scientific areas
(E) The spread of democratic institutions that allowed for more free enterprise

GO ON TO THE NEXT PAGE

39. Which of the following was an important effect of the Haitian Revolution?

    (A) The political marginalization in Haiti of wealthy free people of color
    (B) The overthrow of British colonial rule in Haiti
    (C) The abolition of slavery in Haiti
    (D) The emergence of Haiti as an important producer and exporter of sugar
    (E) The suppression of Vodou and other syncretic religious practices in Haiti

40. The Suez Canal, completed in 1869, had what important effect on Egypt?

    (A) Egypt became a major shipbuilding and naval power.
    (B) The Egyptian economy flourished, boosted by revenue from canal tolls and fees.
    (C) Egypt was drawn further into European colonial rivalries.
    (D) The center of Egyptian agriculture shifted from the Nile delta to the canal zone.
    (E) Egyptian rulers declared complete independence from the Ottoman Empire.

41. "There appeared off our western shore a big ship, carrying a crew whose physical features differed from ours. In their hands they carried something two or three feet long made of a heavy substance. One fills it with powder and small lead pellets. This thing with one blow can smash a mountain of silver and a wall of iron. . . . Lord Tokitaka saw it and thought it was a wonder and he spoke to the [foreigners] through an interpreter: 'Incapable as I am, I should like to learn about it.' They answered: 'If you wish to learn about it, we shall teach you its mysteries.' Tokitaka acquired two pieces of the weapon and studied them. It was he who made our ironworkers learn the method of its manufacture and made it possible for the knowledge to spread over the entire length of the country."

    Japanese chronicle 1500s C.E.

The events described in the passage above contributed to which of the following?

    (A) The conquest of Japan by European colonizers
    (B) The conversion to Shinto by many foreign visitors to Japan
    (C) The unification of Japan by the Tokugawa shoguns
    (D) A series of peasant revolts that led to the granting of political rights to the lower classes
    (E) The growth in the political power of the Japanese emperor

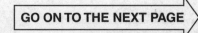
GO ON TO THE NEXT PAGE

42. Which of the following statements about British colonial rule in India is NOT correct?

(A) The Sepoy Mutiny led to the shift from rule by the East India Company to direct rule by the British government.
(B) Most British colonial officers viewed Indian culture as backward and Indians as incapable of self-government.
(C) The British prohibited Indian participation in the colonial bureaucracy or in local government.
(D) Indian princely states were less tightly controlled by the British than were territories under direct British rule.
(E) Access to cotton, opium, and other Indian export commodities was an important motive behind British colonialism in India.

43. Which of the following best characterizes the religious policy of the Ottoman sultans?

(A) They considered themselves the leaders of the Islamic community and insisted that all inhabitants of their empire convert to Islam.
(B) They considered themselves the leaders of the Islamic community, but generally tolerated the existence of large Jewish and Christian populations within their empire.
(C) They refused to profess any religion in public and insisted that all religions be treated equally in their empire.
(D) They considered themselves to be prophets superior to Muhammad and insisted on their absolute authority over the religious affairs of all Muslims in their empire.
(E) They practiced Islam as their personal religion, but insisted on a strict separation between religious affairs and affairs of state.

44. Which of the following undermined the ability of the League of Nations to resolve international disputes and provide collective security?

(A) The mandate system allowed too many former colonies to become independent.
(B) The military forces used for collective security were mostly from the Soviet Union and Germany.
(C) The United States refused to join the organization.
(D) Japan was allowed to have the world's largest navy.
(E) The Soviet Union was allowed to retain numerous client states in Eastern Europe.

45. Which of the following was a common characteristic of the empires founded by the Safavids in Persia, the Ottomans in Turkey, and the Mughals in India?

(A) They all rejected modern military technology, relying instead on traditional means of warfare.
(B) They all were founded with the help of European military alliances.
(C) They all were dominated by Hindu and Buddhist religious traditions.
(D) They all were major participants in overseas shipping trade.
(E) They all were created by Turkic or Mongol military conquests.

46. The Gold Coast of Africa is located on the

(A) Mediterranean coastline of Morocco, Algeria, and Tunisia
(B) coastline of the gold-rich region of South Africa
(C) coasts of Zanzibar and Kenya in the east
(D) Atlantic coastline between the Senegal River and the Niger Delta
(E) Red Sea and Suez Canal in the northeast

GO ON TO THE NEXT PAGE

47. The revolutionary theory of Mao Zedong differed from that of Karl Marx in that Mao

(A) believed class conflict was the driving force of history
(B) did not believe military force was important for successful revolutions
(C) emphasized industrial workers alone as agents of revolution
(D) stressed the revolutionary potential of peasants
(E) sought western European support for his cause

48. Which of the following was a major reason that the Cold War did not lead to a direct military conflict between the United States and the Soviet Union?

(A) The likelihood of mutual destruction by nuclear weapons in the event of a war
(B) The importance of trade between the two countries
(C) The slowing of population growth in both countries
(D) Religious revivals in both countries
(E) The increasing democratization of both countries

49. In India in the late 1500s, the Mughal Emperor Akbar presided over a government that

(A) included both Muslim and Hindu officeholders for political reasons
(B) employed only Hindus for political reasons
(C) employed only Muslims for religious reasons
(D) employed people in government offices strictly according to their talents
(E) required all officeholders to renounce their religion, as a means of reducing conflict

50. Which of the following constitutes a significant continuity in Mesoamerican history from 600 B.C.E. to 600 C.E.?

(A) The reliance of major Mesoamerican societies on long-distance trade with Afro-Eurasia
(B) Adherence to religious beliefs that involved elaborate calendars and human sacrifice
(C) The reliance on potatoes as a staple food for supporting large urban populations
(D) The utilization of copper-based alloys for weapons and tools
(E) The domestication of draft animals for agricultural production

51. Which of the following is true concerning Dutch, English, and French colonization efforts in North America in the seventeenth and eighteenth centuries?

(A) They had very similar goals, methods, and results.
(B) They all focused on trade and neglected permanent settlement.
(C) They differed in that the English focused mainly on fur trading, while the French and Dutch focused on silver mining.
(D) They differed in that the Dutch and French had more difficulty than did the English in attracting permanent settlers of both sexes.
(E) They all generally accommodated the cultures of the indigenous groups in North America.

52. Which of the following early societies had a written language that scholars have not been able to decipher?

(A) The Maya of Mesoamerica
(B) The Harappan of the Indus Valley
(C) The Shang of the Yellow (Huang He) River
(D) The Nubian of the Upper Nile
(E) The Phoenician of the Mediterranean

53. The Western Wall, sometimes also called "The Wailing Wall," is a term used to refer to

(A) an enclosure where the Chinese emperors worshipped their ancestors
(B) part of the sacred route of the pilgrimage to Mecca
(C) the last remaining section of the Jewish Temple in Jerusalem
(D) part of the Inca stronghold of Machu Picchu
(E) the room where condemned prisoners in the Tower of London received last rites

54. The migration of Bantu-speaking peoples into southern Africa and the migration of peoples speaking Indo-European languages into western Europe were similar in that both

(A) were enabled primarily by the domestication of horses
(B) led to the spread of advanced gunpowder weaponry
(C) resulted in the political unification of the regions into which both migrated
(D) were accompanied by the spread of monotheistic religions
(E) led to the spread of ironworking into new regions

55. Nineteenth-century "romantic nationalists" such as Giuseppe Mazzini believed that

(A) the international arena was the site of a Social Darwinist struggle for national predominance
(B) national self-determination for all peoples would guarantee universal human rights
(C) nationalism and liberalism were antithetical
(D) ethnic groups could be unified only by national monarchies
(E) stronger nations should rule over weaker ones

56. The interaction between British settlers and indigenous peoples in Australia in the nineteenth century was most similar to the interaction between

(A) the Portuguese and West Africans in the fifteenth century
(B) the Spanish and Aztecs (Mexica) in the sixteenth century
(C) the British and Chinese in the nineteenth century
(D) the French and Vietnamese in the nineteenth century
(E) White Americans and Native Americans in the United States in the nineteenth century

57. Which of the following statements represents a Confucian view of ethics?

(A) Living a life of faith and moderation ensures entrance into Heaven after death.
(B) Observing norms of proper interpersonal behavior leads to social harmony.
(C) One's actions in life contribute to the cosmic battle between good and evil.
(D) Following society's rules ensures reincarnation into a higher caste in the next life.
(E) The morality of every action must be judged by comparing the number of people it benefits to the number of people it harms.

GO ON TO THE NEXT PAGE

58. Which of the following was a shared characteristic of royal absolutist governments in seventeenth- and eighteenth-century Europe?

    (A) Parliamentary control over matters of fiscal policy and troop recruitment
    (B) Erosion of the power of the feudal aristocracy and the rise of the service aristocracy and bureaucracy
    (C) A policy of universal or near-universal religious toleration
    (D) Written constitutions that enumerated the respective powers of the monarch, the legislature, and the judiciary
    (E) Incorporation of Enlightenment ideas into state policy and royal sponsorship of Enlightenment intellectuals

59. Many scholars believe that early farming communities in the Americas and Australasia domesticated fewer animal species than early farming communities in Afro-Eurasia did because

    (A) most large wild animal species in the Americas and Australasia had migrated to different continents
    (B) most large animal species in the Americas and Australasia had become extinct before the arrival of humans
    (C) an asteroid striking Earth had killed most large animals in the Americas and Australasia
    (D) most large wild animals that lived in the Americas and Australasia were unsuitable for domestication
    (E) American and Australasian peoples considered wild animals sacred and were not willing to harm them

GO ON TO THE NEXT PAGE

© Apaimages/ZUMA Press/Corbis

60. The photo of Mecca best illustrates which of the following Muslim religious
duties?

(A) The giving of alms
(B) Proselytizing
(C) The declaration of faith
(D) Fasting during Ramadan
(E) The hajj

GO ON TO THE NEXT PAGE

61. Which of the following was an important long-term consequence of Arab interaction with South Asia in the ninth and tenth centuries C.E.?

   (A) The spread of the decimal number system to the Middle East and the Mediterranean basin
   (B) The spread of rice-based agriculture to East Africa
   (C) The introduction of slavery to the Middle East
   (D) The decline in the importance of the Silk Roads as a major avenue of East-West trade
   (E) The widespread adoption of Arabic as a spoken language in India

62. The tributary systems of the Aztec empire and Tang China differed most significantly in which of the following ways?

   (A) Aztec rulers depended on tribute as a source of revenue, whereas Tang rulers demanded tribute payments mainly as symbols of foreign rulers' submission.
   (B) Aztec rulers sought only war captives as tribute, whereas Tang rulers did not accept slaves or captives as tribute.
   (C) Aztec rulers collected a wide variety of goods and produce as tribute payments, whereas Tang rulers expected all tribute payments to be made in silver bullion.
   (D) Aztec rulers depended more on tax collection than on tribute payments, whereas Tang rulers depended more on tribute payments than on tax collection.
   (E) Aztec rulers' modest demands for tribute stimulated economic growth in Mesoamerica, whereas Tang rulers' growing demands for tribute inhibited economic growth in East Asia.

63. The term "Shari'a" refers to which of the following?

   (A) The requirement that Muslims pray five times every day
   (B) The opening chapter of the Qur'an
   (C) The circle of philosophers and scientists who translated many Greek scientific works into Arabic in the early ninth century C.E.
   (D) The body of legal norms derived from Islamic religious texts and traditions
   (E) The official title of the religious leader of Shi'ite Muslims

64. Which of the following was the only European country allowed to trade with Japan in the late seventeenth century?

   (A) Britain
   (B) France
   (C) Portugal
   (D) The Netherlands
   (E) Spain

GO ON TO THE NEXT PAGE

NUMBER OF JEWISH HOUSEHOLDS IN SELECTED OTTOMAN CITIES				
	Date	Number	Date	Number
Istanbul	1477 C.E.	1,647	1535 C.E.	8,070
Thessaloniki	1478 C.E.	None	1519 C.E.	3,143

65. Which of the following best explains the population changes in the chart above?

(A) Jews expelled from Portugal and Spain were encouraged to settle in the Ottoman Empire.
(B) Rural Jewish families moved to urban areas after the fall of Constantinople.
(C) The Ottoman Empire imposed forced migration on its Jewish inhabitants.
(D) High Jewish birth rates during the fifteenth and sixteenth centuries increased the number of households.
(E) The population of Thessaloniki grew much faster than the population of Istanbul.

66. Sikhism developed initially as an attempt to bridge the differences between which of the following religions?

(A) Christianity and Judaism
(B) Judaism and Islam
(C) Islam and Buddhism
(D) Buddhism and Hinduism
(E) Hinduism and Islam

67. Chinese influence in Tokugawa Japan was most evident in which of the following areas?

(A) Upper-class dress
(B) Military organization and the samurai warrior code
(C) Confucian influences on official state ideology
(D) Government restrictions on contact with Europeans
(E) Popular forms of entertainment such as Kabuki theater

68. Which of the following features was common to both the Nazi regime in Germany and the Japanese government in the 1930s?

(A) A commitment to the state ownership of all major industries
(B) The glorification of warfare and the military
(C) The belief that the Jews were the source of most of the world's problems
(D) The desire to seek a military alliance with the Soviet Union
(E) The official endorsement of the superiority of the "Aryan race"

69. Which of the following was an important cause of the wars of religion in Europe following the Protestant Reformation?

(A) The pope's abolition of indulgences following Luther's criticism
(B) The expansion of the Russian empire into eastern Europe
(C) The power struggles between individual German princes and the Holy Roman Emperor
(D) The expansion of the Ottoman Empire into the Balkans and central Europe
(E) The conflict between the papacy and the Medici family for control over the Italian city-states

GO ON TO THE NEXT PAGE ⟶

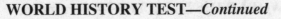

70. "Since . . . whatever a slave acquires becomes the property of his owner and since slave owners do not give their slaves anything more than what is necessary for their nourishment, it is clear that the slave, being the property of his owner, cannot deliver the price of his freedom."

> Slave owners in the Barbacoas goldmines, South America, 1792

The statement above was most likely made in support of which of the following arguments?

(A) That slave owners were being too lax in their treatment of slaves
(B) That slavery was morally justified because slave owners provided nourishment for their slaves
(C) That slave owners were entitled to receive a greater share of their slaves' wealth to cover their expenses
(D) That economic exploitation of slaves went against core Christian values and ought to be discontinued
(E) That the practice of allowing slaves to buy their freedom ought to be abolished

71. In striving for South American independence from Spain, Simón Bolívar was most inspired by the ideas of

(A) the European Enlightenment
(B) the Haitian Revolution
(C) the peninsular administration
(D) the Roman Catholic Church
(E) earlier leaders of the Amerindian resistance to the Spaniards

72. During the period of imperialism from 1880 to 1914, which European country acquired the largest territory in northern and western Africa?

(A) Great Britain
(B) France
(C) Germany
(D) Italy
(E) Spain

73. In nineteenth-century Great Britain, the concept of colonial paternalism was most likely used to justify which of the following?

(A) The expansion of British-controlled territory into southern Africa
(B) The building of railroads and canals in England
(C) Government welfare programs for the working poor
(D) The opening of English-language schools in India
(E) The support for the continued territorial unity of the Ottoman Empire

74. The diplomatic policy before the First World War by which the major European powers acted together to prevent any one of them from becoming too powerful was known as

(A) the Great Tradition
(B) the European Union
(C) the Marshall Plan
(D) the balance of power
(E) free-trade imperialism

GO ON TO THE NEXT PAGE

75. "I order that Mexican tenants immediately pay all rents accumulated to date on lands belonging to the Native Communities . . . so that, being entered in the national Treasury, these lands may be delivered to the said Natives for their cultivation, without being available for rent in the future; it is also my will that such lands be only for the use of the Natives in their respective villages."

> Miguel Hidalgo y Costilla, leader of the Mexican War of Independence, decree, 1810

Miguel Hidalgo's decree quoted above was most likely intended to

(A) assuage Creole fears that the end of Spanish control would bring radical social and economic changes to Mexico

(B) cynically divert attention from more pressing foreign threats by focusing on an unimportant domestic issue

(C) encourage Mexicans of Amerindian descent to participate in the political life of the new nation

(D) implement an equitable system of taxation for all socioeconomic classes in Mexico

(E) use government redistribution of wealth to redress the grievances of Mexico's Amerindian population

76. Which of the following best describes the ideas expressed in Adam Smith's *The Wealth of Nations*?

(A) All real wealth lies in proper use of the land.

(B) Nations should export as much as possible and import as little as possible.

(C) The only forms of wealth worth pursuing are gold and silver.

(D) The workers of the world must unite against capitalist exploitation.

(E) Economies with the fewest restrictions work best.

77. Which of the following was an important unintended effect of Christian missionary activity in China during the nineteenth century?

(A) Empress Dowager Cixi's consolidation of power at the end of the Qing dynasty

(B) The abolition of the custom of foot binding for elite women

(C) The outbreak and initial success of the Taiping Rebellion

(D) The launching of the Self-Strengthening Movement

(E) The decline in Christian missionary activities in other parts of the world, such as Africa

78. Which of the following was central to the thinking of Karl Marx?

(A) All social classes should just get along.

(B) Socialist revolution will overthrow capitalism and establish a fair economic system.

(C) The state usually serves to further the interest of the working class.

(D) The middle class and the working class share common interests.

(E) Profits rightfully belong to the capitalist class, since its members take the most risks.

79. A common characteristic of Latin American political systems in the period from independence to 1900 was the emergence of

(A) Roman Catholic revivalist movements and Native American independence movements

(B) socialist totalitarian regimes in the region

(C) constitutional governments and democratic elections with peaceful transfers of power

(D) liberal parties' successful struggles for women's suffrage

(E) authoritarian leaders who maintained power through military force

GO ON TO THE NEXT PAGE

80. The Japanese constitution adopted in 1947 prohibited the government from resorting to war as an instrument of national policy because

    (A) Japan wanted to lead the world in disarmament
    (B) Japan did not want to be involved in Soviet-American confrontations
    (C) the United States sought to appease strong anti-Japanese feelings in China
    (D) the United States sought to forestall future Japanese aggression
    (E) Japanese leaders decided that diplomacy was a more effective policy instrument

81. In most countries, industrial manufacturing was first introduced in the production of

    (A) foodstuffs
    (B) firearms
    (C) plastics
    (D) textiles
    (E) automobiles

82. "We think that appreciable value must be attached to finding all-British routes [for undersea telegraph cables]; and we regard it as desirable that every important colony of ours should possess one cable to Great Britain which touches only on British territory or on the territory of some friendly neutral."

    British Government Commission on Telegraph Cable Communications, report, 1902

    The recommendation of the report quoted above is best understood in the context of which of the following?

    (A) The growing threat of communist revolution worldwide
    (B) Colonial rivalries and rival alliance building in Europe
    (C) Bureaucratic unease over the introduction of new technologies
    (D) Competition between governments and private companies over telegraph cable installation and use
    (E) A desire to expand the number of British allies in the Third World

83. When countries such as Brazil, India, and Mexico have accepted assistance from the International Monetary Fund and the World Bank, they have been required to

    (A) restructure their economies to allow freer markets
    (B) join the United Nations
    (C) hold democratic elections
    (D) sever diplomatic ties with communist countries
    (E) accept the United States dollar as their principal currency

84. The Young Turks movement, the Boxer Rebellion, and Zionism were all most directly influenced by which of the following?

    (A) Anarchism
    (B) Imperialism
    (C) Existentialism
    (D) Nationalism
    (E) The Enlightenment

85. All of the following are former French colonies EXCEPT

    (A) Haiti
    (B) Vietnam
    (C) Algeria
    (D) Senegal
    (E) Ethiopia

86. "The modern bourgeois society that has sprouted from the ruins of feudal society has not done away with class antagonisms. It has but established new classes, new conditions for oppression, new forms of struggle in place of the old ones."

    Which of the following would most likely have agreed with the statement above?

    (A) Jean-Jacques Rousseau
    (B) Mohandas Gandhi
    (C) Simón Bolívar
    (D) Charles Darwin
    (E) Vladimir Lenin

GO ON TO THE NEXT PAGE

87. Nelson Mandela is best known for his leadership in the movement to

   (A) establish the United Nations
   (B) establish the Organization of African Unity
   (C) end apartheid in South Africa
   (D) overthrow British colonial rule in South Africa
   (E) open South Africa's most productive gold mine

88. During the independence movement in British India, which of the following said that Pakistan was the "only solution to India's constitutional problem"?

   (A) Muhammad Ali Jinnah
   (B) Jawaharlal Nehru
   (C) Mohandas Gandhi
   (D) Lord Mountbatten
   (E) Winston Churchill

89. Which of the following was the most immediate cause of the Iranian revolution in 1979 ?

   (A) The seizure of the American Embassy in Tehran by radical students
   (B) Popular dissatisfaction with the oppressive and corrupt rule of the shah
   (C) Concern among Iranian military officers over Iran's lack of response to the Soviet invasion of Afghanistan
   (D) Resentment among Iranian liberals over the ouster of Iranian Prime Minister Mosaddeq by CIA covert operatives
   (E) The invasion of Iran by Iraqi military forces under Saddam Hussein

90. Pro-communist governments have been formed in nations of all of the following areas of the world EXCEPT

   (A) East Asia
   (B) Central America
   (C) Southern Africa
   (D) the Caribbean
   (E) North America

91. Which of the following was NOT actively promoted by the Chinese Communist Party under the leadership of Mao Zedong?

   (A) Industrialization
   (B) Leader's cult of personality
   (C) Private entrepreneurship
   (D) Vigilance against counterrevolutionary ideas
   (E) Collectivization of agricultural land

92. Which of the following would have been most likely to endorse Mohandas Gandhi's philosophy of nonviolent resistance as a means to achieve political change?

   (A) Lech Walesa
   (B) Ho Chi Minh
   (C) Maximilien Robespierre
   (D) Che Guevara
   (E) Mao Zedong

GO ON TO THE NEXT PAGE

93. Most historians agree that Mikhail Gorbachev's policies of glasnost and perestroika had which of the following effects?

(A) They stabilized the crumbling communist system and prolonged the existence of the Soviet Union.

(B) They allowed Soviet citizens to openly criticize for the first time the policies pursued under Stalin's authoritarian rule.

(C) Their role in the collapse of the Soviet Union was minimal compared to the role of United States economic and military pressure.

(D) They had the unintended effect of hastening the collapse of the Soviet Union.

(E) They had little effect on Soviet satellite countries in Eastern Europe, most of which had already adopted similar policies.

94. Cold War tensions contributed most directly to which of the following?

(A) The partition of British India
(B) The Cuban missile crisis
(C) The Iranian revolution
(D) The Six-Day War
(E) The fall of the Berlin Wall

95. The 1994 genocide in Rwanda can be traced to the eruption of rivalries between

(A) Rwandans and Belgian colonial authorities
(B) the presidents of Rwanda and the Democratic Republic of the Congo
(C) the Hutu and Tutsi peoples of Rwanda
(D) Bantu and non-Bantu ethnic groups
(E) citizens of Rwanda and Uganda

STOP
**If you finish before time is called, you may check your work on this test only.
Do not turn to any other section in the test.**

How to Score the SAT Subject Test in World History

When you take an actual SAT Subject Test in World History, your answer sheet will be "read" by a scanning machine that will record your response to each question. Then a computer will compare your answers with the correct answers and produce your raw score. You get one point for each correct answer. For each wrong answer, you lose one-fourth of a point. Questions you omit (and any for which you mark more than one answer) are not counted. This raw score is converted to a scaled score that is reported to you and to the colleges you specify.

Worksheet 1. Finding Your Raw Test Score

STEP 1: Table A on the following page lists the correct answers for all the questions on the Subject Test in World History that is reproduced in this book. It also serves as a worksheet for you to calculate your raw score.

- Compare your answers with those given in the table.

- Put a check in the column marked "Right" if your answer is correct.

- Put a check in the column marked "Wrong" if your answer is incorrect.

- Leave both columns blank if you omitted the question.

STEP 2: Count the number of right answers.

Enter the total here: _____

STEP 3: Count the number of wrong answers.

Enter the total here: _____

STEP 4: Multiply the number of wrong answers by .250.

Enter the product here: _____

STEP 5: Subtract the result obtained in Step 4 from the total you obtained in Step 2.

Enter the result here: _____

STEP 6: Round the number obtained in Step 5 to the nearest whole number.

Enter the result here: _____

The number you obtained in Step 6 is your raw score.

Answers to Practice Test 1 for World History

Table A
Answers to the Subject Test in World History - Practice Test 1 and Percentage of Students Answering
Each Question Correctly

Question Number	Correct Answer	Right	Wrong	Percent Answering Correctly*	Question Number	Correct Answer	Right	Wrong	Percent Answering Correctly*
1	B			75	26	E			73
2	D			69	27	C			74
3	A			38	28	D			75
4	D			72	29	E			90
5	D			94	30	C			82
6	C			76	31	C			40
7	D			68	32	C			71
8	C			81	33	E			84
9	B			60	34	C			59
10	C			90	35	A			60
11	B			86	36	E			61
12	B			71	37	A			63
13	D			67	38	A			64
14	A			89	39	C			67
15	C			82	40	C			43
16	B			42	41	C			36
17	A			45	42	C			43
18	C			69	43	B			73
19	D			62	44	C			68
20	E			59	45	E			54
21	A			84	46	D			42
22	B			52	47	D			71
23	D			50	48	A			96
24	B			51	49	A			44
25	B			63	50	B			66

Table A continued on next page

Table A continued from previous page

Question Number	Correct Answer	Right	Wrong	Percent Answering Correctly*	Question Number	Correct Answer	Right	Wrong	Percent Answering Correctly*
51	D			34	76	E			52
52	B			64	77	C			40
53	C			50	78	B			79
54	E			50	79	E			55
55	B			48	80	D			56
56	E			38	81	D			85
57	B			75	82	B			47
58	B			34	83	A			48
59	D			67	84	D			73
60	E			87	85	E			66
61	A			51	86	E			49
62	A			39	87	C			86
63	D			65	88	A			45
64	D			49	89	B			43
65	A			62	90	E			84
66	E			58	91	C			81
67	C			58	92	A			43
68	B			75	93	D			48
69	C			53	94	B			91
70	E			59	95	C			84
71	A			53					
72	B			43					
73	D			39					
74	D			65					
75	E			58					

* These percentages are based on an analysis of the answer sheets for a random sample of 12,686 students who took the original administration of this test and whose mean score was 612. They may be used as an indication of the relative difficulty of a particular question. Each percentage may also be used to predict the likelihood that a typical Subject Test in World History candidate will answer correctly that question on this edition of this test.

Finding Your Scaled Score

When you take SAT Subject Tests, the scores sent to the colleges you specify are reported on the College Board scale, which ranges from 200–800. You can convert your practice test score to a scaled score by using Table B. To find your scaled score, locate your raw score in the left-hand column of Table B; the corresponding score in the right-hand column is your scaled score. For example, a raw score of 45 on this particular edition of the Subject Test in World History corresponds to a scaled score of 570.

Raw scores are converted to scaled scores to ensure that a score earned on any one edition of a particular Subject Test is comparable to the same scaled score earned on any other edition of the same Subject Test. Because some editions of the tests may be slightly easier or more difficult than others, College Board scaled scores are adjusted so that they indicate the same level of performance regardless of the edition of the test taken and the ability of the group that takes it. Thus, for example, a score of 500 on one edition of a test taken at a particular administration indicates the same level of achievement as a score of 500 on a different edition of the test taken at a different administration.

When you take the SAT Subject Tests during a national administration, your scores are likely to differ somewhat from the scores you obtain on the tests in this book. People perform at different levels at different times for reasons unrelated to the tests themselves. The precision of any test is also limited because it represents only a sample of all the possible questions that could be asked.

Table B
Scaled Score Conversion Table
Subject Test in World History - Practice Test 1

Raw Score	Reported Score	Raw Score	Reported Score	Raw Score	Reported Score
95	800	55	620	15	430
94	800	54	620	14	420
93	800	53	610	13	420
92	800	52	610	12	410
91	800	51	600	11	410
90	800	50	590	10	400
89	800	49	590	9	400
88	800	48	580	8	390
87	800	47	580	7	390
86	800	46	570	6	380
85	800	45	570	5	380
84	800	44	560	4	370
83	790	43	560	3	370
82	790	42	550	2	360
81	780	41	550	1	360
80	770	40	540	0	350
79	770	39	540	−1	350
78	760	38	530	−2	340
77	760	37	530	−3	330
76	750	36	520	−4	330
75	740	35	520	−5	320
74	740	34	510	−6	310
73	730	33	510	−7	310
72	730	32	500	−8	300
71	720	31	500	−9	290
70	710	30	490	−10	290
69	710	29	490	−11	280
68	700	28	480	−12	270
67	690	27	480	−13	270
66	690	26	470	−14	270
65	680	25	470	−15	260
64	680	24	470	−16	250
63	670	23	460	−17	250
62	670	22	460	−18	250
61	660	21	450	−19	240
60	650	20	450	−20	230
59	650	19	440	−21	220
58	640	18	440	−22	210
57	630	17	440	−23	200
56	630	16	430	−24	200

How Did You Do on the Subject Test in World History?

After you score your test and analyze your performance, think about the following questions:

Did you run out of time before reaching the end of the test?

If so, you may need to pace yourself better. For example, maybe you spent too much time on one or two hard questions. A better approach might be to skip the ones you can't answer right away and try answering all the questions that remain on the test. Then if there's time, go back to the questions you skipped.

Did you take a long time reading the directions?

You will save time when you take the test by learning the directions to the Subject Test in World History ahead of time. Each minute you spend reading directions during the test is a minute that you could use to answer questions.

How did you handle questions you were unsure of?

If you were able to eliminate one or more of the answer choices as wrong and guess from the remaining ones, your approach probably worked to your advantage. On the other hand, making haphazard guesses or omitting questions without trying to eliminate choices could cost you valuable points.

How difficult were the questions for you compared with other students who took the test?

Table A shows you how difficult the multiple-choice questions were for the group of students who took this test during its national administration. The right-hand column gives the percentage of students that answered each question correctly.

A question answered correctly by almost everyone in the group is obviously an easier question. For example, 96 percent of the students answered question 48 correctly. But only 39 percent answered question 73 correctly.

Keep in mind that these percentages are based on just one group of students. They would probably be different with another group of students taking the test.

If you missed several easier questions, go back and try to find out why: Did the questions cover material you haven't yet reviewed? Did you misunderstand the directions?

Answer Explanations

For Practice Test 1

Question 1

Choice (B) is the correct answer. The period circa 4000 B.C.E. falls squarely within the Neolithic period, which was characterized by pottery, agriculture, and grain storage.

Question 2

Choice (D) is the correct answer. Pre-Columbian American civilizations had domesticated dogs, as well as a few small mammals and fowl. The number of domesticated animals, however, was far fewer than in civilizations in Eurasia.

Question 3

Choice (A) is the correct answer. Sargon of Akkad (reigned circa 2340–circa 2284 B.C.E.) conquered the Sumerian city-states and founded the Akkadian dynasty. The Akkadian dynasty ruled parts of modern Iraq, Turkey, Iran, Kuwait, and Syria until circa 2150 B.C.E. Answer choice (B) is incorrect because when Cyrus the Great conquered this region in the sixth century B.C.E., the political and urban centers of Sumer and Akkad had long since disappeared.

Question 4

Choice (D) is the correct answer. An archaeological site that contained large numbers of bronze items without evidence of local casting tools or processes would indicate that the bronze items were brought from other regions that had sources of copper and tin, as well as smelting technologies, through a wider trade network.

Question 5

Choice (D) is the correct answer. Although rivers contributed to brick construction, fortification, sacred geography, and transport in some early cultures, rivers' primary contribution to early civilizations was as a source of water for crop irrigation.

Question 6

Choice (C) is the correct answer. The Hittite chronicle commissioned by King Hattusili I extols his virtues as a strong ruler who sought to curb official corruption.

Question 7

Choice (D) is the correct answer. The passage indicates that King Hattusili recruited, regulated, and punished regional officials in the Hittite kingdom, which demonstrates that the Hittites had created a centralized government.

Question 8

Choice (C) is the correct answer. The hymn praises the economic and social benefits of floods along the Nile River in Egypt. Agricultural production in Egypt depended on the regular floods of the Nile River to fertilize its banks and delta regions.

Question 9

Choice (B) is the correct answer. Spartan women had greater legal, economic, and social status than women in other ancient Greek city-states. Spartan women participated in politics, enjoyed some rights over their marriage and divorce, and had significant independence from their husbands. By contrast Athenian women, choice (A), were highly limited in political and economic activity, property ownership, family law, and access to education.

Question 10

Choice (C) is the correct answer. The causes and transcendence of suffering and desire are central to the Four Noble Truths of the Buddha, which provide a conceptual framework of the central tenets of Buddhist teachings.

Question 11

Choice (B) is the correct answer. Confucianism originated in the late Zhou period. It became a central civic philosophy in China, Korea, Japan, and Vietnam under many ruling dynasties.

Question 12

Choice (B) is the correct answer. The Egyptian *Book of the Dead* is a funerary text that contains a collection of spells whose purpose was to enable a dead person to navigate the afterlife.

Question 13

Choice (D) is the correct answer. Alexander the Great conquered portions of the northern subcontinent. Various Greek kingdoms and empires emerged in the region following Alexander's death and waves of Greek settlers introduced Hellenistic cultural influences. Both sculptures demonstrate the spread of Hellenistic culture in the aftermath of Alexander's conquests. Answer choice (E) is incorrect because it is unclear whether the female figures are wearing silk and because the style similarity derives from the fact that both female figures are covered in the same manner, not because of the choice of cloth.

Question 14

Choice (A) is the correct answer. In the ancient civilizations of Mesopotamia, Egypt, and the Indus Valley, archaeological and historical evidence indicates that the two most powerful hierarchical groups were kings and priests. Merchants, farmers, artists, and even warriors were subordinate to these groups.

Question 15

Choice (C) is the correct answer. The term "foraging" refers to a mode of subsistence in which human populations gather foodstuffs and other materials from the environment.

Question 16

Choice (B) is the correct answer. Linguistic, archaeological, and genetic evidence suggests that Polynesians migrated from Austronesian islands in Southeast Asia across the southern Pacific over a period of several centuries. Their cultures introduced crops and domesticated animals to the islands that they settled. Answer choice (C) is incorrect because other human groups crossed oceans, including the ancient Malays who settled in Madagascar after crossing the Indian Ocean 2,000 years ago.

Question 17

Choice (A) is the correct answer. By the fifth century C.E., the largest and most significant economic and demographic centers of the Roman Empire were located in the eastern Mediterranean region, which was a major contributing factor to the survival of the eastern (Byzantine) portion of the empire.

Question 18

Choice (C) is the correct answer. The Achaemenid Persian Empire expanded to rule regions from Afghanistan to the region of Thrace in northwestern Greece during the period from 550 to 330 B.C.E. before its conquest by Alexander the Great.

Question 19

Choice (D) is the correct answer. The Turkish proverb rejects sedentary agriculture and praises pastoralism and mobility as a path to political power. Choice (D) is the clear analogy to the migrations and conquests of Turkic pastoralists into Anatolia and other regions of the Middle East and Central Asia.

Question 20

Choice (E) is the correct answer. Chastity, poverty, and obedience are core tenets of Christian monasticism.

Question 21

Choice (A) is the correct answer. The Mongols conquered much of Central Asia, China, Persia, the Middle East, and Russia. The Mongols, however, did not conquer Japan or western Europe.

Question 22

Choice (B) is the correct answer. The practices of Sufi Muslims are diverse, but striving for a mystical approach to religious devotion and ritual is central to most Sufi traditions. Answer choice (A) is incorrect because many of the most influential Sufi teachers and orders have rejected strict adherence to a literal interpretation of the Qur'an.

Question 23

Choice (D) is the correct answer. The architecture illustrated in the image derives from the Great Mosque of Djenné in West Africa and was once part of the Mali Empire.

Question 24

Choice (B) is the correct answer. Islam had cemented its religious and political dominance in Central Asia upon the conversion of many Turkic confederations between the mid-tenth and mid-eleventh centuries. By 1500 C.E. the peoples of Central Asia were overwhelmingly Muslim. Answer choice (A) is incorrect because Confucianism's influence in Central Asia was very limited beyond the western provinces of modern China.

Question 25

Choice (B) is the correct answer. During the period 600–1450 C.E., the political features of Japan and western Europe were characterized by decentralization, instability, and the development of numerous small states.

Question 26

Choice (E) is the correct answer. The passage explicitly references the conversion of the king of Kongo and the opportunity to convert the remainder of the country.

Question 27

Choice (C) is the correct answer. The passage suggests that priests sent to sub-Saharan Africa should be allowed to marry, which demonstrates that members within the hierarchy of the Catholic Church were willing to consider modifying traditional church practices to suit local conditions.

Question 28

Choice (D) is the correct answer. Following his issuance of the Edict of Milan in 313 C.E., the Roman Emperor Constantine favored and supported Christianity within the Roman Empire.

Question 29

Choice (E) is the correct answer. The passage describes the Hindu practice of endogamy or marriage only within a social group, a central aspect of the Hindu caste system. Caste groups did not always align directly with professions as the Persian source alleges. However, the principle of endogamy is clearly recognizable within the framework of Hindu caste marital customs.

Question 30

Choice (C) is the correct answer. The passage, a Spanish royal edict from 1593, illustrates mercantilist policies. The edict seeks to regulate and limit trade between Spanish colonial provinces in the Americas and the Philippines and China, most likely to ensure that the Spanish crown could control and tax the lucrative gold and silver trade between the American provinces and China and to ensure that the Crown could secure taxes on expensive luxury goods from China.

Question 31

Choice (C) is the correct answer. The letter from Pope Paschal II in 1099 orders that Christian soldiers be encouraged to hurry eastward to fight in the Crusades and that Christian soldiers must remain there until they succeed. Thus, the inference that Crusaders' numbers were insufficient to hold the territory they had conquered is correct. Between the start of the Crusades in the Levant in 1096 and their end in 1291, historians estimate that only about 150,000 western Europeans settled in the Crusader States, an amount insufficient to maintain long-term political and military dominance. Choice (A) is incorrect because the passage makes no reference to the Muslim inhabitants of conquered territories.

Question 32

Choice (C) is the correct answer. In this negative question requiring the test taker to identify the false option. The Aztec (Mexica) and Inca Empires were not larger than contemporary Eurasian empires such as the Ottoman Empire or Ming China. Since choice (C) is false, it is the correct answer.

Question 33

Choice (E) is the correct answer. In the sixteenth century, the Grand Dukes (*tsars*) of Moscow adopted the concept of the "Third Rome"—originally developed by Bulgarian and Russian Eastern Orthodox monks—to argue that the rulers of Moscow had inherited the imperial legacy of the Roman and Byzantine empires and that Moscow, like Rome and Constantinople before it, served as the imperial capital.

Question 34

Choice (C) is the correct answer. At the time of first contact with Europeans, indigenous Australians were hunter-gatherers who used stone rather than metal tools.

Question 35

Choice (A) is the correct answer. Despite their religious differences, sixteenth-century French Catholic monarchs supported German Lutherans in order to keep the German regions of the Holy Roman Empire politically fragmented and prevent the Habsburg Holy Roman emperors from asserting their dominance over the largely autonomous German princes.

Question 36

Choice (E) is the correct answer. Medieval western European religious elites were most critical of moneylenders because they engaged in usury, the practice of loaning money at interest. Because the Roman Catholic Church published numerous prohibitions against Christian merchants engaging in usury and threatened to excommunicate those who disobeyed, many moneylenders in medieval western Europe were Jews. The association between moneylending and Judaism further stigmatized the practice of moneylending among the Christian clergy.

Question 37

Choice (A) is the correct answer. In 1850 Africans and their descendants, many of whom were of mixed descent, formed the largest part of Brazil's population. Brazil and the Caribbean were the two largest destinations of the Atlantic slave trade.

Question 38

Choice (A) is the correct answer. The availability of coal was the most significant contributing factor to Britain's Industrial Revolution. Choice (E) is incorrect because political institutions in eighteenth-century Great Britain were not very democratic. While members of the House of Commons were elected by a small class of landed property owners and wealthy burghers, the monarchy retained considerable power and nobles held all of the seats in the House of Lords by hereditary right.

Question 39

Choice (C) is the correct answer. The Haitian Revolution (1791–1804) was a successful slave revolt against French rule in Haiti and ended slavery and French colonialism in Haiti.

Question 40

Choice (C) is the correct answer. The Suez Canal was constructed with the support of French engineers and corporate and colonial officers using hundreds of thousands of multinational laborers, including many thousands of forced Egyptian laborers. The British opposed the canal as a threat to their control of the world's transoceanic trade. Thus, the Suez Canal drew Egypt further into European colonial rivalries. Choice (B) is incorrect because Egyptians did not gain control or significantly benefit from the Suez Canal until the mid-twentieth century.

Question 41

Choice (C) is the correct answer. The passage from sixteenth-century Japan describes the arrival of European gunpowder technology and its early spread in Japan. These actions contributed to the unification and centralization of Japan by the Tokugawa shoguns, who subsequently limited the spread and use of firearms in Japan. Choice (A) is incorrect because Japan was not conquered by European colonizers. Choice (E) is incorrect because the growth of the power of the emperor did not begin until after the 1860s and the Meiji Restoration.

Question 42

Choice (C) is the correct answer. The British did not prohibit Indian participation in the colonial bureaucracy. Indeed, the British relied heavily on Indian collaboration in all colonial institutions, which makes choice (C) false and the correct answer. Choice (A) is true and, therefore, incorrect because the Sepoy Mutiny did lead to the transition to direct British rule. Indian princely states were less tightly controlled by the British, making choice (D) true and incorrect.

Question 43

Choice (B) is the correct answer. Since the reign of sultan Murad I (reigned 1362–1389 C.E.) the Ottoman sultans claimed the title of caliph, or spiritual leader of all Muslims. Nevertheless, the Ottoman sultans established policies that tolerated non-Muslim minority groups. The Ottomans granted Christians and Jews *dhimma* status under the *millet* system, which permitted them to practice their religion and retain their traditional laws so long as they paid a poll tax (*jizya*) and submitted to Muslim rule. Although this system was abolished in the nineteenth century, non-Muslim groups continued to be tolerated under Ottoman rule.

Question 44

Choice (C) is the correct answer. The League of Nations was weakened by a variety of factors, one of which was the lack of broad representation beyond the victor nations of the First World War. The United States was the most conspicuous of the missing nations and its unwillingness to join the League of Nations weakened the organization significantly.

Question 45

Choice (E) is the correct answer. The Safavids of Persia, the Ottomans in Turkey, and the Mughals in India were all of Turkic or Mongol descent and established gunpowder conquest states. The Safavid and Mughal governments were not major participants in maritime commerce, making choice (D) incorrect.

Question 46

Choice (D) is the correct answer. The Gold Coast of Africa is located on the Atlantic coastline between the Senegal River and the Niger delta in the region currently occupied by the nation of Ghana in West Africa.

Question 47

Choice (D) is the correct answer. Mao Zedong had to apply Marxist and Leninist theories in China, where industrialization had not yet transformed its economy and where the economy relied on the agricultural production of the peasant population. Thus, Mao stressed that peasants should be the primary revolutionary class of the communist state in China.

Question 48

Choice (A) is the correct answer. The threat of mutually assured destruction through a global nuclear holocaust was the major reason why the Unites States and Soviet Union avoided direct military conflict during the Cold War.

Question 49

Choice (A) is the correct answer. The Mughal emperor Akbar (reigned 1556–1605) pursued a policy of incorporating Hindus into the military and administrative offices of the Mughal state in order to expand its political and economic power. While Akbar emphasized recruiting talented individuals to serve the state, choice (D) is incorrect because he was equally conscious of obtaining support from powerful Muslim and Hindu families regardless of whether they were the most talented people.

Question 50

Choice (B) is the correct answer. Mesoamerican societies strongly emphasized maintaining the cosmic order through ritual. Calendars recorded the times of those rituals, while human sacrifice helped sustain the universe and rewarded the gods that Mesoamericans believed had sacrificed themselves so that humans could live.

Question 51

Choice (D) is the correct answer. Male colonists greatly outnumbered female colonists in the French and Dutch colonial settlements in North America, despite attempts by political authorities to address the gender imbalance. The low number of female settlers limited the potential demographic growth of the French and Dutch colonies and, consequently, the economic, political, and military power of those colonies as well. While the English, French, and Dutch shared many of the same political and economic goals, choice (A) is incorrect because their methods of colonization often differed and because the English colonies were much more politically and economically successful than their French or Dutch counterparts.

Question 52

Choice (B) is the correct answer. Although scholars have hypothesized about the origins of the Harappan language of the Indus Valley and its relationship to other ancient languages such as Sanskrit, Sumerian, and Dravidian languages, they have failed to decipher the language's meaning in the written fragments that survive.

Question 53

Choice (C) is the correct answer. The Western Wall (also known as The Wailing Wall or Kotel) is a segment of the Western Wall of the Second Jewish Temple of Jerusalem, which was constructed by Herod I, the Jewish Roman client king, in 19 B.C.E. The Second Temple and most of the Western Wall were destroyed by the Romans in 70 C.E. following a Jewish revolt against Roman rule.

Question 54

Choice (E) is the correct answer. While scholars debate whether Bantu-speaking peoples were the originators of ironworking in sub-Saharan Africa, archaeological evidence indicates that ironworking spread with the migration of Bantu peoples. Likewise, the migrations of Indo-European peoples such as the Hittites and the Phoenicians also helped spread ironworking techniques throughout Afro-Eurasia.

Question 55

Choice (B) is the correct answer. Romantic nationalists in the nineteenth century argued that the organic cultural, linguistic, and racial unity of the nation provided the state with its authority and gave people the best opportunity to realize their full potential.

Question 56

Choice (E) is the correct answer. As in the nineteenth-century United States, the British Colonial Office refused to recognize the previous territorial claims of indigenous groups. Indigenous peoples in both cases generally lacked large-scale agrarian societies and states, which exacerbated misunderstandings over land use and ownership. In addition, extensive settlement, the clearing of land for agriculture, and the introduction of new species such as horses and cattle severely affected indigenous communities, leading to violence with the European settlers and the forcible relocation of indigenous peoples.

Question 57

Choice (B) is the correct answer. Confucian philosophy stressed that people should preserve their place in the natural order by maintaining their loyalty to their social superiors, honoring and obeying their parents and ancestors, observing traditional customs, and being virtuous in all interpersonal relations.

Question 58

Choice (B) is the correct answer. Seventeenth- and eighteenth-century European monarchs such as Louis XIV of France and Peter the Great of Russia drastically curtailed the authority of their respective nobilities, while creating centralized bureaucracies whose officials were appointed by and dependent on the monarchy. Although some eighteenth-century absolute monarchs such as Frederick II of Prussia and Catherine the Great of Russia embraced certain Enlightenment ideals and patronized some Enlightenment intellectuals, this characteristic was not shared by seventeenth-century absolute monarchs, which makes answer choice (E) incorrect.

Question 59

Choice (D) is the correct answer. While faunal species existed in the Americas and Australasia before the arrival of humans, very few plant or animal species in the Americas or Australasia were suitable for domestication. The north-south axis of, and climatic variations in, the Americas and the oceanic barriers of Australasia also made it difficult for domesticated plants and animals to spread.

Question 60

Choice (E) is the correct answer. The photo shows Muslim pilgrims in the holy city of Mecca participating in the *hajj*, a religious duty that constitutes one of the Five Pillars of Islam.

Question 61

Choice (A) is the correct answer. Following the conquest of parts of the northern Indian subcontinent by Umayyad armies in the early eighth century, Muslims came into contact with Indian science and philosophy. In the early ninth century under the Abbasid Caliphate, two prominent Muslim scholars who studied in the House of Wisdom, Muhammad al-Khwarizmi and Abu Yusuf al-Kindi, wrote treatises on the uses of Indian numerals in mathematical calculations. The Hindu-Arabic numeral system spread to western Europe through contact with Muslim intellectuals in the Mediterranean region and was advocated by famous scholars such as Adelard of Bath and Leonardo de Pisa.

Question 62

Choice (A) is the correct answer. Unlike the Aztecs, the Tang dynasty and many other Chinese dynasties collected tribute from foreign envoys and rulers purely as signs of submission to Chinese hegemony. The gifts presented to the Chinese court frequently were not of great material value. Indeed, after the tribute was presented to the emperor, Chinese emperors often granted gifts to foreign visitors that were of greater material value than the gifts presented to the imperial court.

Question 63

Choice (D) is the correct answer. The term "*Shari'a*" refers to Islamic religious law, which derives its authority and precepts from the Qur'an, the Hadith (sayings of the Prophet Muhammad), the Sunnah (which includes the Hadith and the actions of the Prophet), analogical reasoning (*qiyas*), and the consensus of jurists (*ijma*).

Question 64

Choice (D) is the correct answer. After 1614 the Tokugawa shoguns of Japan suppressed Christianity, expelled most foreigners, and greatly restricted trade with foreign countries. Only Dutch and Chinese vessels were allowed to enter to trade on a small island near Nagasaki.

Question 65

Choice (A) is the correct answer. The chart shows a sharp increase in Jewish populations in Istanbul and Thessaloniki in the period between roughly 1477 and 1535 C.E. This increase is primarily explained by the fact that Ottoman sultans such as Bayezid II resettled Jews expelled from the Iberian Peninsula in 1492 into Ottoman territories.

Question 66

Choice (E) is the correct answer. Sikhism was founded in the late fifteenth century C.E. by Nanak in the Punjab region of India, where both Hindu and Islamic beliefs and cultures came into thorough contact in the period. Sikhism displays Islamic influence in its emphasis on the singularity of God and social equality among all classes. Hindu influence is most evident in the Sikh belief in reincarnation and the need to achieve liberation from it, the emphasis on love (influenced by the Hindu *bhakti* movement), and the numerous references to Hindu gods in the Sikh scriptures.

Question 67

Choice (C) is the correct answer. Chinese influence in Tokugawa Japan was most evident in the influence of Confucian philosophy on the Japanese government. The enactment of the Kansei Edict in 1790 established Neoconfucianism as the state ideology and the ideas of the Chinese Confucian scholar Zhu Xi (died 1200) as the official Confucian philosophy of Japan.

Question 68

Choice (B) is the correct answer. Both the Nazi regime in Germany and the military leaders who controlled Japanese government policy in the 1930s glorified the military capabilities of their states and used war to incite nationalist sentiments and resentments and solidify both regimes' power.

Question 69

Choice (C) is the correct answer. The outbreak of the Protestant Reformation in the early sixteenth century took place at a time when the German princes feared that the powerful emperor Charles V would attempt to usurp their vast privileges and centralize imperial authority. Many princes and nobles in Germany saw Protestantism as an opportunity to resist imperial encroachment and sided with Luther and his allies against Charles V and his supporters. The result was a series of wars that lasted until the Peace of Augsburg in 1555.

Question 70

Choice (E) is the correct answer. In the passage, the slaveholders were arguing that the wealth that slaves used to purchase their freedom was in fact the slaveholder's wealth and, therefore, should not be used to deprive the slaveholder of his "property."

Question 71

Choice (A) is the correct answer. Simón Bolívar was introduced to Enlightenment ideas such as equality, freedom, and the division of powers among different branches of the central government during his studies and travels in Europe between 1800 and 1804. Those ideas and the examples of the American and French revolutions inspired him to lead revolts against Spanish rule in South America in the early nineteenth century. Although Bolívar condemned slavery and received military help from Haitian troops during his struggle against Spain, choice (B) is not the best answer. Bolívar's strongest influences came from the writings of European Enlightenment authors such as Adam Smith, Voltaire, and Montesquieu.

Question 72

Choice (B) is the correct answer. Beginning around 1881 and continuing after the Berlin Conference of 1884 intensified what historians commonly refer to as the Scramble for Africa, French colonial possessions in northern and western Africa expanded considerably to include regions such as Tunisia, Morocco, Sudan, and Nigeria.

Question 73

Choice (D) is the correct answer. The concept of colonial paternalism refers to the arguments made by colonial officials in European colonies in Asia and Africa that European rule was necessary to promote progress and civilization. British officials touted the opening of English language schools in India as a way of improving education across India and thereby reducing social barriers between classes and bridging the linguistic divides caused by India's linguistic diversity. British officials contended that such a measure was necessary for preparing India for eventual independence. Answer choice (A) is incorrect because the justification of the expansion of British rule in southern Africa was not

the result of ideas associated with colonial paternalism. Rather, the British cited the need to protect their settlers, expand their business interests in southern Africa's gold and diamond mines, and secure the Cape of Good Hope's strategic maritime route to India.

Question 74

Choice (D) is the correct answer. Before the First World War, European states entered into often complex political alliances, which historians commonly refer to as the "balance of power system," to attempt to prevent one state from becoming too powerful and dominating others. This system was evident during conflicts such as the Thirty Years' War (1618–1648) and the Napoleonic Wars (1803–1815) and was also prominent in the intricate and often overlapping secret agreements between European powers in the period between German unification and the First World War.

Question 75

Choice (E) is the correct answer. Miguel Hidalgo y Costilla was a prominent leader of Mexico's revolt against Spanish rule, which lasted from 1810 to 1821. Hidalgo was an advocate for Mexico's poor, and the passage demonstrates his attempts to address social inequality through such measures as the introduction of land reforms.

Question 76

Choice (E) is the correct answer. Adam Smith was an Enlightenment economist and intellectual whose book *The Wealth of Nations* further developed the concept of laissez-faire capitalism from the ideas of eighteenth-century French physiocrats such as Vincent de Gournay. Smith argued that the economic marketplace was governed by the "invisible hand" of natural laws and that government intervention not only would hurt commercial enterprise but also would deprive people of liberty.

Question 77

Choice (C) is the correct answer. The Taiping Rebellion (1850–1864) was led by Hong Xiuquan, who was exposed to Christianity in the mid-1830s by European and Chinese missionaries. It was not until the early 1840s that Hong became interested in Christianity, and it was not until the late 1840s that he gained a large following that he would eventually lead into rebellion against the Qing dynasty.

Question 78

Choice (B) is the correct answer. In works such as *Das Kapital* and *The Communist Manifesto*, the German philosopher Karl Marx argued that capitalist exploitation of the working class would lead to a

proletarian revolution, the overthrow of the capitalist system, and the establishment of a communist society that would create a system of economic equality and abolish class distinctions.

Question 79

Choice (E) is the correct answer. Social and political instability in Latin America following the end of Spanish rule throughout most of the region in the nineteenth century led to numerous internal and regional conflicts. Military leaders seized power and used force to attempt to suppress dissent, which contributed to a cycle of revolts, coups, and regional wars that typically ended with another military leader seizing power.

Question 80

Choice (D) is the correct answer. Following its defeat of Japan during the Second World War, the United States drafted and imposed a pacifist constitution on Japan in 1947 that temporarily abolished the Japanese armed forces and forbade the use of war to settle international disputes.

Question 81

Choice (D) is the correct answer. Beginning in Great Britain in the mid-eighteenth century, industrial manufacturing was first introduced in the production of textiles, particularly cotton. Textile production was an easier process to mechanize, and it offered the possibility of developing an export-led economy and a large trade surplus. Finally, because prior cotton manufacturing was relatively small and lacked strong guild organizations, there were fewer labor barriers to reorganizing the production process.

Question 82

Choice (B) is the correct answer. The British government report's recommendation occurred in the context of fierce colonial rivalries between European powers in Asia and Africa and the creation of strategic alliances between European powers, who vowed to defend each other in case of war in Europe.

Question 83

Choice (A) is the correct answer. Nation-states typically turn to international organizations such as the International Monetary Fund (IMF) and the World Bank when they face severe macroeconomic challenges. Accepting a loan from the IMF or the World Bank typically requires economic restructuring based on neoliberal economic principles that stress privatization of state-owned enterprises, trade liberalization, and eliminating price controls, state subsidies, and burdensome regulations.

Question 84

Choice (D) is the correct answer. The Young Turks movement that sought to overthrow the Ottoman Empire and replace it with a constitutional government in the early twentieth century, the Boxer Rebellion (1899–1901) that sought to expel foreign forces from China, and the Zionist movement that sought to create a homeland for Jews in Palestine were all most heavily influenced by nationalist ideas.

Question 85

Choice (E) is the correct answer. Ethiopia was never a French colony, though it lost its independence to Italy between 1936 and 1941. Haiti, Vietnam, Algeria, and Senegal were all former French colonies.

Question 86

Choice (E) is the correct answer. The quotation comes from *The Communist Manifesto*, which was written by Karl Marx and Frederich Engels in 1848. Of the people listed in the answer choices, the one most likely to agree with that statement would have been Vladimir Lenin. Lenin led communist forces during the Russian Revolution of 1917, which resulted in the overthrow of the czarist government and the creation of the Soviet Union as a communist state.

Question 87

Choice (C) is the correct answer. Nelson Mandela became a leader of the African National Congress, a South African political organization that sought to end apartheid in South Africa. After being released from prison in 1990, Mandela worked with South African president F. W. de Klerk to negotiate an end to apartheid. In 1994 Mandela was elected president of South Africa following the nation's first multiracial elections.

Question 88

Choice (A) is the correct answer. On August 11, 1947, Muhammad Ali Jinnah, the leader of the Muslim League of India and the first governor-general of Pakistan, addressed the newly formed constituent assembly of Pakistan in Karachi. Jinnah claimed, as he had previously, that although the partition of India was not necessarily desirable, it was the only practical method for resolving the "constitutional problem" of how to create a politically and religiously equitable state for Hindus and Muslims.

Question 89

Choice (B) is the correct answer. The Iranian Revolution (January 1978 to February 1979) emerged in response to the oppressive and corrupt state of the Pahlavi dynasty of Iran. The revolution resulted in the establishment of a theocratic government in Iran.

Question 90

Choice (E) is the correct answer. Although radical leftist movements emerged in Nicaragua and El Salvador in the 1980s and early 1990s, none of those movements were purely communist and none ever led to the establishment of a communist government in North America.

Question 91

Choice (C) is the correct answer. The Chinese Communist Party under Mao Zedong collectivized agriculture and private property and concentrated all industry under state control. However, the Chinese Communist Party under Mao Zedong did not promote private entrepreneurship.

Question 92

Choice (A) is the correct answer. Lech Walesa became the leader of the trade union movement called Solidarity that utilized nonviolent tactics to pressure the Polish communist government to agree to social and economic reforms. Solidarity's efforts contributed to the introduction of parliamentary elections in 1989 and the end of communist rule in Poland.

Question 93

Choice (D) is the correct answer. Mikhail Gorbachev's introduction of the policies of *perestroika* ("restructuring") and *glasnost* ("openness") intended to reform the Soviet economy and society by introducing free-market reforms and allowing individuals and the press more freedom. However, the reforms exacerbated Soviet economic uncompetitiveness, unleashed social and ethnic tensions within the Soviet state, and contributed to the loss of Soviet satellite states in Eastern Europe. These developments led to the collapse of the Soviet Union in 1991.

Question 94

Choice (B) is the correct answer. The Cuban missile crisis of 1962 resulted from Cold War tensions between the United States and the Soviet Union. The Soviet Union had installed ballistic missiles in Cuba, and the United States attempted to prevent further missile deliveries and the withdrawal of missiles already in place in Cuba through a naval blockade.

Question 95

Choice (C) is the correct answer. The 1994 genocide in Rwanda, which led to the deaths of 800,000 people, was the result of conflict between Hutu and Tutsi ethnic groups.

World History – Practice Test 2

Practice Helps

The test that follows is an actual, previously administered SAT Subject Test in World History. To get an idea of what it's like to take this test, practice under conditions that are much like those of an actual test administration.

- Set aside an hour when you can take the test uninterrupted.

- Sit at a desk or table with no other books or papers. Dictionaries, other books, or notes are not allowed in the test room.

- Tear out an answer sheet from the back of this book and fill it in just as you would on the day of the test. One answer sheet can be used for up to three Subject Tests.

- Read the instructions that precede the practice test. During the actual administration, you will be asked to read them before answering test questions.

- Use a clock or kitchen timer to time yourself.

- After you finish the practice test, read the sections "How to Score the SAT Subject Test in World History" and "How Did You Do on the Subject Test in World History?"

- The appearance of the answer sheet in this book may differ from the answer sheet you see on test day.

WORLD HISTORY TEST

The top portion of the page of the answer sheet that you will use to take the World History Test must be filled in exactly as illustrated below. When your supervisor tells you to fill in the circle next to the name of the test you are about to take, mark your answer sheet as shown.

○ Literature	○ Mathematics Level 1	○ German	○ Chinese Listening	○ Japanese Listening
○ Biology E	○ Mathematics Level 2	○ Italian	○ French Listening	○ Korean Listening
○ Biology M	○ U.S. History	○ Latin	○ German Listening	○ Spanish Listening
○ Chemistry	● World History	○ Modern Hebrew		
○ Physics	○ French	○ Spanish		

Background Questions: ① ② ③ ④ ⑤ ⑥ ⑦ ⑧ ⑨

After filling in the circle next to the name of the test you are taking, locate the Background Questions box on your answer sheet (as shown above). This is where you will answer the following Background Questions on your answer sheet.

BACKGROUND QUESTIONS

Please answer the two questions below by filling in the appropriate circle in the Background Questions box on your answer sheet. <u>The information you provide is for statistical purposes only and will not affect your test score.</u>

Question I

How many semesters of world history, world cultures, or European history have you taken from grade 9 to the present? (If you are taking a course this semester, count it as a full semester.) Fill in only <u>one</u> circle of circles 1- 4.

- One semester or less   —Fill in circle 1.
- Two semesters   —Fill in circle 2.
- Three semesters   —Fill in circle 3.
- Four or more semesters   —Fill in circle 4.

Question II

For the courses in world history, world cultures, or European history you have taken, which of the following geographical areas did you study? Fill in <u>all</u> of the circles that apply.

- Africa   —Fill in circle 5.
- Asia   —Fill in circle 6.
- Europe   —Fill in circle 7.
- Latin America   —Fill in circle 8.
- Middle East   —Fill in circle 9.

When the supervisor gives the signal, turn the page and begin the World History Test. There are 100 numbered circles on the answer sheet and 95 questions in the World History Test. Therefore, use only circles 1 to 95 for recording your answers.

Directions: Each of the questions or incomplete statements below is followed by five suggested answers or completions. Select the one that is best in each case and then fill in the corresponding circle on the answer sheet.

Note: The World History Test uses the chronological designations B.C.E. (before common era) and C.E. (common era). These labels correspond to B.C. (before Christ) and A.D. (anno Domini), which are used in some world history textbooks.

1. Which of the following features of human societies in the Paleolithic era has left NO direct physical evidence?

   (A) Burial customs
   (B) Big game hunting
   (C) The making of stone tools
   (D) Family and kinship structures
   (E) The creation of art

2. Which of the following geographic features was the most important to the development of the first urbanized societies?

   (A) Mountain ranges
   (B) Rain forests
   (C) Lakes and streams
   (D) River valleys
   (E) Deserts

3. Major shifts in population patterns in northern and central Africa circa 3000–1000 B.C.E. occurred mostly as a result of which of the following?

   (A) The formation of Lake Chad
   (B) The desertification of the Sahara
   (C) The fall of the Bantu dynasty
   (D) The spread of the tsetse fly from Asia
   (E) The beginning of the Egyptian slave trade

4. Which of the following describes a difference between the Egyptian and Mesopotamian civilizations?

   (A) Egyptian city-states were loosely bound by shared cultural traditions, whereas Mesopotamian rule was maintained by a centralized authority.
   (B) Egyptian pharaohs considered themselves to be living gods, whereas Mesopotamian rulers considered themselves to be intermediaries between humans and the gods.
   (C) Egyptian engineers constructed vast irrigation channels to water crops, whereas Mesopotamian rivers were easily predictable in their flooding.
   (D) Egyptian pyramids were primarily used for ancestor worship, whereas Mesopotamian ziggurats were primarily used for mass burials.
   (E) Egyptians traded across broad expanses to gain goods and ideas, whereas Mesopotamians had limited trade because of geographic barriers.

GO ON TO THE NEXT PAGE

5. Which of the following was a major consequence of the domestication of plants and animals during the Neolithic Revolution?

   (A) Dramatic increases in food production that led to larger human populations
   (B) Increased leisure time, since less time was needed to procure food
   (C) Increased tendency to live in extended family units in order to protect livestock and work the land
   (D) Decreased levels of conflict due to the greater availability of food supplies
   (E) Decreased levels of disease due to better nutrition

6. Most of what is known of the ancient Indus River valley civilizations comes from

   (A) the Harappan written language
   (B) excavations of cities like Mohenjo Daro
   (C) the earliest Hindu religious works
   (D) Buddhist sutras
   (E) Egyptian trade records dealing with the area

7. Isolated regions of the premodern world may have had a better chance than well-connected areas to avoid which of the following?

   (A) Soil depletion
   (B) Oppressive rule
   (C) Famine
   (D) Epidemics
   (E) Gender inequalities

8. The discovery of oracle bones was significant for the study of China during the Shang dynasty because

   (A) they confirmed the existence of many earlier dynasties
   (B) they showed dramatic evidence of human sacrifice
   (C) they helped to explain the extinction of many large mammals
   (D) they contained the earliest examples of the Chinese writing system
   (E) they laid the groundwork for the Confucian belief system

© Art Resource, NY # ART133009

9. Monumental basalt heads, such as the one above, are characteristic of which of the following civilizations?

   (A) Byzantine
   (B) Babylonian
   (C) Mauryan
   (D) Olmec
   (E) Qin

10. Which of the following statements is one of the Buddha's Four Noble Truths?

   (A) Know that life is full of suffering.
   (B) Be willing to sacrifice your life for your children.
   (C) Remember the importance of filial piety.
   (D) Pursue moderation in all things.
   (E) Love your neighbor as yourself.

GO ON TO THE NEXT PAGE ➡

11. "According as a man acts and walks in the path of life, so he becomes. He that does good becomes good; he that does evil becomes evil."

    From the Upanishads, a Hindu religious text, first millennium B.C.E.

    The passage above illustrates which of the following basic concepts in Hinduism?

    (A) Atman
    (B) Dharma
    (C) Karma
    (D) Moksha
    (E) Samsara

12. Sanskrit, Persian, Greek, and Latin belong to which of the following language groups?

    (A) Altaic
    (B) Dravidian
    (C) Indo-European
    (D) Semitic
    (E) Sinitic

Copyright German Archaeological Institute Cairo

13. The sculpture above, from the Temple of Luxor in Egypt, was commissioned by Alexander the Great of Macedon after his conquest of Egypt in 332 B.C.E. and depicts Alexander (left) in the presence of the god Amun (right). The image suggests that

    (A) Alexander imposed Macedonian religious practices on his Egyptian subjects
    (B) Egyptians worshipped Alexander as the greatest deity in their pantheon
    (C) Macedonians and Egyptians cooperated as equals in the overthrow of their common Persian enemies
    (D) Alexander used local religious symbols and artistic imagery to legitimize his rule over Egypt
    (E) Greek artistic forms replaced Egyptian ones as a result of the Macedonian conquest

GO ON TO THE NEXT PAGE

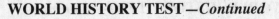

14. The Maya civilization flourished in which of the following present-day countries?

    (A) Mexico, Guatemala, and Honduras
    (B) The United States, Mexico, and Guatemala
    (C) Mexico, Cuba, and Belize
    (D) Guatemala, Belize, and Peru
    (E) Guatemala, Belize, and Brazil

Questions 15-16 refer to the passage below.

If anyone presumes to kill a native freeman of our people or a servant of the king, let him make restitution for the crime by the shedding of his blood . . . If anyone kills a slave, a trained house servant or messenger, let him pay compensation of sixty gold pieces and a fine of twelve. If anyone kills a slave who is either a ploughman or a swineherd, let him pay thirty gold pieces . . . For killing a skilled goldsmith, let him pay two hundred. For killing a silversmith, one hundred. For killing a blacksmith, fifty. For killing a carpenter, forty.

> Laws of King Gundobad of the Burgundians, Western Europe, ca. 475 C.E.

15. The law code quoted above asserts the principle that

    (A) everyone is equal before the law
    (B) house servants are more valuable than metalworkers
    (C) farmers are more valuable than herders
    (D) free people are innocent until proved guilty
    (E) native freemen rank above skilled slaves

16. The provisions of the law code quoted above resemble the earlier Code of Hammurabi in that

    (A) capital punishment is replaced with monetary compensation
    (B) crimes against women are punished more severely than are crimes against men
    (C) the state is removed from the resolution of capital crimes
    (D) punishment is based on the status of the victim
    (E) punishment is based on the status of the criminal

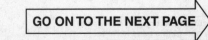
GO ON TO THE NEXT PAGE

17. "For [the last] three thousand years China
[has] lived in seclusion, early developing and
long retaining a distinct type of civilization.
A fairly unified Chinese Empire existed as early
as 1000 B.C.E. The Chinese system of writing was
being developed as early."

    World History Today, a survey of world history
    published in the United States, 1927

    For most world historians today, the passage
    above would appear

    (A) factually correct and still widely accepted as
    an interpretation of early Chinese history
    (B) wrong in its treatment of China as a "distinct
    type of civilization"
    (C) characteristic of views currently held by most
    Chinese historians of China
    (D) to be a surprisingly uncommon assumption
    about Chinese history
    (E) factually incorrect in its view that China
    existed in seclusion for 3,000 years

18. Which of the following was a major food source
for the pre-Columbian societies of the Andes, the
Yucatán, and the Central Valley of Mexico?

    (A) Wheat
    (B) Potatoes
    (C) Maize
    (D) Cattle
    (E) Rice

19. In the period from 1000 C.E. to 1500 C.E., the
largest states in sub-Saharan Africa were located

    (A) in the savannas of West Africa
    (B) along the coasts of the Indian Ocean
    (C) in tropical rain forests
    (D) in the Great Lakes region of East Africa
    (E) along the southern Atlantic coast

20. Compared to other empires of the same period
(circa 200 B.C.E.–500 C.E.), the Roman Empire
was unusual because

    (A) it granted conquered peoples partial or full
    citizenship
    (B) it mandated primary education for children
    (C) the head of the state was also the chief priest
    of the state religion
    (D) the aristocracy was expected to make
    substantial sacrifices for the good of
    the state
    (E) the government was frequently concerned
    about land tenure and the plight of small
    farmers

21. The state religion of the Sasanid Empire
in Persia was

    (A) Shinto
    (B) Zoroastrianism
    (C) Islam
    (D) Buddhism
    (E) Eastern Orthodox Christianity

22. In Dutch and German, oranges are called
"Chinese apples"; in French and English, the
word for "peach" derives from the Latin word
meaning "Persian." These linguistic facts suggest
which of the following?

    (A) Oranges and apples are of Middle Eastern
    origin.
    (B) Oranges and apples are of Chinese origin.
    (C) Chinese and Persians were the great fruit
    sellers of medieval Europe.
    (D) Both peaches and oranges originated in the
    same place.
    (E) The Silk Road helped spread the cultivation
    of fruits.

GO ON TO THE NEXT PAGE

23. Which of the following is a major difference between Islam and Hinduism?

    (A) Islam sanctions a hierarchical stratum of priests, while Hinduism stresses the direct relationship between believers and God.
    (B) The Muslim community has remained unified and free of sectarian conflict, while Hinduism is beset by sectarian divisions.
    (C) Islam rejects the idea of proselytizing, while Hinduism encourages its practitioners to convert nonbelievers.
    (D) Islam stresses the equality of all believers, while Hinduism embraces social stratifications.
    (E) In most cases, Islam has spread to new areas through migration, while Hinduism has spread to new areas through conquest and commercial exchange.

24. One reason that early Buddhism and Christianity were particularly appealing to women was that both religions

    (A) had female goddesses
    (B) taught that women could attain the same spiritual rewards as men could
    (C) granted women a dominant role in spiritual matters
    (D) allowed women to preside over public rituals as priestesses
    (E) offered strong critiques of the male-dominated governments in their areas of origin

25. The Council of Chalcedon in 451 C.E. resulted in declarations that

    (A) the use of human images in Christian churches was heretical
    (B) the patriarch of Constantinople had authority superior to that of the pope of Rome
    (C) Jesus Christ had both a human and a divine nature
    (D) St. Paul should be venerated as the second founder of Christianity
    (E) the Catholic Church should organize expeditions to combat Islam

26. In which of the following did the majority of people convert from one religion to another as a result of a political change?

    (A) In northern India under the Delhi Sultanate
    (B) In Palestine under Roman rule
    (C) In Persia under Mongol rule
    (D) In Greece under Ottoman rule
    (E) In Egypt under 'Abbasid and Fatimid rule

27. The introduction of silk production to the Byzantine Empire in the sixth century is an example of what historical process?

    (A) Rediscovery of lost technology
    (B) Independent technological invention
    (C) Spread of new technology by military conquest
    (D) Cross-cultural transfer of technology
    (E) Spread of new technology as a result of demographic change

28. Beginning in the 1200s C.E., Arab merchant influence in Southeast Asia was particularly strong in the

    (A) Irrawaddy delta
    (B) Central Highlands of Vietnam
    (C) Mekong delta
    (D) Strait of Malacca
    (E) northern Philippines

29. Which of the following dynasties is credited with the revival of ancient learning in eighth- and ninth-century Western Europe?

    (A) Merovingian
    (B) Carolingian
    (C) Angevin
    (D) Macedonian
    (E) Capetian

GO ON TO THE NEXT PAGE

30. The geographical placement of Teotihuacán, Tenochtitlán, and Mexico City suggests which of the following?

   (A) Sites that were especially suitable for cities attracted new settlements over and over again.
   (B) The Spanish built cities in Mexico that were larger than any that had come before.
   (C) Defense against invasion was the most important consideration for the Native Americans and the Spanish.
   (D) Early Native American cities were usually constructed along the banks of major rivers.
   (E) Native Americans learned their architectural skills from the Spanish.

31. The Byzantine emperor Justinian's accomplishments included

   (A) establishing new trade routes to India and China
   (B) defeating the Huns
   (C) conquering the Holy Land
   (D) founding the Holy Roman Empire
   (E) codifying Roman civil law

32. The great extent and speed of the Muslim conquests during the seventh century C.E. can be explained by all of the following EXCEPT

   (A) popular dissatisfaction with Byzantine rule in Syria and Egypt
   (B) conflict between the Byzantine and Persian empires
   (C) Muslim rulers' policy of religious tolerance vis-à-vis their Christian and Jewish subjects
   (D) religious sanction for territorial conquest exemplified by the idea of *jihad*
   (E) lack of sectarian and doctrinal divisions among adherents of Islam

33. The most important deity of the Inca rulers was the

   (A) fertility goddess
   (B) mother goddess
   (C) sun god
   (D) moon god
   (E) wind god

Questions 34-35 are based on the following passage.

First they did their homage thus, the count [of Flanders] asked if he was willing to become completely his man, and the other replied, "I am willing," and with clasped hands, surrounded by the hands of the count, they were bound together by a kiss. Secondly, he who had done homage gave his fealty to the representative of the count in these words, "I promise on my faith that I will in future be faithful to Count William, and will observe my homage to him completely against all persons in good faith and without deceit." Thirdly, he took his oath to this upon the relics of the saints.

Chronicle, northern France, 1127 C.E.

34. The passage suggests that French society in the twelfth century was organized and governed primarily through

   (A) bureaucratic routine
   (B) obedience to religious figures
   (C) democratic assemblies
   (D) personal bonds
   (E) absolute monarchy

35. The relationship established by the ceremony in the passage is most similar to the relationship between

   (A) an Athenian citizen and the archon
   (B) a Roman senator and the consul
   (C) a mandarin and the Chinese emperor
   (D) an American plantation slave and master
   (E) a samurai and daimyo in Japan

36. From its consolidation in the third century B.C.E., the Great Wall of China's primary purpose was to serve as a

   (A) demarcation line between agricultural and pastoral China
   (B) defense against nomadic invaders
   (C) boundary between China and neighboring states to the south
   (D) location for international markets
   (E) testing site for new Chinese weapons

GO ON TO THE NEXT PAGE

© Bruno Morandi/Age Fotostock # F33-588586

37. Which of the following belief systems is reflected in the architecture of the Javanese temple of Borobodur, shown above?

    (A) Islam
    (B) Hinduism
    (C) Orthodox Christianity
    (D) Buddhism
    (E) Confucianism

GO ON TO THE NEXT PAGE

© Erich Lessing / Art Resource, NY

38. The architecture of the building pictured above
    shows a mixture of which two religious traditions?

    (A) Christian and Hindu
    (B) Christian and Jewish
    (C) Christian and Muslim
    (D) Muslim and Hindu
    (E) Muslim and Jewish

GO ON TO THE NEXT PAGE

39. The political and intellectual influences of the Tang dynasty (618–907 C.E.) were most conspicuous in which of the following?

    (A) East Africa
    (B) Carolingian Europe
    (C) Gupta India
    (D) Nara Japan
    (E) Sasanid Persia

40. The 'Abbasid caliphate differed from the Umayyad caliphate in that the 'Abbasids

    (A) were Arabs and used Arabic in their court
    (B) incorporated more Persian influence in their government
    (C) treated Medina and Mecca as holy places
    (D) controlled the lands of the former Persian Empire
    (E) saw Islam as their source of political legitimacy

41. "The island of Java is becoming more and more famous for its blessed state throughout the world. 'Only Jambudwipa and Java,' so people say, 'are mentioned for their superiority, good countries as they are, because of the multitude of men experienced in the doctrine'. . . . First comes the Illustrious Brahmarajah, the excellent brahmin, an irreproachable, great poet and expert of the religious traditions; he has complete knowledge of the speculative as well as all the other philosophies. . . . Then comes the holy Shamana, very pious, virtuous, experienced in the Vedas and the six pure activities."

    The *Nagarakertagama*, Javanese epic poem, circa 1360 C.E.

    The passage above is evidence of

    (A) China's cultural and religious influence in Korea and Vietnam
    (B) Islam's spread over the Malay Peninsula
    (C) Buddhism's spread to Tibet and Central Asia
    (D) India's cultural and religious influence in Southeast Asia
    (E) India's military and political influence in Sri Lanka

42. Which of the following best describes a policy pursued by the emperors of the Song dynasty in China?

    (A) They continued the Tang emperors' support for foreign religions.
    (B) They strengthened China's political control over Korea.
    (C) They attempted to invade and conquer Japan.
    (D) They reinvigorated state support for Chinese cultural and philosophical traditions.
    (E) They completely overhauled China's existing trade relationships with the outside world.

43. Which of the following best describes a unique aspect of the worldview of the Jains?

    (A) Compassion for fellow human beings
    (B) Fasting frequently
    (C) Giving of alms regularly
    (D) Reverence for all life
    (E) Social justice for all

44. The kinds of scholarly activities pursued by Muslim scientists in the early 'Abbasid period (800–1000 C.E.) were most closely paralleled by the kinds of scholarly activities pursued by scientists in which of the following?

    (A) The Tokugawa shogunate at its height
    (B) The late Byzantine Empire
    (C) The Inca Empire before the arrival of the Spanish
    (D) Ancient Egypt before the Hyksos invasions
    (E) The European Renaissance

GO ON TO THE NEXT PAGE

© Mary Evans Picture Library/Alamy # AY2M7F

45. The image above was most probably made in response to which of the following?

(A) Peasant revolts in France and England in the fourteenth century
(B) The decimation of the population in France during the Hundred Years' War
(C) The European experience of the Black Death
(D) The spread of smallpox among the Amerindians
(E) A famine caused by the Little Ice Age in the early fourteenth century

GO ON TO THE NEXT PAGE

46. Based on the geographic extent of their migrations, which of the following groups were the most successful colonizers of new territories in the period before 1500 C.E.?

    (A) Spaniards
    (B) Vikings
    (C) Polynesians
    (D) Chinese
    (E) Indonesians

47. In the period 1500 to 1800, European merchants paid for Chinese goods primarily with

    (A) slaves
    (B) opium
    (C) tea
    (D) silver
    (E) firearms and ammunition

48. The coming of Islam to India marked a major historical change in that

    (A) it coincided with the final decline of Buddhism in the region
    (B) it coincided with the decline of Christianity in the region
    (C) Islam quickly became the majority religion in most regions of South Asia
    (D) Islam quickly became the most important cultural element in Indian civilization
    (E) Islam faced no competition from other religious practices and faiths in the region

49. In the fifteenth century, the building of roads paved with stone was most characteristic of which of the following Amerindian societies?

    (A) Inca
    (B) Maya
    (C) Anasazi
    (D) Mississippian
    (E) Iroquois

50. Vasco da Gama was a European explorer who

    (A) conquered the Inca Empire and made it part of New Spain
    (B) searched for the fountain of youth in Florida
    (C) circumnavigated the world before dying in the Philippines
    (D) helped establish Portugal as a dominant commercial power in the Indian Ocean
    (E) explored the coast of Brazil

51. Which of the following places the navigators in proper chronological order?

    (A) Columbus, Magellan, Zheng He
    (B) Zheng He, Magellan, Columbus
    (C) Zheng He, Columbus, Magellan
    (D) Magellan, Columbus, Zheng He
    (E) Magellan, Zheng He, Columbus

52. All of the following societies were heavily influenced by Chinese culture EXCEPT

    (A) Mongol
    (B) Russian
    (C) Japanese
    (D) Korean
    (E) Vietnamese

53. Martin Luther, John Calvin, and Henry VIII of England had which of the following in common?

    (A) They all rejected the authority of the Pope.
    (B) They all stressed the authority of the clergy over individual conscience.
    (C) They all demanded that the clergy be celibate.
    (D) They all forbade divorce.
    (E) They all allied themselves with the common people against their rulers.

54. Which of the following most weakened the Spanish Empire in the sixteenth century?

    (A) The conquest of Mexico
    (B) The defeat of the Armada
    (C) The union with Portugal
    (D) The creation of the Jesuit order
    (E) The development of effective, mobile artillery

55. The Tokugawa shogunate in Japan (1603–1867) enforced a period of isolation from the rest of the world primarily in response to

    (A) a heavy deficit in its trade with European nations
    (B) fear of Chinese immigration
    (C) fear of political and religious influence of European powers
    (D) piracy along its coastline
    (E) the expulsion of Japanese Buddhist missionaries from Europe

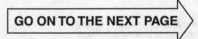
GO ON TO THE NEXT PAGE

Warriors of the Esmeraldas, 1599 (oil on canvas) by Adrian Sanchez Galque (fl. 16th century)
Museo de America, Madrid, Spain/The Bridgeman Art Library

56. The painting of the leaders of the Maroon settlement of
Esmeraldas (in present-day Ecuador) suggests all of the
following EXCEPT:

(A) They have removed their hats indicating their economic
dependence on Spain.

(B) They are adorned with Native American jewelry to
demonstrate their wealth.

(C) They are wearing European upper-class clothing to assert
their equality with Spanish colonial authorities.

(D) They are bearing spears in order to demonstrate their
military prowess.

(E) They are interested in presenting themselves as worthy of
being negotiated with.

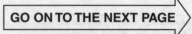GO ON TO THE NEXT PAGE

57. Which of the following food crops native to the Americas came to be most widely cultivated in Africa in the period from 1600 to 1900 ?

(A) Manioc and maize
(B) Sweet potatoes and beans
(C) Potatoes and tomatoes
(D) Peanuts and pineapples
(E) Chilies and squashes

58. Between 1600 and 1900 which religion spread most rapidly among residents of Africa?

(A) Buddhism
(B) Christianity
(C) Hinduism
(D) Islam
(E) Judaism

59. Who led the Roundheads in the English Civil War and set up a Commonwealth in place of the monarchy?

(A) Charles I
(B) Oliver Cromwell
(C) Thomas More
(D) James I
(E) William of Orange

60. "The decline of the Safavids and Mughals [in the first half of the eighteenth century] let loose a great wave of turbulence which stretched from Mesopotamia in the west to Thailand in the east. The main beneficiaries were the European powers, perched hungrily on the periphery."

        C. A. Bayly, British historian, 2004

Which of the following best summarizes the implicit argument made in the passage?

(A) European imperialism caused the collapse of the Safavid and Mughal empires.
(B) European imperialists gobbled up the Safavid and Mughal empires.
(C) For two centuries the Safavid and Mughal empires had fought a losing battle against Europeans.
(D) After 1750, Muslim states were no match militarily against Christian states.
(E) Only after the decline of the Safavid and Mughal empires were Europeans in a position to expand in southern Asia.

61. The culture of Russian elites was dramatically altered by the introduction of western European practices during the reign of

(A) Ivan the Terrible
(B) Nicholas II
(C) Peter the Great
(D) Alexander I
(E) Prince Yaroslav of Kiev

62. The French Revolutionary governments of 1789 to 1799 accomplished all of the following EXCEPT:

(A) They reformed government finances.
(B) They reorganized the army.
(C) They redrew the administrative districts of France.
(D) They granted political equality to women.
(E) They created a republican form of government.

63. In the eighteenth century, the most financially profitable European colonies were located in

(A) the Caribbean
(B) North America
(C) Central America
(D) East Asia
(E) Africa

64. Which of the following was the largest Muslim empire between 1750 and 1900 C.E.?

(A) 'Abbasid
(B) Umayyad
(C) Mongol
(D) Manchu
(E) Ottoman

GO ON TO THE NEXT PAGE

65. The storming of the Bastille in 1789 in Paris was historically significant primarily because

(A) it gave the rioting crowds in Paris access to weapons and ammunition with which to fight King Louis XVI's soldiers

(B) it enabled the working-class residents of Paris to establish a commune with shared property and guaranteed wages

(C) the capture of the fortress represented a symbolic attack on King Louis XVI's authority as an absolute monarch

(D) the prisoners held in the dungeons were freed after unfair prosecutions by Maximilien Robespierre during the Reign of Terror

(E) Napoleon Bonaparte gained fame in the fighting around the Bastille

66. Which of the following former European colonies had economies that depended strongly on African slave labor in the decades after independence?

(A) Guatemala and Mexico

(B) Brazil and the United States

(C) Canada and Colombia

(D) Bolivia and Peru

(E) Argentina and Chile

67. All of the following statements describe significant effects of Napoleon Bonaparte's rule EXCEPT:

(A) Conservative governments across Europe joined forces to defeat Napoleon.

(B) Napoleon's campaigns brought the ideas of the French Revolution to many parts of Europe.

(C) Napoleon's wars allowed some colonies to rebel against their European rulers.

(D) Napoleon's codification of French laws had a long-term impact on many European legal systems.

(E) Napoleon's support for legal emancipation for women inspired the early feminist movement.

68. Which of the following most accurately describes a trend in world population during the period 1750–1914 ?

(A) It increased slowly.

(B) It only increased in nonindustrialized areas.

(C) It showed a net decrease.

(D) It remained about the same.

(E) It increased rapidly.

69. Which of the following countries won its independence without warfare in the early nineteenth century?

(A) Mexico

(B) Peru

(C) The United States

(D) Haiti

(E) Brazil

GO ON TO THE NEXT PAGE

Questions 70-71 are based on the passage below.

The coffee plant was first introduced by the Dutch early in the eighteenth century and has since formed one of the articles of their exclusive monopoly. The labor by which it is planted and its produce collected is included among the oppressions of forced services of the natives. . . . [T]his shrub usurped the soil destined for the subsistence of the people, and every other kind of cultivation was made subservient to it. The coffee culture in the Sunda districts has sometimes been so severely exacted that it deprived the unfortunate peasants of the time necessary to raise food. Many thus perished by famine while others have fled to the mountains, where, raising a scanty subsistence, or dependent on the roots of the forests, they congratulated themselves on their escape from the reach of their oppressors.

Thomas Raffles, British official, early 1800s

70. The passage is referring to coffee production in

(A) Brazil
(B) India
(C) Indonesia
(D) Jamaica
(E) Ethiopia

71. The agricultural labor system described by Raffles most closely resembles the system used in the production of

(A) potatoes in Ireland in the early 1800s
(B) wheat on the Great Plains of North America in the late 1800s
(C) rice in Japan in the late 1800s
(D) rubber in the Congo Free State in the early 1900s
(E) wool in Australia in the early 1900s

72. In the first half of the nineteenth century, which of the following political developments occurred in both Great Britain and the United States?

(A) A major expansion of voting rights for men
(B) The rapid growth of anti-immigrant parties
(C) The abolition of slavery
(D) Growing demands for regional autonomy
(E) The establishment of an independent judiciary

73. Which of the following authors wrote vivid portraits of the economic miseries of the factory system in nineteenth-century England?

(A) Mary Wollstonecraft
(B) William Wordsworth
(C) Percy B. Shelley
(D) Jane Austen
(E) Charles Dickens

74. All of the following strongly contributed to Hitler's rise to power EXCEPT

(A) German resentment over the terms of the Treaty of Versailles
(B) the economic suffering of Germans in the period after the First World War
(C) fear of communism
(D) the growth of a pacifist movement in Germany
(E) the spread of radio technology

GO ON TO THE NEXT PAGE

75. Which of the following is an accurate statement concerning European imperialism in Africa in the late nineteenth century?

(A) Very little of the African continent was actually claimed by European states.

(B) The European powers scrambled for control over African territory.

(C) Africans put up little resistance to colonial rule.

(D) The only nations that claimed African territories were Britain, France, and Germany.

(E) The European powers generally tried to establish representative governments in their African colonies.

76. The Meiji Restoration involved the overthrow of which of the following ruling governments?

(A) The Qing dynasty in China

(B) The Tokugawa shogunate in Japan

(C) The Le dynasty in Vietnam

(D) The Gupta dynasty in India

(E) The Safavid dynasty in Iran

77. Ethiopia, Japan, and Siam had which of the following in common during the period of European imperialism in the late 1800s and early 1900s?

(A) They all rejected Christianity and Christian influences.

(B) They all attempted to expand their territory to better defend themselves against European imperialism.

(C) They all developed elites that owed their positions to European support.

(D) They all managed to avoid direct European domination.

(E) They all abandoned their traditional monarchies and replaced them with representative governments.

78. The Russian Bolshevik Revolution of 1917 and the Chinese Revolution of 1911 were both immediately followed by

(A) a long period of civil war

(B) a period of repression

(C) an adoption of an expansionist foreign policy

(D) an opening of trade relations

(E) an eventual rehabilitation of the deposed elites

79. The Balfour Declaration of 1917 promised British support for

(A) Mustafa Kemal to secularize Turkey after the First World War

(B) the establishment of a Saudi kingdom in Arabia

(C) the establishment of a Jewish homeland in Palestine

(D) self-determination among the peoples in Southwest Asia

(E) the League of Nations to establish mandates out of territories of the former Ottoman Empire

80. Aung San Suu Kyi was awarded the Nobel Peace Prize in 1991 for her

(A) humanitarian efforts against the communist regime of Myanmar (Burma)

(B) nonviolent struggle for democracy and human rights in Myanmar (Burma)

(C) revolution to overthrow the military dictatorship of Myanmar (Burma)

(D) leadership of the nonaligned movement during the Cold War

(E) success in leading peaceful political change in Myanmar (Burma)

GO ON TO THE NEXT PAGE

81. The economy of the Soviet Union was largely unaffected by the Great Depression of the 1930s because it

   (A) had few economic ties to the global capitalist economy
   (B) had an unlimited supply of labor, which allowed it to grow despite the Depression
   (C) was in the process of extreme militarization that created jobs and stimulated its industry
   (D) had an agriculture-based economy and therefore was not affected by downturns in the global industrial economy
   (E) was largely dependent on the export of petroleum, which remained in strong demand

82. The Mexican Revolution of 1910 and the Russian Bolshevik Revolution of 1917 were similar in that both

   (A) contributed to the fall of strongly authoritarian governments
   (B) began following national defeats in war
   (C) were started by outside powers
   (D) had leaders who sought to imitate the goals of the American Revolution
   (E) immediately led to other revolutions in neighboring countries

83. Which of the following most accurately describes a major effect of the First World War (1914–1918) in European colonies?

   (A) The war contributed to the establishment of many anticolonial movements.
   (B) The war resulted in the immediate success of several anticolonial movements in achieving independence.
   (C) The war led to decreased support for most anticolonial movements as colonial inhabitants rallied in support of their ruling countries.
   (D) The war led to the establishment of anticolonial movements among the colonies of the Central Powers, but not of the Entente Powers.
   (E) The United States insisted on the recognition of anticolonial movements as a condition for its entry into the war on the Entente side.

GO ON TO THE NEXT PAGE

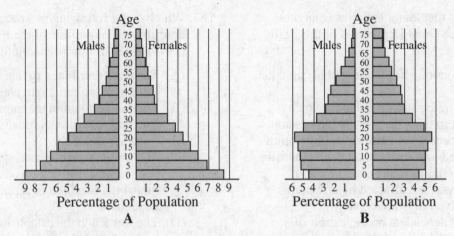

Percentage of Population

A

Percentage of Population

B

84. The population pyramids A and B shown above illustrate, respectively, the age distribution of a

(A) poor, underdeveloped country and a wealthy, developed country

(B) wealthy, developed country and a poor, underdeveloped country

(C) medieval European country suffering from bubonic plague and one free of the plague

(D) country of high birth rates and low death rates and a country of low birth rates and high death rates

(E) country of low birth rates and low death rates and a country of high birth rates and high death rates

85. In the 1980s and 1990s, far-right political parties in many Western European countries gained support because of their

(A) opposition to immigration from Africa, Asia, and Eastern Europe

(B) support for dialogue with communist countries

(C) resistance to pressure from the United States on foreign policy issues

(D) calls for the abolition of the welfare state

(E) attempts to reduce military spending

GO ON TO THE NEXT PAGE

Dr. Seuss Collection, Mandeville Special Collections Library,
University of California, San Diego.

86. The United States cartoon above, published shortly after the
beginning of the Nazi invasion of Russia in June 1941, was
intended to suggest that

(A) the Russians were racially inferior to the Germans and
deserved to be conquered

(B) Russia's communist government would not be able to
resist Hitler's armies

(C) Hitler's invasion of Russia was making him unpopular
among Germans

(D) Hitler intended to treat Russia differently than other
countries conquered by Nazi Germany

(E) Hitler would find it much more difficult to defeat Russia
than his earlier conquests

GO ON TO THE NEXT PAGE

87. After the British withdrawal from the Palestine Mandate in 1947, the United Nations plan for the future of the region provided for the

   (A) establishment of Palestine as an Arab state with guaranteed rights for the Jewish minority
   (B) partition of Palestine between Egypt and Israel
   (C) establishment of a single Jewish state over all of Palestine with guaranteed rights for the Arab majority
   (D) establishment of one Jewish state and one Arab state in Palestine
   (E) partition of Palestine between Lebanon and Israel

88. Which of the following African leaders was the first to lead a newly independent African country in the period of decolonization?

   (A) Julius Nyerere of Tanzania
   (B) Jomo Kenyatta of Kenya
   (C) Robert Mugabe of Zimbabwe
   (D) Kwame Nkrumah of Ghana
   (E) Nelson Mandela of South Africa

_____

Indira Gandhi

Margaret Thatcher

Corazón Aquino

Golda Meir

89. All four women named above have which of the following in common?

   (A) They won the Nobel Peace Prize.
   (B) They were among the top ten best-selling nineteenth-century novelists.
   (C) They were political leaders of their nations in the twentieth century.
   (D) They were the wives of important twentieth-century political and religious leaders.
   (E) They led social reform movements in their countries during the nineteenth century.

90. The Berlin Airlift of 1948 came as a result of

   (A) French occupation of the Ruhr industrial areas in Germany
   (B) Soviet acquisition of the atomic bomb
   (C) Soviet blockade of land access to West Berlin
   (D) American and British attempts to get around the Berlin Wall
   (E) American, British, and French attempts to invade East Germany

91. Most leaders of successful nationalist and independence movements in Asia in the twentieth century had which of the following in common?

   (A) They were traditional religious leaders.
   (B) They had received Western-style educations.
   (C) They were members of the armed forces.
   (D) They were members of the indigenous ruling class.
   (E) They had served in the highest levels of the colonial administration.

92. Fidel Castro and Gamal Abdel Nasser had which of the following in common?

   (A) Both used nationalization of foreign-owned assets to advance their political goals.
   (B) Both relied on China as their primary ally in the struggle against Western imperialism.
   (C) Neither had traveled outside his own country before seizing power.
   (D) Both had upper-class family backgrounds.
   (E) Both had been firm believers in Marxism before assuming power.

93. During the 1960s, the idea that if the United States failed to intervene militarily in Vietnam, then more countries in Southeast Asia might join the Soviet camp was commonly known as

   (A) the Marshall Plan
   (B) mutual assured destruction (MAD)
   (C) the domino theory
   (D) détente
   (E) Vietnamization

GO ON TO THE NEXT PAGE

94. Which of the following was the most important factor in the growing appeal of Islamic fundamentalism in the late twentieth-century Middle East?

(A) The fear of communist expansion into the Middle East
(B) The perception that many Middle Eastern governments were unresponsive and corrupt
(C) Restrictions placed on Middle Eastern Muslims attempting to emigrate to Europe
(D) Increased funding for Muslim religious institutions from Muslims in the United States
(E) The increasing influence of the Arab League in world affairs

Far Eastern Economic Review, @Dow Jones & Co., Inc.

95. Published after the Tiananmen Square incident in June 1989, the cartoon above is probably intended to depict Chinese Communist Party leader Deng Xiaoping as

(A) struggling to preserve China's historic monuments from flood damage
(B) resisting pressures to open China to large-scale immigration from other countries
(C) trying to protect the communist regime from powerful forces of change
(D) defending the democratic reform movements that were active in China at the time
(E) ignoring the threat of Japanese military aggression against China

STOP
**If you finish before time is called, you may check your work on this test only.
Do not turn to any other section in the test.**

How to Score the SAT Subject Test in World History

When you take an actual SAT Subject Test in World History, your answer sheet will be "read" by a scanning machine that will record your response to each question. Then a computer will compare your answers with the correct answers and produce your raw score. You get one point for each correct answer. For each wrong answer, you lose one-fourth of a point. Questions you omit (and any for which you mark more than one answer) are not counted. This raw score is converted to a scaled score that is reported to you and to the colleges you specify.

Worksheet 1. Finding Your Raw Test Score

STEP 1: Table A on the following page lists the correct answers for all the questions on the Subject Test in World History that is reproduced in this book. It also serves as a worksheet for you to calculate your raw score.

- Compare your answers with those given in the table.

- Put a check in the column marked "Right" if your answer is correct.

- Put a check in the column marked "Wrong" if your answer is incorrect.

- Leave both columns blank if you omitted the question.

STEP 2: Count the number of right answers.

Enter the total here: _____

STEP 3: Count the number of wrong answers.

Enter the total here: _____

STEP 4: Multiply the number of wrong answers by .250.

Enter the product here: _____

STEP 5: Subtract the result obtained in Step 4 from the total you obtained in Step 2.

Enter the result here: _____

STEP 6: Round the number obtained in Step 5 to the nearest whole number.

Enter the result here: _____

The number you obtained in Step 6 is your raw score.

Answers to Practice Test 2 for World History

Table A
Answers to the Subject Test in World History - Practice Test 2 and Percentage of Students Answering
Each Question Correctly

Question Number	Correct Answer	Right	Wrong	Percent Answering Correctly*	Question Number	Correct Answer	Right	Wrong	Percent Answering Correctly*
1	D			66	26	E			27
2	D			80	27	D			74
3	B			48	28	D			35
4	B			66	29	B			37
5	A			66	30	A			40
6	B			49	31	E			47
7	D			73	32	E			28
8	D			50	33	C			70
9	D			62	34	D			49
10	A			59	35	E			57
11	C			65	36	B			90
12	C			65	37	D			28
13	D			80	38	C			57
14	A			65	39	D			52
15	E			83	40	B			25
16	D			82	41	D			69
17	E			47	42	D			38
18	C			73	43	D			37
19	A			35	44	E			53
20	A			66	45	C			81
21	B			51	46	C			17
22	E			70	47	D			41
23	D			69	48	A			34
24	B			85	49	A			53
25	C			24	50	D			34

Table A continued on next page

Table A continued from previous page

Question Number	Correct Answer	Right	Wrong	Percent Answering Correctly*	Question Number	Correct Answer	Right	Wrong	Percent Answering Correctly*
51	C			41	76	B			55
52	B			83	77	D			57
53	A			79	78	A			35
54	B			76	79	C			43
55	C			80	80	B			47
56	A			46	81	A			59
57	A			35	82	A			55
58	D			46	83	A			37
59	B			56	84	A			51
60	E			50	85	A			26
61	C			58	86	E			92
62	D			72	87	D			39
63	A			37	88	D			17
64	E			73	89	C			46
65	C			63	90	C			66
66	B			82	91	B			50
67	E			61	92	A			37
68	E			74	93	C			78
69	E			43	94	B			36
70	C			31	95	C			77
71	D			39					
72	A			24					
73	E			46					
74	D			64					
75	B			71					

* These percentages are based on an analysis of the answer sheets for a random sample of 3,350 students who took the original administration of this test and whose mean score was 590. They may be used as an indication of the relative difficulty of a particular question. Each percentage may also be used to predict the likelihood that a typical Subject Test in World History candidate will answer correctly that question on this edition of this test.

Finding Your Scaled Score

When you take SAT Subject Tests, the scores sent to the colleges you specify are reported on the College Board scale, which ranges from 200–800. You can convert your practice test score to a scaled score by using Table B. To find your scaled score, locate your raw score in the left-hand column of Table B; the corresponding score in the right-hand column is your scaled score. For example, a raw score of 45 on this particular edition of the Subject Test in World History corresponds to a scaled score of 590.

Raw scores are converted to scaled scores to ensure that a score earned on any one edition of a particular Subject Test is comparable to the same scaled score earned on any other edition of the same Subject Test. Because some editions of the tests may be slightly easier or more difficult than others, College Board scaled scores are adjusted so that they indicate the same level of performance regardless of the edition of the test taken and the ability of the group that takes it. Thus, for example, a score of 500 on one edition of a test taken at a particular administration indicates the same level of achievement as a score of 500 on a different edition of the test taken at a different administration.

When you take the SAT Subject Tests during a national administration, your scores are likely to differ somewhat from the scores you obtain on the tests in this book. People perform at different levels at different times for reasons unrelated to the tests themselves. The precision of any test is also limited because it represents only a sample of all the possible questions that could be asked.

Table B
Scaled Score Conversion Table
Subject Test in World History - Practice Test 2

Raw Score	Reported Score	Raw Score	Reported Score	Raw Score	Reported Score
95	800	55	660	15	430
94	800	54	660	14	430
93	800	53	650	13	420
92	800	52	640	12	420
91	800	51	630	11	410
90	800	50	630	10	400
89	800	49	620	9	400
88	800	48	610	8	390
87	800	47	600	7	390
86	800	46	600	6	380
85	800	45	590	5	370
84	800	44	590	4	360
83	800	43	580	3	360
82	800	42	570	2	350
81	800	41	570	1	340
80	800	40	560	0	330
79	800	39	550	−1	320
78	800	38	550	−2	310
77	800	37	540	−3	290
76	790	36	540	−4	280
75	790	35	530	−5	270
74	780	34	520	−6	250
73	770	33	520	−7	240
72	770	32	510	−8	240
71	760	31	510	−9	230
70	760	30	500	−10	230
69	750	29	490	−11	220
68	750	28	490	−12	220
67	740	27	480	−13	220
66	740	26	480	−14	220
65	730	25	480	−15	220
64	720	24	470	−16	210
63	720	23	470	−17	210
62	710	22	460	−18	210
61	700	21	460	−19	210
60	700	20	450	−20	210
59	690	19	450	−21	200
58	680	18	440	−22	200
57	680	17	440	−23	200
56	670	16	430	−24	200

How Did You Do on the Subject Test in World History?

After you score your test and analyze your performance, think about the following questions:

Did you run out of time before reaching the end of the test?

If so, you may need to pace yourself better. For example, maybe you spent too much time on one or two hard questions. A better approach might be to skip the ones you can't answer right away and try answering all the questions that remain on the test. Then if there's time, go back to the questions you skipped.

Did you take a long time reading the directions?

You will save time when you take the test by learning the directions to the Subject Test in World History ahead of time. Each minute you spend reading directions during the test is a minute that you could use to answer questions.

How did you handle questions you were unsure of?

If you were able to eliminate one or more of the answer choices as wrong and guess from the remaining ones, your approach probably worked to your advantage. On the other hand, making haphazard guesses or omitting questions without trying to eliminate choices could cost you valuable points.

How difficult were the questions for you compared with other students who took the test?

Table A shows you how difficult the multiple-choice questions were for the group of students who took this test during its national administration. The right-hand column gives the percentage of students that answered each question correctly.

A question answered correctly by almost everyone in the group is obviously an easier question. For example, 90 percent of the students answered question 36 correctly. But only 43 percent answered question 79 correctly.

Keep in mind that these percentages are based on just one group of students. They would probably be different with another group of students taking the test.

If you missed several easier questions, go back and try to find out why: Did the questions cover material you haven't yet reviewed? Did you misunderstand the directions?

Answer Explanations

For Practice Test 2

Question 1

Choice (D) is the correct answer. While the other choices have left behind artifacts that can be studied by scholars, family and kinship structures, being social relationships, have left behind no direct physical evidence for scholars to examine.

Question 2

Choice (D) is the correct answer. River valleys, providing consistent and reliable sources of water for crop irrigation, were key to the development of the majority of early urbanized societies. Examples include the Nile valley, the Huang He valley, and the Tigris and Euphrates river system.

Question 3

Choice (B) is the correct answer. The long-term climatic shift in northern Africa that created and expanded the Sahara desert forced migrations of human populations, both pastoral and agricultural, out of the region.

Question 4

Choice (B) is the correct answer. (B) is the accurate comparison, as the Egyptian pharaohs considered themselves divine and were worshipped by their subjects. Mesopotamian rulers did not claim divinity but claimed favor from the gods in order to justify their kingship.

Question 5

Choice (A) is the correct answer. The key development of the Neolithic Revolution was the beginning of settled farming, following the domestication of various types of food plants and herd animals, leading to the expansion of human populations where agriculture took hold.

Question 6

Choice (B) is the correct answer. As the written language of the Harappan civilization has not been deciphered, most of what scholars have learned about the early Indus valley agricultural civilization has come from the excavation of urban sites such as Mohenjo Daro.

Question 7

Choice (D) is the correct answer. As epidemic diseases flourish in larger populations, people in isolated areas would have a better chance of avoiding contact with carriers of epidemic disease, and those diseases would be less likely to become endemic within the population, reducing the chance of outbreak.

Question 8

Choice (D) is the correct answer. The inscriptions carved on the oracle bones of the Shang period (fourteenth to eleventh centuries B.C.E.) are the earliest documented examples of the writing system that would develop into Chinese.

Question 9

Choice (D) is the correct answer. Giant carved stone heads such as the one depicted are characteristic of the Mesoamerican Olmec culture circa 1500 to 400 B.C.E.

Question 10

Choice (A) is the correct answer. That "life is suffering" is the first of the Four Noble Truths of Buddhism. The admonition to pursue moderation is part of the Noble Eightfold Path that leads to the end of suffering, but is not explicitly called out as one of the Four Truths.

Question 11

Choice (C) is the correct answer. The quote best illustrates the principle of Karma in Hinduism, where a person's actions have an impact on their soul (the atman) and determine the soul's fate in the cycle of rebirth. Dharma (choice B), in Hinduism, is the guide by which one's actions are considered to be good or evil, primarily based on the expectations of caste, which is not explicitly mentioned in the passage, making (C) the best choice.

Question 12

Choice (C) is the correct answer. Sharing common linguistic roots, Sanskrit, Persian, Greek, and Latin all derive from a common ancestor, the Proto-Indo-European language spoken by migrants coming from the central Asian steppe after 4000 B.C.E.

Question 13

Choice (D) is the correct answer. The sculpture is best seen in light of Alexander's efforts to govern Egypt in such a way as not to provoke widespread discontent. By using local religious symbolism and having himself depicted as a pharaoh, Alexander could legitimize his rule over Egypt by incorporating himself into a framework of governance and religious belief familiar to Egyptians.

Question 14

Choice (A) is the correct answer. The classical Maya civilization was located primarily on the Yucatan peninsula, in the modern day countries of Mexico, Guatemala, and Honduras.

Question 15

Choice (E) is the correct answer. Based on the principles outlined in the passage, the Burgundians, a Germanic tribe settling in what was Roman territory, valued freemen over slaves, regardless of how skilled the slave happened to be and regardless of the economic status of the freeman.

Question 16

Choice (D) is the correct answer. As in the more famous Code of Hammurabi, which specified a variety of punishments for a particular crime, the laws of the Burgundians considered the social status of the victim as an important factor in determining the punishment for a crime committed against that person.

Question 17

Choice (E) is the correct answer. While Europeans of the late nineteenth century, whose view was largely influenced by the Industrial Revolution, came to see the Chinese as a backward and isolated society, the stereotype of China as a secluded kingdom is almost entirely rejected by contemporary historians, making (E) the correct characterization of how world historians would view the passage.

Question 18

Choice (C) is the correct answer. While potatoes were grown in the Andes, they did not spread to the rest of the Americas until after the voyages of Columbus. Maize was predominant in Mesoamerica and was also grown in Andean societies starting approximately 5,000 to 7,000 years ago.

Question 19

Choice (A) is the correct answer. While there were significant coastal trading cities and numerous small states in sub-Saharan Africa from 1000 to 1500 C.E., the savannas of West Africa were home to the large imperial states of Mali and Songhay, the largest states in Africa during the period.

Question 20

Choice (A) is the correct answer. One of the major governing strategies of the Roman Republic and the later the empire was to incorporate conquered peoples by offering them citizenship and implicit legal equality with Romans from central Italy.

Question 21

Choice (B) is the correct answer. While the Sasanid empire did allow other faiths, such as Christianity, within Persian territory, Zoroastrianism remained the official faith of the Sasanid rulers, who followed the earlier Achaemenid and Parthian dynasties in endorsing Zoroastrianism, actively promoting the Zurvanite form of the faith.

Question 22

Choice (E) is the correct answer. Oranges and peaches are both native to China, though earlier varieties of oranges may have originated in South or Southeast Asia. Peaches are recorded as arriving in Greece by 300 B.C.E., likely as a result of contacts with the Persians. Oranges appear to have arrived in Europe through contacts with Muslims in the Mediterranean by the tenth century. The spread of both oranges and peaches likely followed trade routes across Eurasia by the Silk Roads and sea routes in the Indian Ocean.

Question 23

Choice (D) is the correct answer. Hinduism incorporates a concept of caste status as part of the belief in reincarnation, resulting in varying degrees of social stratification based on an individual's birth into a particular caste group. Islam stresses the religious equality of all of those who follow the tenets of the faith.

Question 24

Choice (B) is the correct answer. Though women were not treated as absolute equals, early Buddhism and Christianity achieved success in gaining converts by offering women a prominent place within the faith, particularly through monasticism.

Question 25

Choice (C) is the correct answer. The Council of Chalcedon was called to settle doctrinal disputes over the nature of Jesus Christ, and ruled that he was both human and divine, a ruling accepted by both the Catholic and Eastern Orthodox Churches, but rejected by the Coptic Orthodox Church.

Question 26

Choice (E) is the correct answer. While the other examples highlight instances where political change did not result in religious change, the conquest of Egypt by the Arab armies of the caliphate brought a long-lasting change to Islam for the majority of Egyptians, though smaller communities of Jews and Christians remained. In northern India, while the Delhi Sultanate (choice A) was Muslim, prior waves of Muslim invasion had established Islamic communities, and the Sultanate itself practiced a form of religious tolerance in order to keep political order among its Hindu subjects, instead subjecting non-Muslims to the *jizya*, or head tax, as the Ottomans would later do in Greece (choice D).

Question 27

Choice (D) is the correct answer. The introduction of silk production into the Byzantine Empire is an example of cross-cultural exchange facilitated by the Silk Roads.

Question 28

Choice (D) is the correct answer. The Strait of Malacca, a narrow sea channel dividing the Indonesian island of Sumatra from the Malay Peninsula, was one of the most important trade routes in the overseas trade between the Indian Ocean and China, attracting many Muslim traders who sought access to the trade in luxury goods from China.

Question 29

Choice (B) is the correct answer. Starting with the crowning of Charlemagne as Holy Roman emperor, the Carolingians are widely credited with reviving ancient learning in Western Europe by establishing political order and forging ties with the Roman Catholic Church in Italy.

Question 30

Choice (A) is the correct answer. The close proximity of the sites of Teotihuacán, Tenochtitlán, and modern Mexico City in the Valley of Mexico suggests that the valley's geographical features are especially suited for urban development. Although the valley was not located along the banks of any significant rivers, a lake system provided the valley with abundant food and a basis for agricultural development.

Question 31

Choice (E) is the correct answer. Emperor Justinian's major long-term accomplishment was the consolidation of Roman civil law into a collection of laws and legal interpretations that became known as the Code of Justinian.

Question 32

Choice (E) is the correct answer. Although sectarian and political divisions between Sunni and Shi'a emerged early on, the Muslim conquests, fueled by religious fervor, were greatly facilitated by the internal weaknesses of the Persian and Byzantine Empires. After centuries of conflict, the populations of both empires were willing to accept new rulers, and Muslim policies of religious tolerance aided in assimilating conquered peoples into the caliphate.

Question 33

Choice (C) is the correct answer. Inti, the Inca Sun god, was considered the patron deity of the Inca Empire, and was the center of many of the empire's religious rituals.

Question 34

Choice (D) is the correct answer. The passage best illustrates the reciprocal bonds of personal loyalty that defined the feudal system in medieval Europe.

Question 35

Choice (E) is the correct answer. The bonds illustrated by the passage are very similar to the feudal relations created in Tokugawa Japan between the daimyo and samurai, where personal loyalty was the contractual bond.

Question 36

Choice (B) is the correct answer. The primary purpose of the system of fortifications known as the Great Wall of China was to serve as a barrier to nomadic incursions from pastoral steppe nomads such as the Xiongnu and the Mongols.

Question 37

Choice (D) is the correct answer. The stupa, a common feature of Buddhist temples, reflect the influence of Indian architecture on the island of Java, and the temple complex of Borobudur is the world's largest Buddhist temple.

Question 38

Choice (C) is the correct answer. The Hagia Sophia was initially constructed during the Byzantine Empire as a Christian cathedral. Following the Ottoman conquest in 1453, the cathedral was converted into a mosque, and the distinctive Islamic minarets were added to the building.

Question 39

Choice (D) is the correct answer. Because of its close proximity and extensive trade contacts with China, Nara Japan was most conspicuously influenced by the intellectual and political developments of the Tang period in China.

Question 40

Choice (B) is the correct answer. Although the two groups had much in common, after the 'Abbasid revolt against the Umayyad caliphate, the 'Abbasid caliphs incorporated much more of the Persian traditional government bureaucracy into their political system than the Umayyads had done.

Question 41

Choice (D) is the correct answer. As Java is geographically considered part of Southeast Asia, and the poem refers to the Hindu Vedas and Brahmins, the passage is best seen as evidence of India's influence over Southeast Asia.

Question 42

Choice (D) is the correct answer. One of the most significant cultural and political developments of the Song period was the increasing support for Neoconfucian ideals, as the influence of Buddhism and other foreign ideas were seen as causes of the collapse of the Tang dynasty.

Question 43

Choice (D) is the correct answer. One of the central tenets of Jainism is nonviolence and respect for all living things.

Question 44

Choice (E) is the correct answer. A common feature of Renaissance Europe and the 'Abbasid Caliphate was the scholarly engagement with classical Greek and Roman texts, with scholars in both cultures commenting and expanding upon their writings.

Question 45

Choice (C) is the correct answer. The image, with its dancing skeletons symbolizing death, was a common motif of artwork produced during the Black Death in Europe during the 1300s.

Question 46

Choice (C) is the correct answer. In terms of covering the widest geographical area, the Polynesian migrations and colonization of the islands of the Pacific provided the most successful example of colonization before European efforts that occurred after 1500.

Question 47

Choice (D) is the correct answer. Primarily mined in the Americas, silver was the primary trade item that Europeans exchanged for Chinese goods in the period 1500 to 1800. Opium (choice B), did not become a significant trade good until after 1800, when the British East India Company developed plantations in India in order to access the illicit market for opium in China.

Question 48

Choice (A) is the correct answer. Though Buddhism was founded in what is today northern India, it steadily lost ground to devotional Hinduism during the Gupta dynasty and after the invasions of northern India by the White Huns at the end of that dynasty destroyed many temples. By the time of the Muslim invasions circa 1200, Buddhism was a minority faith, and Islam largely displaced Buddhism as an alternative to Hinduism.

Question 49

Choice (A) is the correct answer. The Inca state invested significant resources in building stone roads so that its messengers, armies, and traders could more easily travel the Andes highlands.

Question 50

Choice (D) is the correct answer. Vasco da Gama is best known for circumnavigating Africa and establishing a Portuguese presence in the Indian Ocean.

Question 51

Choice (C) is the correct answer. Zheng He's voyages took place in the early fifteenth century. Columbus's four voyages to the New World took place between 1492 and 1502. Magellan's voyage began in 1519.

Question 52

Choice (B) is the correct answer. Because of their geographic proximity to China, Mongol, Japanese, Korean, and Vietnamese societies were all profoundly influenced by Chinese cultural traditions, adopting, at various points and to various degrees, elements of Chinese traditions such as Confucianism, Daoism, writing systems, agricultural and artisanal techniques, and political systems. By contrast, Russian culture developed in relative isolation from Chinese influences, in northwestern Eurasia.

Question 53

Choice (A) is the correct answer. The rejection of the authority of the Roman pontiff and the established Catholic Church hierarchy was the common strand that united Luther and Calvin's reformation with Henry VIII's break with Rome, which led to the establishment of the Church of England.

Question 54

Choice (B) is the correct answer. Not only was the defeat of Philip II's Armada in 1588 a significant military loss for Spain but, more importantly, it solidified the Protestant succession in England (under Elizabeth I). England's rise as a maritime rival to Spain in the Atlantic was one of the most important factors in Spain's subsequent decline as an imperial power.

Question 55

Choice (C) is the correct answer. European ships began arriving in Japan in the mid-sixteenth century, and Catholic missionaries successfully converted tens of thousands of Japanese to Christianity in the following decades. After the establishment of the Tokugawa Shogunate in 1600, European merchants and missionaries as well as the Japanese converts to Christianity were increasingly viewed with suspicion by the state. The process culminated with the adoption of policies of persecution of Christians (beginning in the 1610s) and drastic restrictions on European merchants' access to Japan (beginning in the 1630s).

Question 56

Choice (A) is the correct answer. Maroon communities in Spanish colonial America tended to be largely economically self-sufficient. Their trade contacts were often limited to neighboring Native American communities, not Spanish colonial societies. Therefore it is unlikely that the leaders of Esmeraldas shown in the painting would have been economically dependent on Spain. By contrast, the remaining four answer choices all describe behaviors that the Esmeraldas leaders would have been likely to adopt in their dealings with Spanish

colonial authorities. Their choice of European-style clothing in particular (choice C), would have been a deliberate attempt to assert their position of equality relative to Spanish colonial officials.

Question 57

Choice (A) is the correct answer. Because they flourish in warm, tropical climates, both manioc (cassava) and maize began to be cultivated in Africa as early as the sixteenth century. First grown in in Portuguese African colonies but soon spreading over most of the continent, manioc and maize became the most important staple crops in Africa by the 1800s. Although the crops listed in the remaining four answer choices are all currently cultivated extensively in Africa, especially sweet potatoes (choice B), their spread is relatively more recent and not as historically significant as the impact of manioc and maize.

Question 58

Choice (D) is the correct answer. Although Christianity (choice B), spread by contact with Europeans, made considerable inroads in Africa during this period, Islam spread even more extensively. The period after 1600 saw the lasting Islamization of most of the societies in the Sahel (or historic Sudan) region south of the Sahara, further expansion of Islam into West Africa, including present-day Senegal, Guinea, and northern Nigeria, and the growth of Islam along the Swahili coast of East Africa and in the Horn of Africa region (present-day Eritrea).

Question 59

Choice (B) is the correct answer. Oliver Cromwell was the leader of Parliament's army, also known as Roundheads, in the conflict against Charles I's pro-monarchy forces during the English Civil War. After the execution of the king in 1649, Cromwell helped establish the republican Commonwealth government, in which he ultimately came to hold dictatorial power as lord protector.

Question 60

Choice (E) is the correct answer. It can be inferred from the passage that the author contends that the Safavid and the Mughal empires, at their height of power, had brought a measure of political stability to South and Southwest Asia. With the decline of the empires, political instability ("a great wave of turbulence") engulfed the region, providing the opportunity for early European imperial expansion in the region.

Question 61

Choice (C) is the correct answer. The reign of Peter the Great (1682–1725) was the first period of sustained and deliberate Westernization policies in the history of Russia. Peter's reforms substantially undermined the autonomy of traditional military and landed elites in Russia and shifted power to a new service nobility that was largely pro-Western in outlook and values.

Question 62

Choice (D) is the correct answer. Despite the radicalism of most of their reforms, the leaders of the French revolution did not grant women the right to vote or consider them equal in citizenship to men. This failure led to numerous criticisms by revolutionary women, most notably Olympe de Gouges' 1791 *Declaration of the Rights of Woman and the Female Citizen*.

Question 63

Choice (A) is the correct answer. The sugar islands in the Caribbean were widely considered to be the most profitable European colonial possessions in the Americas, especially after the loss of the thirteen British North American colonies in the American Revolutionary War. As an illustration of that view, French negotiators at the Treaty of Paris, which ended the Seven Years' War (1763), were more willing to cede all of French Canada to Britain than to lose the Caribbean sugar island of Guadeloupe.

Question 64

Choice (E) is the correct answer. The Ottoman Empire is the only one of the answer choices that was a Muslim empire in existence during the period specified in the question.

Question 65

Choice (C) is the correct answer. At the time of the outbreak of the French Revolution, the prison fortress the Bastille in Paris had become a largely symbolic structure representing, in the eyes of many Parisians, the abuses of power of the Old Regime. On the eve of the storming, the Bastille held only a handful of prisoners and had been largely emptied of gunpowder and military supplies.

Question 66

Choice (B) is the correct answer. Neither Brazil nor the United States abolished slavery upon achieving independence, and both countries had extensive plantation economy sectors that relied on African slave labor to produce cash crops.

Question 67

Choice (E) is the correct answer. Napoleon is not usually considered to have been a champion of women's rights, and many of his domestic reforms, including the Civil Code promulgated under his rule (in 1804), are seen by most historians as setbacks for the cause of women's rights. Napoleon did not support full legal emancipation for women and was not seen as a champion by early feminists.

Question 68

Choice (E) is the correct answer. Although the period 1750–1914 was generally one of continued high mortality and relatively low life expectancy in most of the world, it also saw significant improvements in food availability and economic development in many areas, notably Western Europe, North America, and parts of East Asia. With the effective end of the old Malthusian cycles of famine and recovery in such areas, the overall world population rose rapidly and steadily.

Question 69

Choice (E) is the correct answer. The Portuguese royal family had fled to Brazil when Napoleonic France invaded Portugal (1807), and the Portuguese king ruled from Brazil the remaining Portuguese imperial possessions around the world. In 1815 Brazil was proclaimed a coequal kingdom with Portugal within the Portuguese empire. In 1822, following a constitutional revolution in Portugal, the Brazilian regent Prince Pedro (son of the reigning Portuguese king) proclaimed the country's independence. While Portugal attempted to contest Pedro's independence declaration and a few minor armed skirmishes ensued, Brazilian independence was effectively achieved without major warfare.

Question 70

Choice (C) is the correct answer. The references to the Dutch introducing coffee in the region, the mention of Sunda (a historical region on the island of Java), and Raffles' general association with developments in Southeast Asia all point toward the passage referring to territory in present-day Indonesia.

Question 71

Choice (D) is the correct answer. Raffles' description of coffee growing as an economic activity forced on native laborers by European colonial authorities and pursued with a relentless and oppressive determination that often left workers hungry and destitute most directly resembles the rubber-producing European monopoly system introduced in Belgian King Leopold II's Congo Free State in Central Africa.

Question 72

Choice (A) is the correct answer. The early nineteenth century saw major expansions of voting rights for men in both England (most notably in the Great Reform Act of 1832, which lowered property qualifications for voters and made electoral districts more representative of population density) and in the United States (most notably through the gradual reduction and abolition of state-imposed property qualifications for voters as part of the Jacksonian Democracy movement). The abolition of slavery (choice C) took place in Great Britain within the time period specified in the question (with formal abolition across the British empire enacted in 1838), but not in the

United States, where slavery was abolished in the second half of the nineteenth century (1863, with Abraham Lincoln's Emancipation Proclamation).

Question 73

Choice (E) is the correct answer. Many of Charles Dickens' novels, such as *Oliver Twist*, *Little Dorrit*, and *Great Expectations* explore the difficult lives of the lower socioeconomic classes in Victorian England.

Question 74

Choice (D) is the correct answer. Pacifist sentiment did rise in Germany in the immediate aftermath of the country's defeat in the First World War, but by the early 1930s pacifist voices had become largely irrelevant. The economic devastation of the Great Depression (choice B) and lingering resentment over the terms of the Treaty of Versailles (choice A) made radical and militaristic political platforms (most notably that of National Socialists) more popular and contributed to Hitler's rise to power.

Question 75

Choice (B) is the correct answer. The late nineteenth century was a period of rapid European imperial expansion in the interior of the African continent. The process, often termed the Scramble for Africa by historians, was formalized and given a veneer of legality at the 1884–1885 Berlin Conference.

Question 76

Choice (B) is the correct answer. The term "Meiji Restoration" refers to the political events in Japan in 1866–1867 that led to the end of Tokugawa shogunate and the resumption of effective political power by the Japanese emperor, Mutsuhito (who is better known by his traditional regnal name, the Meiji Emperor).

Question 77

Choice (D) is the correct answer. Ethiopia, Japan, and Siam all managed to retain their independence in this period either because of a combination of internal reforms and military victories over European powers (as in the case of Ethiopia and Japan) or because of fortuitous geostrategic circumstances (as in the case of Siam, which was in a position to serve as a buffer state between French and British imperial possessions in Southeast Asia).

Question 78

Choice (A) is the correct answer. Both revolutions plunged their respective countries into long periods of civil war. In Russia, the war pitted the Bolshevik government and the Red Army (the Reds) against

numerous White enemies that fought either for the restoration of the monarchy or for various non-Bolshevik forms of government. The war lasted until 1922–1923. In China, the 1911 revolution overthrew the monarchy but failed to effectively unify the country, resulting in the effective establishment of regional governments and statelets as well as two rival national governments. This warlord era ended in 1926 with a victory of the Guomindang, but a new challenge arose in 1927 with the rise of Communists under Mao Zedong, effectively prolonging China's civil war into the late 1930s. Answer choice (B) describes a longer-term (not immediate) effect of both revolutions.

Question 79

Choice (C) is the correct answer. The declaration was part of a 1917 letter sent by British Foreign Secretary Arthur Balfour to Baron Rothschild, a leader of the Jewish community in England. In order to solidify support for the British war effort, Balfour pledged that, in the event of a victory for the Allies, Great Britain would support the establishment of a "national home for the Jewish people" in Palestine (which, at the time of the declaration, was part of the Ottoman Empire).

Question 80

Choice (B) is the correct answer. At the time she received the Nobel Peace Prize, Aung San Suu Kyi was being held under house arrest by Burma's military government, despite being the leader of the political party that had won the most recent general election in Burma. From her house arrest, she called on the Burmese people to oppose military rule through peaceful, nonviolent means.

Question 81

Choice (A) is the correct answer. Because Soviet leaders pursued a policy of economic autarky (with limited foreign trade and no foreign investments) and had effectively abolished private economic enterprise, the Soviet Union remained relatively insulated from the economic upheavals of the Great Depression. In fact, the Depression years in the West coincided with a period of rapid state-led industrialization in the Soviet Union.

Question 82

Choice (A) is the correct answer. The Bolshevik Revolution in Russia ensured the irreversible nature of the abolition of the autocratic Russian monarchy (former Tsar Nicholas II and his family were executed on the orders of the Bolshevik government). The Mexican revolution led to the deposition and exile (in 1911) of the Mexican authoritarian leader General Porfirio Díaz.

Question 83

Choice (A) is the correct answer. Disillusionment with European treatment of colonial resources during the war, including European use of colonial troops, as well as a general reassessment of the notion of European cultural and political superiority as a result of the devastation of the war led many colonial subjects to embrace the cause of independence. Answer choice B is chronologically incorrect— European colonial holdings actually expanded in the period between 1918 and 1939.

Question 84

Choice (A) is the correct answer. Population pyramid A shows a pattern typical of a poor, underdeveloped country, with high birth rates and a considerable drop between the earliest two age cohorts, suggesting relatively high childhood mortality rates. Population pyramid B shows a pattern typical of a wealthy developed country, with low birth rates and an aging population.

Question 85

Choice (A) is the correct answer. Western European far-right parties in the 1980s and 1990s were characterized primarily by their opposition to immigration from outside Western Europe. While some far-right groups did express opposition to the welfare state (choice D), most did not. In fact, many far-right parties justified their opposition to immigration by claiming that immigrants placed an undue strain on the benefits provided by welfare programs, which these parties claimed they wished to preserve for native-born citizens.

Question 86

Choice (E) is the correct answer. The size and fearsomeness of the animal symbolizing Russia clearly suggests that the cartoonist intended to convey the idea that by attacking the Soviet Union, Nazi Germany had set itself a military challenge quite out of proportion to its earlier conquests.

Question 87

Choice (D) is the correct answer. According to the 1947 United Nations partition plan, the British Palestine mandate was to be divided into a Jewish state and an Arab state, with the city of Jerusalem being placed under international administration. The United Nations plan did not call for the establishment of a single Jewish state in the area of the mandate (choice C).

Question 88

Choice (D) is the correct answer. Ghana gained independence from Great Britain in 1957, and Kwame Nkrumah became the first Ghanaian prime minister postindependence. Decolonization occurred later in Tanzania, Kenya, and Zimbabwe (Options A, B, and C) than in Ghana. Nelson Mandela became president of South Africa (Option E) only in 1994, after the end of the apartheid regime and the first election in which all South Africans, regardless of skin color, could participate.

Question 89

Choice (C) is the correct answer. All four women on the list were elected political leaders in their respective countries: India (Indira Gandhi), Great Britain (Margaret Thatcher), the Philippines (Corazón Aquino), and Israel (Golda Meir).

Question 90

Choice (C) is the correct answer. Because of its location in eastern Germany, the city of Berlin was located within the Soviet occupation zone after the end of the Second World War. By the terms of the Potsdam Agreement, however, the city was also internally divided into four zones, only one of which was under Soviet control. As Cold War tensions increased, the Soviet Union imposed a land blockade on the three Western zones of occupation in June of 1948. The Western powers retaliated by dramatically increasing the number of commercial supply flights into West Berlin, a practice that became known as the Berlin Airlift.

Question 91

Choice (B) is the correct answer. Some of the most prominent leaders of nationalist and/or independence movements in Asia had received Western educations, either in Western countries or in Western-run institutions of learning in their own countries. Notable examples include Mohandas K. Gandhi and Jawaharlal Nehru (India), Muhammad Ali Jinnah (Pakistan), Ho Chi Minh (Vietnam), Sun Yat-sen (China), and Sukarno (Indonesia).

Question 92

Choice (A) is the correct answer. Once in power, both Castro and Nasser nationalized foreign-held property, notably United States–owned assets in the case of the Castro's Cuba and the Anglo-French-held Suez Canal and Suez Canal company holdings in Nasser's Egypt. Adherence to Marxism before assuming power (choice E) was characteristic of Castro, but not of Nasser.

Question 93

Choice (C) is the correct answer. Originating in the 1950s, the domino theory referred to the belief in United States foreign policy circles that friendly Third World countries must be defended from communist takeover to prevent Soviet influence from spreading further and further. The domino theory was used to justify military intervention in Vietnam to prop up the South Vietnamese against communist North Vietnam.

Question 94

Choice (B) is the correct answer. The growth of Islamic fundamentalism in the Middle East in the late twentieth century was directly related to the authoritarian nature and perceived corruption of many Middle Eastern governments. Notable examples include Iran under Reza Shah Pahlavi, Egypt under Anwar Sadat and Hosni Mubarak, Syria under Hafiz al-Assad, and Saudi Arabia under the Saudi royal family.

Question 95

Choice (C) is the correct answer. The cartoon depicts Deng Xiaoping trying to plug a minor leak in China's Great Wall by using his finger, oblivious to the deluge on the other side of the wall. The imagery clearly suggests that the cartoonist believed that the regime's suppression of the Tiananmen Square protests would not be sufficient to save communist China from the forces of popular discontent.

World History – Practice Test 3

Practice Helps

The test that follows is an actual, previously administered SAT Subject Test in World History. To get an idea of what it's like to take this test, practice under conditions that are much like those of an actual test administration.

- Set aside an hour when you can take the test uninterrupted.

- Sit at a desk or table with no other books or papers. Dictionaries, other books, or notes are not allowed in the test room.

- Tear out an answer sheet from the back of this book and fill it in just as you would on the day of the test. One answer sheet can be used for up to three Subject Tests.

- Read the instructions that precede the practice test. During the actual administration, you will be asked to read them before answering test questions.

- Use a clock or kitchen timer to time yourself.

- After you finish the practice test, read the sections "How to Score the SAT Subject Test in World History" and "How Did You Do on the Subject Test in World History?"

- The appearance of the answer sheet in this book may differ from the answer sheet you see on test day.

WORLD HISTORY TEST

The top portion of the page of the answer sheet that you will use to take the World History Test must be filled in exactly as illustration below. When your supervisor tells you to fill in the circle next to the name of the test you are about to take, mark your answer sheet as shown.

◯ Literature	◯ Mathematics Level 1	◯ German	◯ Chinese Listening	◯ Japanese Listening
◯ Biology E	◯ Mathematics Level 2	◯ Italian	◯ French Listening	◯ Korean Listening
◯ Biology M	◯ U.S. History	◯ Latin	◯ German Listening	◯ Spanish Listening
◯ Chemistry	● World History	◯ Modern Hebrew		
◯ Physics	◯ French	◯ Spanish	**Background Questions:** ①②③④⑤⑥⑦⑧⑨	

After filling in the circle next to the name of the test you are taking, locate the Background Questions box on your answer sheet (as shown above). This is where you will answer the following Background Questions on your answer sheet.

BACKGROUND QUESTIONS

Please answer the two questions below by filling in the appropriate circle in the Background Questions box on your answer sheet. The information you provide is for statistical purposes only and will not affect your test score.

Question I

How many semesters of world history, world cultures, or European history have you taken from grade 9 to the present? (If you are taking a course this semester, count it as a full semester.) Fill in only one circle of circles 1- 4.

- One semester or less   —Fill in circle 1.
- Two semesters   —Fill in circle 2.
- Three semesters   —Fill in circle 3.
- Four or more semesters   —Fill in circle 4.

Question II

For the courses in world history, world cultures, or European history you have taken, which of the following geographical areas did you study? Fill in all of the circles that apply.

- Africa   —Fill in circle 5.
- Asia   —Fill in circle 6.
- Europe   —Fill in circle 7.
- Latin America   —Fill in circle 8.
- Middle East   —Fill in circle 9.

When the supervisor gives the signal, turn the page and begin the World History Test. There are 100 numbered circles on the answer sheet and 95 questions in the World History Test. Therefore, use only circles 1 to 95 for recording your answers.

WORLD HISTORY TEST

Directions: Each of the questions or incomplete statements below is followed by five suggested answers or completions. Select the one that is best in each case and then fill in the corresponding circle on the answer sheet.

Note: The World History Test uses the chronological designations B.C.E. (before common era) and C.E. (common era). These labels correspond to B.C. (before Christ) and A.D. (anno Domini), which are used in some world history textbooks.

1. Which of the following was true of both Greece and China in the period around 500 B.C.E.?

    (A) Both fostered vibrant philosophical schools that debated the human condition.
    (B) Both were threatened by more powerful neighboring civilizations.
    (C) Both experienced economic revolutions brought on by the discovery of iron.
    (D) Both underwent social revolutions that led to the seclusion of women.
    (E) Both suffered from overpopulation that led to class warfare and massive emigration.

2. Which of the following is true of the epic poems the *Mahabharata*, the *Iliad*, and the *Tales of the Heike* ?

    (A) All three were influenced by Chinese literary forms.
    (B) All three stress the exploits of a warrior elite.
    (C) All three were written down at first and later transmitted orally.
    (D) All three stress humanity's independence from the influence of the gods.
    (E) Historians have conclusively identified the authors of the three works.

3. Which of the following statements about the effects of Muhammad's teaching is true?

    (A) Islam initially attracted many followers, but gradually became less popular.
    (B) Muhammad believed that social differences needed to be preserved, which encouraged divisions in society.
    (C) Islam affected every aspect of life and encouraged unity among converts with widely diverse backgrounds.
    (D) Muhammad believed that wealth should be renounced; thus Islam did not attempt to expand.
    (E) Muslims set up a complex priesthood that mediated the contact between Allah and individual believers.

4. The military campaigns of the Huns under Attila contributed to which of the following?

    (A) The introduction of the bubonic plague to Asia
    (B) The fall of the western Roman Empire
    (C) The division of Charlemagne's empire
    (D) The introduction of horse domestication into western Europe
    (E) The defeat of the Muslims in Spain

GO ON TO THE NEXT PAGE

5. After the fall of the Han dynasty, the nomadic peoples who invaded China did which of the following?

(A) They attempted to restore the Han dynasty to power.
(B) They tried unsuccessfully to convert the Chinese to Islam.
(C) They outlawed the use of the Chinese language by governing officials.
(D) They launched an invasion of Japan.
(E) They adopted Chinese culture and customs.

6. Mahavira and Buddha were similar in that both

(A) were successful military leaders who conquered most of India
(B) resisted the spread of Islam in India
(C) were theorists who pioneered new mathematical concepts
(D) led religious movements that challenged the social order of Hinduism
(E) were martyred for their beliefs

7. "Warfare in nineteenth-century southern Africa was revolutionized with the development of the short, stabbing spear, the body shield, and a tactical formation known as the ox's horns."

The above describes innovations developed by the

(A) Zulu
(B) Xhosa
(C) Sotho
(D) Shona
(E) Ibo

8. All of the following are central to the practice of Islam EXCEPT

(A) Observation of Ramadan through fasting
(B) Monotheism
(C) Prayer five times a day facing Mecca
(D) Making a pilgrimage to Mecca at least once
(E) Realistic representations of people in art

9. Which of the following is a pair of neighboring countries both of which had acquired the capability of exploding nuclear weapons by the late 1990's?

(A) Argentina and Chile
(B) Mexico and the United States
(C) The Czech Republic and Germany
(D) India and Pakistan
(E) North Korea and South Korea

10. Which of the following best describes the economic strategy of the Soviet Union under Stalin?

(A) Development of a mixed economy
(B) Creation of a landowning peasant class
(C) Production for export
(D) Centralized economic planning
(E) Government encouragement of free enterprise

11. Historiography is

(A) a single, accurate account of events in past time
(B) the study of how historical accounts are produced
(C) a chronological chart of historical events
(D) a historical account based only on written records
(E) the official record of past events, usually produced by a government

12. Which of the following describes the primary role of the scholar-gentry in imperial China?

(A) The mainstay of the imperial bureaucracy
(B) The development of political revolution
(C) The education of China's peasantry
(D) The dissemination of European culture in China
(E) The advancement of engineering and agricultural science

GO ON TO THE NEXT PAGE

13. The Japanese victory in the Russo-Japanese War demonstrated to other non-Western peoples that

   (A) successful modernization was not a strictly Western phenomenon
   (B) countries that held traditional values could not defeat a European power
   (C) passive resistance could be effectively employed in the defeat of a European power
   (D) the distance between Asia and Europe would make Asian industrialization difficult
   (E) further expansion by Russia in Asia was inevitable

14. The defeat of the Umayyads by the Abbasids in 750 C.E. led to the relocation of the caliphate and of the primary center of Islamic culture from

   (A) Mecca to Medina
   (B) Jerusalem to Cairo
   (C) Damascus to Baghdad
   (D) Constantinople to Beirut
   (E) Córdoba to Alexandria

15. Which of the following is an example of an ancient megalithic structure?

   (A) Stonehenge
   (B) The Coliseum
   (C) Angkor Wat
   (D) The Acropolis
   (E) Great Zimbabwe

16. The Aztec viewed the Toltec as

   (A) barbarians who lacked culture
   (B) slaves, fit only for conquest
   (C) the givers of civilization
   (D) heretics who practiced a forbidden religion
   (E) the greatest rivals to the Aztec dominance of the valley of Mexico

17. The terms Indo-European and Bantu were created to describe

   (A) biological races
   (B) language groups
   (C) religious movements
   (D) artistic styles
   (E) ancient empires

18. According to one theory of state formation, large states first developed in river valleys because

   (A) coordination of large-scale irrigation projects created the need for more complex organizations
   (B) the healthier climates of river valleys allowed large populations to develop there
   (C) river valleys provided the best natural defensive barriers for growing states
   (D) river valleys were the only sources of drinking water large enough to support concentrated populations
   (E) river valleys were the best sources of metal ores for weapons and tools

19. In England in the late nineteenth century it was socially acceptable for young working-class women to take jobs as domestic servants because

   (A) many of their employers allowed them to do volunteer work among the urban poor on evenings and weekends
   (B) this work was believed to contribute to habits of hard work, cleanliness, and obedience, which were seen as good preparation for marriage
   (C) such jobs provided opportunities for them to meet and marry men from higher social classes
   (D) the training they received in household management provided them with skills needed for later careers in business
   (E) residence in middle- or upper-class homes contributed to their political education

20. In Chinese history, the phrase "Mandate of Heaven" refers to the

   (A) divine selection of China as the holiest place in the world
   (B) obligation of each individual to obey religious teachings
   (C) divine favor enjoyed by wise and benevolent rulers
   (D) Chinese version of the Ten Commandments
   (E) most important of the Confucian writings

GO ON TO THE NEXT PAGE

21. Which of the following is the commonly accepted meaning of the term *Homo sapiens*?

    (A) The southern apes
    (B) The upright-walking humans
    (C) The consciously thinking humans
    (D) The animal with a large brain
    (E) The missing link

22. In their original form, all of the following major religions focused on humanity's relationship to a god or gods EXCEPT

    (A) Buddhism
    (B) Christianity
    (C) Hinduism
    (D) Islam
    (E) Judaism

23. Social Darwinism is most closely associated with the idea that

    (A) government should provide support for disadvantaged members of society
    (B) competition is natural to society
    (C) revolution is inevitable
    (D) imperialistic expansion will increase economic pressures on citizens
    (E) technological development will decrease the gap between rich and poor

24. Which of the following led Great Britain and France to declare war on Germany in 1939?

    (A) Hitler established a fascist dictatorship in Germany.
    (B) Germany occupied France.
    (C) Germany annexed Austria.
    (D) Germany invaded Poland.
    (E) Germany passed anti-Semitic laws.

25. The pyramids in ancient Egypt were built to function primarily as

    (A) temples
    (B) tombs
    (C) watchtowers
    (D) astronomical observatories
    (E) sundials

26. In the Hindu caste system, members of the Brahman caste originally served as

    (A) priests
    (B) farmers
    (C) warriors
    (D) merchants
    (E) herders

27. Which of the following is attributed to Alexander the Great?

    (A) Three centuries of political stability in the Middle East
    (B) The establishment of the basic political forms of the Roman Empire
    (C) The concept of kingship limited by elected representatives
    (D) The spread of Greek cultural forms into western Asia
    (E) The extension of property and inheritance rights to women

28. Prior to the Roman conquests of Gaul, Spain, and Britain, these areas were inhabited primarily by

    (A) Celts
    (B) Goths
    (C) Greeks
    (D) Mongols
    (E) Scythians

29. Which of the following major ancient civilizations did NOT originate along a river valley?

    (A) Chinese
    (B) Indian
    (C) Egyptian
    (D) Mesopotamian
    (E) Greek

GO ON TO THE NEXT PAGE

30. Which of the following changes best characterizes the commercial revolution that accelerated during the 1400's and continued throughout the Age of Exploration?

    (A) The growth of capitalism as an economic system
    (B) The shift of the center of trading from the Mediterranean Sea to the Indian Ocean
    (C) The development and application of communism
    (D) The decline in the production of consumer goods
    (E) The loss of overseas empires by western European nations

31. The words "alchemy," "algebra," "assassin," "sugar," "zenith," and "zero" entered the English language as a result of the influence on Europe of which of the following cultures?

    (A) Arabic
    (B) Turkish
    (C) Indian
    (D) Aramaic
    (E) Hebrew

32. The principal development during the Neolithic Age was the

    (A) disappearance of the Neanderthals
    (B) invention of writing
    (C) beginning of metallurgy
    (D) domestication of animals and plants
    (E) appearance of craft specialization

33. Cultivation of which of the following crops most drastically changed the geographical distribution of human populations?

    (A) Sugar
    (B) Opium
    (C) Tobacco
    (D) Tea
    (E) Cotton

34. Which of the following crops originated in Mesoamerica and spread to South America and the present-day United States in the pre-Columbian period?

    (A) Maize
    (B) Oats
    (C) Peanuts
    (D) Potatoes
    (E) Wheat

35. The African kingdoms of Mali and Ghana acquired much of their wealth from

    (A) trade across the Sahara
    (B) trade with Portuguese ships along the Atlantic coast
    (C) trade across the Atlantic with the Maya and Aztec
    (D) production of food for export to Europe
    (E) tribute from the Islamic states north of the Sahara

GO ON TO THE NEXT PAGE

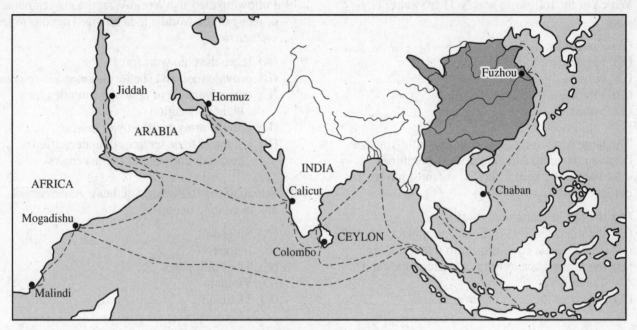

36. The map above shows the route of

   (A) Marco Polo on his travels to the court of Kublai
       Khan
   (B) Ibn Battutah on his travels through Dar al-Islam
   (C) Zheng He in his seafaring voyages from China
   (D) the Arab slave traders
   (E) the Buddhist pilgrim Xuanzang

GO ON TO THE NEXT PAGE

37. Which of the following was NOT a Swahili city-state?

    (A) Zimbabwe
    (B) Mogadishu
    (C) Kilwa
    (D) Mombasa
    (E) Sofala

38. The large earthen mounds built in North America between the tenth and the thirteenth centuries C.E., such as those at Cahokia, are most likely evidence of

    (A) the use of communal dwellings
    (B) the importance of trade and commerce
    (C) a large-scale commitment to road-building
    (D) the importance of religious ceremonies and rituals
    (E) a democratic form of government

39. Following the First World War, the governments of many of the world's industrialized nations urged women to

    (A) leave the paid workforce
    (B) provide food and shelter for disabled veterans
    (C) take advantage of new opportunities for higher education
    (D) join the army to offset war losses
    (E) volunteer their services in understaffed hospitals and rehabilitation centers

40. Which of the following Southeast Asian nations has an Islamic majority?

    (A) Singapore
    (B) Indonesia
    (C) The Philippines
    (D) Vietnam
    (E) Thailand

GO ON TO THE NEXT PAGE

EURASIA, 1300 C.E.

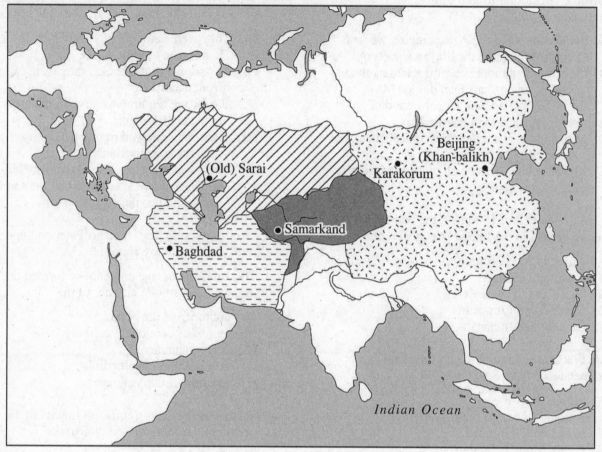

41. The four differently shaded land regions on the map
    above were collectively known as the

    (A) Quadruple Alliance
    (B) Hellenistic Kingdoms
    (C) Mongol Khanates
    (D) Mamluk Sultanates
    (E) Tetrarchy

GO ON TO THE NEXT PAGE

42. Mayan civilization differed from Aztec civilization in that

 (A) nobles governed the Aztec empire, whereas priests dominated the Mayan society
 (B) the Aztec had more peaceful relations with neighboring groups than did the Maya
 (C) the Aztec had a much longer period of predominance than did the Maya
 (D) Mayan cities were generally independent, but Aztec cities were not
 (E) Mayan society was much more expansionist than Aztec society

43. In the period before 1500 C.E., the two primary trading groups in the Indian Ocean were the

 (A) Africans and Portuguese
 (B) Arabs and Indians
 (C) Arabs and Portuguese
 (D) Chinese and Europeans
 (E) Chinese and Indians

44. The first armed attempt to gain Mexican independence from Spain was led by

 (A) Simón Bolívar
 (B) Antonio López de Santa Anna
 (C) Bernardo O'Higgins
 (D) Father Miguel Hidalgo
 (E) José de San Martín

45. The feudal periods in Japan and western Europe were similar in that both

 (A) coincided with a period of growth in the money economy
 (B) were characterized by frequent warfare
 (C) saw the development of strong monarchies
 (D) were marked by greater freedom for women than had existed previously
 (E) were dominated by religious strife

46. Which of the following cities had the largest population in 1000 C.E.?

 (A) Constantinople
 (B) London
 (C) Paris
 (D) Rome
 (E) Toledo

47. Which of the following is true of the legal status of Jews and Christians in early Islamic society?

 (A) They were categorically forbidden from holding any public office.
 (B) As "people of the book," they were exempt from taxation.
 (C) They were required to serve in the army in place of Muslims.
 (D) They were allowed to practice their religions with some restrictions.
 (E) They were treated as equals of Muslim citizens and were accorded all the same rights and privileges as Muslims.

48. "And I say unto thee, thou art Peter and upon this rock I will build my church."

The Biblical passage cited above formed the basis in the early Catholic church for the

 (A) authority of the pope
 (B) emphasis on clerical celibacy
 (C) seven sacraments
 (D) construction of cathedrals
 (E) location of the Vatican

49. What was the most significant impact of the period of the Mongol rule on Russia?

 (A) The period of Mongol rule reinforced the isolation of Russia from western Europe.
 (B) The Mongols aided the Russians in gaining political dominance over the peoples of the Central Asian steppes.
 (C) The period of Mongol rule introduced many Muslims into the region of Russia.
 (D) The Mongol domination resulted in the destruction of Eastern Orthodoxy and the rise of Nestorian Christianity.
 (E) Russians' admiration of Mongol culture led them to abandon their Byzantine roots.

GO ON TO THE NEXT PAGE

50. Which of the following was an important characteristic of the Inca road system?

   (A) It was well equipped for even the heaviest wheeled wagons.
   (B) It was kept up by privately owned commercial companies.
   (C) It required frequent repair because of the high tides and salt water of the Pacific.
   (D) It facilitated transportation among the towns of the high Andes mountains.
   (E) It linked independent city-states.

51. As a result of the defeats of China in the first Anglo-Chinese war (1839-1842) and in later conflicts with Westerners, the Chinese were forced to do all of the following EXCEPT

   (A) allow Western missionaries to seek converts in China
   (B) cede Hong Kong territory to the British
   (C) open numerous port cities to foreign traders
   (D) grant Westerners in China the privilege of extraterritoriality
   (E) ban the import of opium into China

52. In 750 C.E., a major political difference between China and Europe was that, unlike Europe, China

   (A) was a unified empire
   (B) was a theocracy
   (C) was controlled by rulers who came from outside its borders
   (D) was under threat of invasion from all sides
   (E) had a republican form of government

53. "When the personal life is cultivated, the family will be regulated; when the family is regulated, the state will be in order; and when the state is in order, there will be peace throughout the world."

   The quotation above reflects a key tenet of which of the following teachings?

   (A) Taoism
   (B) Zen Buddhism
   (C) Mahayana Buddhism
   (D) Shinto
   (E) Confucianism

54. Early Roman religious ritual was heavily influenced by the religious practices of the

   (A) Scythians
   (B) Gauls
   (C) Etruscans
   (D) Carthaginians
   (E) Druids

55. After amassing the largest land empire ever known, most of the Mongols and Turks who invaded central and south Asia converted to

   (A) Confucianism
   (B) Christianity
   (C) Buddhism
   (D) Judaism
   (E) Islam

56. In the seventeenth century, European maritime trade was dominated by the

   (A) English
   (B) Dutch
   (C) French
   (D) Swedes
   (E) Spanish

57. The failure of Europe's potato crop in the late 1840's spurred mass emigration from

   (A) Sweden
   (B) Spain
   (C) Ireland
   (D) Italy
   (E) Russia

58. Which of the following became important New World contributions to the world's food crops?

   (A) Wheat and barley
   (B) Rice and sugarcane
   (C) Oats and millet
   (D) Maize and potatoes
   (E) Bananas and melons

GO ON TO THE NEXT PAGE

59. Alexander II emancipated the serfs and introduced government reforms following Russia's defeat in the

(A) Balkan Wars
(B) Crimean War
(C) First World War
(D) Russo-Turkish Wars
(E) Russo-Japanese War

60. After independence, India pursued a foreign policy that led to which of the following?

(A) Its membership in the Soviet-backed Warsaw Pact
(B) Its membership in the Southeast Asia Treaty Organization
(C) Its signing of a mutual defense pact with the People's Republic of China
(D) Its emergence as a leader of the Nonaligned Movement
(E) Its avoidance of armed conflict with its neighbors

61. Which of the following best characterizes the classical economic theory of Adam Smith?

(A) The demands of consumers are met most cheaply by competition among individual producers.
(B) Since land is the source of value, the whole economy will benefit if small holdings are consolidated into large estates.
(C) An increase in wages will increase the demand for manufactured goods, making the economy as a whole grow.
(D) Since the interests of businessmen and workers are necessarily in conflict, the interests of one can thrive only at the expense of the other.
(E) To encourage the growth of infant national industries, government should protect them from unfair foreign competition by imposing tariffs.

62. Which of the following countries are members of the Organization of Petroleum Exporting Countries (OPEC) ?

(A) Argentina, Mexico, and Turkey
(B) China, Egypt, and the United States
(C) Great Britain, Canada, and Morocco
(D) The Soviet Union, Syria, and Kenya
(E) Venezuela, Nigeria, and Iraq

63. The navigator James Cook was most famous for

(A) being the first to sail around the world
(B) charting a northwest passage
(C) exploring the Antarctic continent
(D) scientific observation on Caribbean islands
(E) charting the seas around Australia and New Zealand

64. In closing Japan to Europeans, the Tokugawa shogunate was motivated primarily by a desire to limit

(A) the influence of Westerners on Japanese government and society
(B) a large influx of European immigrants
(C) widespread intermarriage between Japanese and Europeans
(D) the despoiling of Japan's pristine natural environment by Europeans
(E) the spread of industrialization to Japan

65. Which of the following was a major consequence of the opening of large silver mines in Spanish colonies in the Americas during the 1500's?

(A) The production of goods in Spain for export to its colonies in America was greatly stimulated.
(B) The increased wealth circulating in Spain's colonies fueled a resurgence of Native American culture.
(C) The European economy experienced an extended period of price inflation.
(D) The Spanish colonies where the mines were located were successful in declaring their independence from Spain.
(E) Other European powers succeeded in capturing the mines from Spain.

GO ON TO THE NEXT PAGE

66. Which of the following societies was the LEAST dependent on livestock?

    (A) Aztec society
    (B) Chinese society
    (C) Persian society
    (D) Tartar society
    (E) Roman society

67. Which of the following was called "the Sick Man of Europe" in the nineteenth century?

    (A) Italy
    (B) Spain
    (C) The Netherlands
    (D) The Ottoman Empire
    (E) Russia

68. The eighteenth-century philosophy of Deism was strongly denounced by

    (A) Voltaire and his followers
    (B) the Roman Catholic church
    (C) essayists in Diderot's *Encyclopédie*
    (D) Locke and his followers
    (E) Frederick the Great of Prussia

69. Which of the following was one of the major effects of the spread of gunpowder technology in Europe in the 1400's and 1500's C.E.?

    (A) The superior firepower of European armies led to the reconquest of most lands that had been lost to the Ottoman Turks.
    (B) The widespread use of guns in hunting led to a virtual extermination of game animals and game birds in Europe.
    (C) The high cost of equipping armies with guns led to a strengthening of some centralized monarchies at the expense of feudal lords.
    (D) Fear of the new technology led to religious revivals in many areas of Europe.
    (E) Many European countries sought to avoid conflicts with each other because gunpowder made wars more destructive.

70. Which of the following factors contributed to the success of independence movements in Latin America during the early 1800's?

    (A) Military and economic aid from the United States
    (B) An increase in the production of precious metals from Latin American mines
    (C) The establishment of universities throughout Latin America
    (D) The drain on Spain's resources caused by the Napoleonic Wars
    (E) Intervention by professional revolutionaries from France

71. In the sixteenth and seventeenth centuries, the primary interest of the European powers in the East Indies was to

    (A) buy rice and other food grains
    (B) obtain wood for shipbuilding
    (C) obtain spices for trading
    (D) seek markets for exports
    (E) exploit silver mines in the area

72. The most characteristic feature of Enlightenment thought was

    (A) opposition to slavery
    (B) antimaterialism
    (C) opposition to religious belief
    (D) an emphasis on reason
    (E) a belief in sexual equality

73. Mazzini, Cavour, and Garibaldi are most often associated with

    (A) parliamentary democracy in Italy
    (B) Italian unification
    (C) the rebuilding of Rome
    (D) Italian imperialism in Ethiopia
    (E) Italian industrialization

GO ON TO THE NEXT PAGE

74. When Siddhartha Gautama (the Buddha) embarked on his spiritual quest in the sixth century B.C.E., his primary concern was

    (A) whether there is one God or many
    (B) whether there is life after death
    (C) why humans suffer
    (D) how to convert nonbelievers
    (E) the relationship between religion and the state

75. Which of the following best explains ancient Egypt's ability to support a large population?

    (A) Its strategic location on the Mediterranean Sea
    (B) The approval its religious leaders gave to the concept of large families
    (C) The yearly flooding of the Nile River
    (D) The early introduction of technology from Mesopotamia
    (E) The use of the three-field crop rotation system

76. Which of the following best characterizes demographic change in eighteenth century England?

    (A) Destruction of the nuclear family during the Industrial Revolution caused the population to decline.
    (B) Unhealthy conditions in crowded cities caused the population to decline.
    (C) Pressures of the enclosure movement caused the population to decline.
    (D) Dramatically rising birth rates caused the population to increase.
    (E) Falling death rates caused the population to increase.

GO ON TO THE NEXT PAGE

77. The cartoon above shows President Gamal Abdel
    Nasser (1956–1970) encouraging Egyptians to see
    the advantages of

    (A) maintaining equality in the workplace
    (B) curbing population growth
    (C) reducing consumption
    (D) increasing savings
    (E) legalizing unions

GO ON TO THE NEXT PAGE

78. Of the following Southeast Asian countries, which is NOT matched with the colonial power that dominated it during the colonial period?

   (A) Vietnam   <------>   France
   (B) Burma   <------>   Germany
   (C) Indonesia <------>   the Netherlands
   (D) Malaya   <------>   Great Britain
   (E) The Philippines <---> the United States

79. The Boxer Rebellion was a revolt of

   (A) Indian soldiers against British domination
   (B) Vietnamese against French domination
   (C) Arabs against the Ottoman Empire
   (D) Chinese against Western imperialism
   (E) Koreans against Japanese rule

Mansell Collection

80. The picture above, which depicts the symbolic crowning of a twelfth-century king of Sicily by Christ, reveals the cultural influence of

   (A) Russia
   (B) Scandinavia
   (C) Spain
   (D) Islam
   (E) Byzantium

GO ON TO THE NEXT PAGE ⟩

81. The political and religious center at Great Zimbabwe, which reached its height in the fifteenth century, was characterized by all of the following EXCEPT

    (A) long-distance trading
    (B) gold mining
    (C) significant population expansion
    (D) a written epic tradition
    (E) copper and bronze ornament making

82. Which of the following art forms originated in the United States?

    (A) Impressionism
    (B) Surrealist poetry
    (C) Social realism
    (D) Jazz
    (E) Atonal music

83. The Provisional Government failed to keep the support of the Russian people in 1917 because it

    (A) executed the entire royal family
    (B) collectivized agriculture and industry
    (C) allowed Nicholas II to rule as a constitutional monarch
    (D) suffered a humiliating defeat by the Japanese
    (E) continued Russia's participation in the First World War

84. Which of the following best describes the Indian National Congress?

    (A) The first national political organization in India to challenge British rule
    (B) The first all-Indian legislative body formed after independence in 1947
    (C) An organization formed by Hindus that primarily preached tolerance of Indian Muslims
    (D) An organization formed by Hindus and Muslims that sought social reform within India
    (E) A conference of Muslim religious leaders that convened to discuss Indian statehood

85. Of all the dictatorial regimes established in Europe between the First and Second World Wars, the one that held power the longest was that of

    (A) Hitler
    (B) Stalin
    (C) Mussolini
    (D) Pilsudski
    (E) Franco

86. One of the principal strengths of the Byzantine empire was its

    (A) constitutional monarchy
    (B) sound economic base
    (C) preference for decentralized government
    (D) close relationship with the Roman Catholic church
    (E) orderly system of succession to the throne

87. The first significant test of the ability of the League of Nations to respond when a major nation acted as an aggressor occurred when

    (A) Japan invaded Manchuria
    (B) the Soviet Union invaded Poland
    (C) Japan declared war on China
    (D) Franco's rebels attacked Spanish loyalists
    (E) Hitler incorporated Austria into the Third Reich

88. In the 1980's, which of the following Muslim countries most actively promoted Islamic fundamentalism?

    (A) Morocco
    (B) Iran
    (C) Iraq
    (D) Indonesia
    (E) Turkey

89. Mao Zedong revolutionized Chinese Marxist doctrine in the 1920's by advocating that the

    (A) Chinese Communist Party sever its ties with the Soviet Union to preserve its independence
    (B) Chinese Communist Party allow its rival, the Kuomintang, to reform a separate government on the island of Taiwan
    (C) Chinese Communist Party renounce the use of violence to achieve revolution
    (D) rural peasants, not the urban proletariat, lead the revolution in China
    (E) landlord and capitalist classes be allowed to survive even after the communists took power

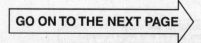

90. The economies of China, North Korea, and North Vietnam were relatively isolated from the world economy during much of the third quarter of the twentieth century primarily because of their

(A) adherence to a planned Marxist economy
(B) inability to recover from the devastation of the Second World War
(C) subjection to a trade embargo enforced by the United Nations
(D) subjection to almost continual civil wars
(E) enduring extended droughts due to global climate change

91. The partition of Korea at the end of the Second World War in 1945 was primarily the result of

(A) rivalry between the United States and the Soviet Union
(B) Japanese dominance of important sectors of the Korean economy
(C) the emergence of China as a major world power
(D) the inability of the Koreans to agree on a form of government
(E) sharp cultural differences between northern and southern Korea

92. During the American occupation of Japan following the Second World War, authorities seeking to restructure Japanese society received the strongest support from which of the following Japanese groups?

(A) Socialist leaders
(B) Business leaders
(C) Military leaders
(D) Expatriates returning to Japan
(E) Members of the imperial court

93. Many historians believe that the end of the French Revolutionary era was the

(A) execution of King Louis XVI
(B) Reign of Terror
(C) storming of the Bastille prison
(D) defeat of Napoleon in Russia
(E) peace settlement at the Congress of Vienna

94. The nations that signed and confirmed the 1975 Helsinki Accords agreed to

(A) establish uniform prices for crude oil
(B) establish peace in the Middle East
(C) cooperate among themselves and respect human rights
(D) end the Vietnam conflict and withdraw all foreign troops
(E) end the Cold War

95. In the late twentieth century, experts began to question the value of building large dam projects in the developing world primarily because these projects tend to

(A) reduce the cost of electric power in the countries in which they are built
(B) displace people from their homes and disturb the ecology of the regions in which they are built
(C) encourage separatist movements in the areas in which they are built
(D) conflict with the development plans of the central governments of the countries in which they are built
(E) disrupt road and rail communications across the rivers on which the dams are built

S T O P

**If you finish before time is called, you may check your work on this test only.
Do not turn to any other section in the test.**

How to Score the SAT Subject Test in World History

When you take an actual SAT Subject Test in World History, your answer sheet will be "read" by a scanning machine that will record your responses to each question. Then a computer will compare your answers with the correct answers and produce your raw score. You get one point for each correct answer. For each wrong answer, you lose one-quarter of a point. Questions you omit (and any for which you mark more than one answer) are not counted. This raw score is converted to a scaled score that is reported to you and to the colleges you specify.

Worksheet 1. Finding Your Raw Test Score

STEP 1: Table A on the following page lists the correct answers for all the questions on the Subject Test in World History that is reproduced in this book. It also serves as a worksheet for you to calculate your raw score.

- Compare your answers with those given in the table.

- Put a check in the column marked "Right" if your answer is correct.

- Put a check in the column marked "Wrong" if your answer is incorrect.

- Leave both columns blank if you omitted the question.

STEP 2: Count the number of right answers.

Enter the total here: _____

STEP 3: Count the number of wrong answers.

Enter the total here: _____

STEP 4: Multiply the number of wrong answers by .250.

Enter the product here: _____

STEP 5: Subtract the result obtained in Step 4 from the total you obtained in Step 2.

Enter the result here: _____

STEP 6: Round the number obtained in Step 5 to the nearest whole number.

Enter the result here: _____

The number you obtained in Step 6 is your raw score.

Answers to Practice Test 3 for World History

Table A
Answers to the Subject Test in World History - Practice Test 3 and Percentage of Students Answering Each Question Correctly

Question Number	Correct Answer	Right	Wrong	Percentage of Students Answering the Question Correctly*	Question Number	Correct Answer	Right	Wrong	Percentage of Students Answering the Question Correctly*
1	A			66	26	A			73
2	B			59	27	D			68
3	C			76	28	A			46
4	B			49	29	E			77
5	E			65	30	A			48
6	D			79	31	A			73
7	A			61	32	D			56
8	E			93	33	A			41
9	D			57	34	A			64
10	D			76	35	A			50
11	B			35	36	C			52
12	A			54	37	A			24
13	A			80	38	D			59
14	C			41	39	A			33
15	A			51	40	B			71
16	C			21	41	C			69
17	B			43	42	D			19
18	A			29	43	B			37
19	B			81	44	D			37
20	C			71	45	B			55
21	C			47	46	A			67
22	A			73	47	D			51
23	B			85	48	A			36
24	D			82	49	A			60
25	B			95	50	D			55

Table A continued on next page

Table A continued from previous page

Question Number	Correct Answer	Right	Wrong	Percentage of Students Answering the Question Correctly*	Question Number	Correct Answer	Right	Wrong	Percentage of Students Answering the Question Correctly*
51	E			69	76	E			20
52	A			65	77	B			80
53	E			65	78	B			39
54	C			45	79	D			74
55	E			62	80	E			67
56	B			32	81	D			49
57	C			89	82	D			88
58	D			65	83	E			52
59	B			43	84	A			41
60	D			35	85	E			12
61	A			46	86	B			31
62	E			65	87	A			41
63	E			46	88	B			53
64	A			83	89	D			56
65	C			53	90	A			55
66	A			27	91	A			47
67	D			63	92	B			54
68	B			50	93	E			38
69	C			36	94	C			26
70	D			52	95	B			77
71	C			71					
72	D			82					
73	B			60					
74	C			77					
75	C			65					

* These percentages are based on an analysis of the answer sheets of a representative sample of 9,745 students who took the original administration of this test and whose mean score was 611. They may be used as an indication of the relative difficulty of a particular question.

Finding Your Scaled Score

When you take SAT Subject Tests, the scores sent to the colleges you specify are reported on the College Board scale, which ranges from 200 to 800. You can convert your practice test raw score to a scaled score by using Table B. To find your scaled score, locate your raw score in the left-hand column of Table B; the corresponding score in the right-hand column is your scaled score. For example, a raw score of 39 on this particular edition of the SAT Subject Test in World History corresponds to a scaled score of 580.

Raw scores are converted to scaled scores to ensure that a score earned on any one edition of a particular Subject Test is comparable to the same scaled score earned on any other edition of the same Subject Test. Because some editions of the tests may be slightly easier or more difficult than others, College Board scaled scores are adjusted so that they indicate the same level of performance regardless of the edition of the test taken and the ability of the group that takes it. Thus, for example, a score of 400 on one edition of a test taken at a particular administration indicates the same level of achievement as a score of 400 on a different edition of the test taken at a different administration.

When you take the SAT Subject Tests during a national administration, your scores are likely to differ somewhat from the scores you obtain on the tests in this book. People perform at different levels at different times for reasons unrelated to the tests themselves. The precision of any test is also limited because it represents only a sample of all the possible questions that could be asked.

Table B
Scaled Score Conversion Table
Subject Test in World History Test – Practice Test 3

Raw Score	Scaled Score	Raw Score	Scaled Score	Raw Score	Scaled Score
95	800	55	670	15	440
94	800	54	660	14	440
93	800	53	660	13	430
92	800	52	650	12	420
91	800	51	640	11	420
90	800	50	640	10	410
89	800	49	630	9	410
88	800	48	630	8	400
87	800	47	620	7	400
86	800	46	620	6	390
85	800	45	610	5	380
84	800	44	610	4	380
83	800	43	600	3	370
82	800	42	590	2	370
81	800	41	590	1	360
80	800	40	580	0	360
79	800	39	580	−1	350
78	800	38	570	−2	350
77	790	37	570	−3	340
76	790	36	560	−4	340
75	780	35	560	−5	330
74	770	34	550	−6	330
73	770	33	550	−7	330
72	760	32	540	−8	320
71	760	31	530	−9	320
70	750	30	530	−10	310
69	750	29	520	−11	310
68	740	28	520	−12	300
67	740	27	510	−13	300
66	730	26	510	−14	300
65	720	25	500	−15	290
64	720	24	490	−16	280
63	710	23	490	−17	280
62	710	22	480	−18	270
61	700	21	480	−19	260
60	690	20	470	−20	250
59	690	19	470	−21	250
58	680	18	460	−22	240
57	680	17	450	−23	230
56	670	16	450	−24	220

How Did You Do on the Subject Test in World History?

After you score your test and analyze your performance, think about the following questions:

Did you run out of time before reaching the end of the test?

If so, you may need to pace yourself better. For example, maybe you spent too much time on one or two hard questions. A better approach might be to skip the ones you can't answer right away and try answering all the remaining questions on the test. Then if there's time, go back to the questions you skipped.

Did you take a long time reading the directions?

You will save time when you take the test by learning the directions to the Subject Test in World History ahead of time. Each minute you spend reading directions during the test is a minute that you could use to answer questions.

How did you handle questions you were unsure of?

If you were able to eliminate one or more of the answer choices as wrong and guess from the remaining ones, your approach probably worked to your advantage. On the other hand, making haphazard guesses or omitting questions without trying to eliminate choices could cost you valuable points.

How difficult were the questions for you compared with other students who took the test?

Table A shows you how difficult the multiple-choice questions were for the group of students who took this test during its national administration. The right-hand column gives the percentage of students that answered each question correctly.

A question answered correctly by almost everyone in the group is obviously an easier question. For example, 82 percent of the students answered question 24 correctly. However, only 19 percent answered question 42 correctly.

Keep in mind that these percentages are based on just one group of students. They would probably be different with another group of students taking the test.

If you missed several easier questions, go back and try to find out why: Did the questions cover material you haven't yet reviewed? Did you misunderstand the directions?

Answer Explanations

For Practice Test 3

Question 1

Choice (A) is the correct answer. Philosophical schools flourished in both Greece and China around 500 B.C.E. In Greece, during the sixth and fifth centuries B.C.E., many influential philosophers, including Pythagoras, Parmenides, Heraclitus, Socrates, and Plato debated the human condition. At the same time in China, Lao Tzu wrote *Tao Te Ching*, in which he outlined a new philosophical understanding and practice of human life, eventually known as Taoism. Also in China, the philosophy of Confucianism took shape at this time.

Question 2

Choice (B) is the correct answer. The central characters of these three epic poems are all from the elite class of warriors of their respective civilizations. The *Mahabharata* recounts the battle between two branches of the same Indian warrior family, the Kauravas and the Pandavas. The *Iliad* focuses on the battle between the Trojan and the Achaean (or Greek) warriors. The *Tales of the Heike* is an account of the struggle between two Japanese samurai clans, the Taira and the Minamoto.

Question 3

Choice (C) is the correct answer. Islam, founded on Muhammad's teaching, stresses the influence of Allah (God) on every aspect of human life. As such, Islam's teachings and decrees affected the entire life of its converts, thus establishing similarity and unity among followers of diverse backgrounds.

Question 4

Choice (B) is the correct answer. Attila led his empire and armies of the Huns from 434 C.E. until his death in 453 C.E. Although he never gained full control over the area covered by the Western Roman Empire, in the 450s, Attila invaded and ravaged much of the Empire, entirely destroying several cities. This damage by Attila contributed to the deterioration of the Western Roman Empire and its eventual fall in 476.

Question 5

Choice (E) is the correct answer. After the fall of the Han dynasty, northern China eventually came to be ruled by nomadic peoples. They were far fewer than the Chinese people they governed. As a result, they tended to assimilate or adopt the customs of the larger Chinese population.

Question 6

Choice (D) is the correct answer. Both Mahavira and Buddha led religious movements in India sometime between the sixth and fourth centuries B.C.E. They both came from prominent families in Hindu society and developed religious systems that challenged that social order. Mahavira impoverished himself and spread teachings that became the basic tenets of Jainism. Buddha developed the religious system that has come to be known as Buddhism.

Question 7

Choice (A) is the correct answer. In 1816, Shaka took over leadership of the Zulu. Shaka reorganized the Zulu army and instituted the use of short spears that forced close warfare. He also developed military tactics that utilized several groups of warriors, some of which encircled the foe from the sides like a set of ox's horns. Under Shaka, the Zulu were incredibly successful warriors who dominated southern Africa throughout the nineteenth century.

Question 8

Choice (E) is the correct answer. Realistically representing people in art is not central to Islamic faith and is generally considered to go against the teachings of Muhammad. The five central pillars of Islam are fasting during Ramadan (A); professing faith in the one God, Allah (B); praying five times daily facing Mecca (C); making a pilgrimage to Mecca at least once (D); and giving alms to the poor.

Question 9

Choice (D) is the correct answer. In the late 1990s, Pakistan acquired the capability of exploding nuclear weapons. India had acquired this capability in 1974. The two countries share a border and historically have had a strained relationship, especially with respect to the disputed territory of Kashmir, so the acquisition of nuclear weapons by both countries is a matter of global concern.

Question 10

Choice (D) is the correct answer. The main tenet of Stalin's governing strategy was to centralize as much control of the Soviet Union as possible. A major strategy for achieving strong central control was to centralize economic planning. Soviet economic decisions under Stalin were made by a central State authority; companies were not allowed to make private economic decisions.

Question 11

Choice (B) is the correct answer. Historiography is the study of different ways historical events are interpreted and recorded, not the study of the events themselves. Historiography is also the study of the methodology and practices used when writing history. Its elements include inquiry into the nature and credibility of the source, evolving views of history, and the specific perspective from which a particular history or historical narrative has been written.

Question 12

Choice (A) is the correct answer. In imperial China, the scholar-gentry (sometimes referred to as scholar-officials or mandarins) composed the most important part of the official bureaucracy. The members of the scholar-gentry usually came from landowner families and were the imperial civil servants. They were well educated and, by the Tang dynasty (618–907 C.E.), had to pass civil service exams to receive a position. At this time, wealthy merchants paid to educate their sons so they could pass the exam and become imperial bureaucrats.

Question 13

Choice (A) is the correct answer. Japan's defeat of Russia in the Russo-Japanese War (1904–1905) demonstrated that modernization was not limited to Western nations. Japan was able to defeat the massive Russian navy and much of the Russian army. By using its newly modernized forces, Japan's victory established it as a world power in the modern era and was a source of inspiration for anti-colonial movements throughout the world.

Question 14

Choice (C) is the correct answer. After defeating the Umayyads at the Battle of the Zab River in 750 C.E., the Abbasids moved the caliphate from Damascus to Baghdad. The Umayyad caliphs had ruled the Islamic world since 661 C.E. The Abbasids relied on Persian support to overthrow the Umayyads and incorporated Persian methods of government in their caliphate.

Question 15

Choice (A) is the correct answer. A megalithic structure is a structure made of large rocks that may be free-standing or may be connected without the use of cement or mortar. Stonehenge is the most famous megalithic structure. Located near Amesbury, England, Stonehenge is a circular arrangement of stone monuments that was constructed between 3100 B.C.E. and 2000 B.C.E.

Question 16

Choice (C) is the correct answer. The Toltec were a Native American people who thrived in central Mexico between the tenth and twelfth century C.E. When the Aztec came to power in the fourteenth century, they claimed that they had descended from the Toltec, whom they regarded as the givers of civilization. The Aztec did, in fact, speak Nahuatl, the language of the Toltec, and the two peoples shared many customs and rituals.

Question 17

Choice (B) is the correct answer. Indo-European and Bantu are both terms historians use to describe language groups. Indo-European refers to the large language group now found throughout much of Europe and Asia that includes many modern languages such as English, Persian (or Farsi), Russian, Spanish, and Hindi. The Bantu language family, which includes Zulu, Xhosa, Kongo, Swahili, and Sotho, is found throughout much of Sub-Saharan Africa.

Question 18

Choice (A) is the correct answer. One historical theory proposes that the need for flood protection and irrigation in river valleys caused civilizations in these areas to develop large bureaucratic, impersonal, and often despotic governments. Agricultural-based civilizations relied on the irrigation of water and large-scale irrigation projects required a strong centralized government to be successful. These river-valley civilizations (called "hydraulic civilizations" by Karl Wittfogel) developed a complex social organization, usually with forced labor, a bureaucratic government, and a powerful emperor who was often identified with the gods.

Question 19

Choice (B) is the correct answer. Working-class women in nineteenth-century England had limited social and employment opportunities. Many young working-class women were encouraged by their parents to take jobs as domestic servants in higher-class homes, not for future professional training (D) or with the hopes of marrying wealthier men (C), but primarily to make extra money for their families, while learning habits and skills they could apply later on as wives.

Question 20

Choice (C) is the correct answer. Beginning in the Zhou dynasty, emperors of China used the concept of the Mandate of Heaven to justify their power. According to the Mandate of Heaven, as long as an emperor ruled wisely and justly, he enjoyed divine blessing. If he began to misuse his position, he would lose the Mandate. Throughout Chinese history, the Mandate of Heaven was used to justify the passing of power from one dynasty to the next. As one dynasty began to misuse its power, the next claimed the authority of the Mandate to avoid suffering any disasters or disturbances.

Question 21

Choice (C) is the correct answer. It is commonly accepted that the term *Homo sapiens* classifies humans who can consciously think. In evolutionary theory, *Homo sapiens* (translated from Latin as "wise or thinking man") are distinguished from their closest ancestors or related species by the advanced form of conscious thinking that their large brain allows. Other related species, like *Homo erectus*, may have walked upright, but probably lacked the level of conscious thinking of *Homo sapiens*.

Question 22

Choice (A) is the correct answer. Although some later branches of Buddhism include belief in a god, Buddhism, in its original form, is a religious system that focuses on humanity's correct path through life without making reference to any god or gods. Buddhism originated in the late sixth century B.C.E. in northeastern India as a belief system centered on the religious and philosophical teachings of the Buddha. The wider tradition of Hinduism includes belief in many different deities (C). Christianity (B), Islam (D), and Judaism (E) are all religions that are centered on the belief in one god.

Question 23

Choice (B) is the correct answer. Social Darwinism applies Charles Darwin's theory of natural selection in plant and animal development to the development of human societies. According to Social Darwinism, social groups follow the same natural law of "survival of the fittest" as plants and animals. Social groups naturally compete for power and resources and the strongest, most fit societies will be the ones that survive. In the late nineteenth and early twentieth century C.E., the theory of Social Darwinism was used to justify the competition of laissez-faire capitalism and class stratification, arguing that it was in the best interest of human development for weaker societies and classes to be eliminated in favor of stronger, more fit humans.

Question 24

Choice (D) is the correct answer. The Second World War officially started on September 3, 1939, when Great Britain and France declared war on Germany in response to the German invasion of Poland. Germany had invaded Poland on September 1. Six days earlier, on August 25, Great Britain had signed a treaty with Poland pledging assistance in the event of a German invasion.

Question 25

Choice (B) is the correct answer. The pyramids of ancient Egypt were built primarily to be huge monumental tombs. The Pyramids of Giza, located on the west bank of the Nile River in northern Egypt, were built as tombs for three kings—Khufu, Khafre, and Menkaure—who reigned during the Fourth dynasty (circa 2575–2465 B.C.E.).

Question 26

Choice (A) is the correct answer. The term "caste system," often used to describe Hindu society, is characterized as a rigid socially stratified society. While the term "caste" itself does not originate in Hinduism, Hindu society was traditionally divided into four levels. The Brahman enjoy the highest position in society and were originally the priests and teachers of the Hindu scriptures.

Question 27

Choice (D) is the correct answer. From his ascent to the Macedonian throne in 336 B.C.E. until his death in 323 B.C.E., Alexander the Great led continuous successful military expeditions that expanded the Greek Empire beyond the Middle East and into Asia. In 333 B.C.E., he defeated the main Persian army, and eventually gained control over the Persian Empire throughout western Asia. As he took control of lands with different cultures, Alexander encouraged the intermingling of Greek and non-Greek peoples and customs. By the time of his death, he had spread Greek cultural forms from the Mediterranean to India, laying the foundation for the Hellenistic Age.

Question 28

Choice (A) is the correct answer. The Celts are a group of ancient Indo-European peoples who inhabited the British Isles and western Europe from prehistory until their eventual absorption into the Roman Empire. In the first century B.C.E., Julius Caesar led the Roman conquests over the Celts in Gaul. Britain was conquered by the Romans a century later, thus ending the history of Celtic political power in Europe.

Question 29

Choice (E) is the correct answer. Greek civilization did not originate along a river valley, but around the Aegean Sea, a branch of the Mediterranean Sea. The other four civilizations all originated in river valleys: the Chinese (A), along the Huang He (Yellow) River; the Indian (B), along the Indus and Ganges rivers; the Egyptian (C), along the Nile River; and the Mesopotamian (D), between the Tigris and Euphrates rivers.

Question 30

Choice (A) is the correct answer. Beginning in the 1400s C.E., European states underwent a commercial revolution in which the capitalistic trade of goods became more central to their economies. In the developing capitalistic economies, the European states competed for new trade routes, products, and partners. With the invention of larger and stronger ships capable of navigating the Atlantic Ocean, European explorers expanded the reach of these economies to the Americas and Africa, during what has come to be called the Age of Exploration.

Question 31

Choice (A) is the correct answer. All of these English words are derivations of Arabic words and reflect the intermingling of Arab and European cultures.

Question 32

Choice (D) is the correct answer. The term "Neolithic" refers to the period in human technological development characterized by the domestication of plants and animals. Originally associated with the end of the Old Stone Age in Europe, Asia, and Africa, "Neolithic" is now more commonly used to refer to the developmental period of any culture when plant and animal domestication occurs. Metallurgy, or the development of metal tools, marks the end of the Neolithic Age.

Question 33

Choice (A) is the correct answer. The spread of sugar cultivation to the Americas was accompanied by a major shift in human population. Sugar cultivation was labor intensive, and the Europeans who established plantations on Caribbean islands and the mainland relied on enslaved Africans to do most of the work. Though exact numbers are unobtainable, millions of Africans were transported to the Americas during the sixteenth through nineteenth centuries. Probably more than three-quarters of them were sent to sugar plantations.

Question 34

Choice (A) is the correct answer. Domestic cultivation of maize, or corn, probably began to spread from the Oaxaca Valley of Mexico (part of Mesoamerica) around 3500 B.C.E. Maize spread widely during the pre-Columbian era, becoming a staple food in many pre-Columbian cultures throughout North and South America.

Question 35

Choice (A) is the correct answer. The West African Muslim kingdoms of Ghana (eighth to thirteenth century C.E.) and Mali (fourteenth to sixteenth century C.E.) acquired vast amounts of wealth through the trans-Saharan trade routes to the North African cities along the Mediterranean Sea. The West African kingdoms desired the salt of the Mediterranean regions and, in return, provided gold and slaves.

Question 36

Choice (C) is the correct answer. This map shows the routes of Zheng He's seafaring voyages from China across the Indian Ocean to Africa, Arabia, India, Ceylon, and Southeast Asia. Zheng He, a Chinese Muslim, commanded massive expeditions of up to 30,000 men on more than 300 ships for the Ming emperors during the fifteenth century C.E.

Question 37

Choice (A) is the correct answer. Mogadishu, Kilwa, Mombasa, and Sofala were all Swahili city-states along the coast of East Africa. Starting around 1000 C.E., numerous Swahili city-states developed along Africa's eastern coast through successful trading with one another and with landlocked African regions like Zimbabwe. Although it interacted with the Swahili city-states, Zimbabwe was an interior empire, not a Swahili city-state.

Question 38

Choice (D) is the correct answer. Between the tenth and thirteenth centuries C.E., mound-building cultures thrived in North America. These cultures built large earthen mounds that were most likely used as sites for religious ceremonies and burials. The largest of these mounds was built in the 1000s C.E. in the Native American city of Cahokia, in present-day Illinois.

Question 39

Choice (A) is the correct answer. During the First World War, many women in Europe and the United States filled industrial jobs left vacant by the men who were fighting. By including women, who were previously excluded, in the workforce, industrial nations were able to maintain and increase productivity during the war. When the men returned at the end of the war, many women were asked to leave their jobs to make room for the unemployed veterans.

Question 40

Choice (B) is the correct answer. Islam is the dominant religion in Indonesia. Arab merchants brought Islam to Indonesia beginning around the twelfth century C.E. Indonesia is now the most populous Muslim nation in the world.

Question 41

Choice (C) is the correct answer. The shaded areas on the map together comprise the extent of the Mongol Khanates. The Mongol Empire, began by Genghis Khan, spread throughout Europe and Asia during the thirteenth and fourteenth centuries. At its height, it was the largest empire in world history, stretching, as the map indicates, from the Pacific Ocean to the Middle East. After the reign of Kublai Khan, the empire was divided into four Khanates as shown.

Question 42

Choice (D) is the correct answer. The Maya civilization, which originated in Mesoamerica around 1500 B.C.E., was characterized by large cities that were politically independent of one another. In contrast, the Aztecs, a Mesoamerican civilization during the fourteenth to sixteenth centuries C.E., were governed by powerful emperors who ruled from the capital city of Tenochtitlán.

Question 43

Choice (B) is the correct answer. In the period before 1500 C.E., the Indian Ocean was used primarily by Indian and Arab merchants. After 1500 C.E., Europeans, including many successful Portuguese merchants, began to use the Indian Ocean for trade. Chinese admiral Zheng He had sailed throughout the Indian Ocean before 1500 C.E., but he was primarily interested in diplomacy and exploration rather than trade.

Question 44

Choice (D) is the correct answer. On September 16, 1810, Father Miguel Hidalgo began Mexico's long war with Spain to gain independence. A parish priest from the town of Dolores, Hidalgo roused his parishioners to arms with the famous Grito de Dolores (Cry of Dolores). Hidalgo's armed group was able to capture some towns, but failed to take Mexico City. It was not until 1821, in part under the leadership of Antonio López de Santa Anna (B), that Mexico gained its independence from Spain. José de San Martín (E) was an Argentine revolutionary leader; Bernardo O'Higgins (C) was a Chilean revolutionary leader; and Simón Bolívar (A) was a South American revolutionary hero.

Question 45

Choice (B) is the correct answer. The feudal periods in both Japan and western Europe were characterized by frequent warfare. In feudal Japan (eleventh to nineteenth centuries C.E.), feudal families were led by daimyo (warlords) who fought both among each other as well as with outside invaders like the Mongols. The feudal period in western Europe (fifth to sixteenth centuries C.E.) was also characterized by warfare among small feudal principalities. In both Japan and Europe, the frequent warfare hindered the development of a money economy and a centralized monarchy.

Question 46

Choice (A) is the correct answer. In 1000 C.E., Constantinople, now the Turkish city of Istanbul, was the capital of the Eastern Roman, or Byzantine, Empire and the largest city in Europe. At that time, London, Paris, Rome, and Toledo, although important cities in their own right, were all smaller than Constantinople.

Question 47

Choice (D) is the correct answer. In early Islamic society, Jews and Christians were allowed to practice their own religions but were subject to some restrictions within society. Jews and Christians were allowed to hold some public offices, but could not be rulers (A). They were exempt from the Muslim *zakat* tax, but were required to pay the poll tax, *jizya*, which was often higher (B). They were exempt from serving in the army (C) and were tolerated, but they were considered second-class citizens (E).

Question 48

Choice (A) is the correct answer. This Biblical passage (Matthew 16:19) was used in the early Catholic Church to argue for the authority of the pope. As Bishop of Rome, the pope traces his authority back to Peter the Apostle, who was martyred and buried in Rome. According to the doctrine of "the apostolic primacy of Peter," the Bishops of Rome had authority over the other bishops who traced their authority to other apostles of Jesus. This passage, in which Jesus states that he will build his church on Peter, was used as the Biblical basis for that doctrine.

Question 49

Choice (A) is the correct answer. The period of Mongol rule over Russia during the thirteenth century reinforced Russia's isolation from western Europe. Under Mongol rule, large sections of Russia were unified, but because the Mongol Empire did not extend into western Europe, the political and cultural lines dividing Russia and western Europe became more defined. The Mongols did not force most Russians to adopt Mongol culture or Islam. As a result, when Mongol rule ended, Eastern Christian Orthodoxy was still thriving.

Question 50

Choice (D) is the correct answer. The Inca road system was a series of foot trails traversing the high Andes Mountains in Peru and linking the towns of the Inca Empire. Unfit for wheeled vehicles, the roads were used by travelers on foot to carry messages and goods between distant Incan towns.

Question 51

Choice (E) is the correct answer. British merchants were able to continue importing harmful opium into China. After losing the first Anglo-Chinese War (also known as the First Opium War) to the United Kingdom, the Chinese signed the Treaty of Nanking in 1842. This treaty, along with settlements after other defeats, ceded Hong Kong to the British (B), opened numerous ports to foreign traders (C), allowed Western missionaries in China (A), and granted Westerners the privilege of extraterritoriality (D). Additionally, China lost the power to ban the import of opium into China.

Question 52

Choice (A) is the correct answer. Unlike Europe, China was a unified empire in 750 C.E. At this time, China was unified under the Tang dynasty, which is often considered to be a high point in China's cultural history. In contrast, in 750 C.E., Europe was undergoing a period of political division. After the fall of the Western Roman Empire in the fifth century C.E., Europe was subject to continual invasion from various peoples such as the Goths and the Huns.

Question 53

Choice (E) is the correct answer. This quotation reflects a key tenet of the Chinese philosophy of Confucianism. Confucianism, developed from the teachings of Chinese philosopher Confucius (551–479 B.C.E.), draws a connection between the private lives of individuals and wider political stability. Much of Confucius' teachings centered on cultivating a personal life in line with principles of righteousness. Confucianism holds that wider political order rests on the order achieved by individuals in their own families.

Question 54

Choice (C) is the correct answer. Many early Roman religious rituals and beliefs were influenced by the religious practices of the Etruscans. The Etruscans, who inhabited ancient Italy before the rise of Roman civilization, believed that there were many gods who interacted intimately with humans. Religious rituals were used to persuade the gods to act favorably toward humans. The Romans adopted the same system, appeasing and consulting the gods in all important affairs through religious rituals.

Question 55

Choice (E) is the correct answer. The Mongol and Turkish people who made up the armies of the Mongol Khans who invaded central and south Asia later converted to Islam. Securing control over these territories, the Mongols and Turks helped define and defend the Islamic world against European Christian crusaders.

Question 56

Choice (B) is the correct answer. During the seventeenth century, the Dutch dominated European maritime trade. In 1602, the Dutch East India Company, promoting Dutch colonization and trade throughout Asia, was established. The company gained European monopolies, often violently, on the trade of many spices throughout modern-day Indonesia. The Dutch West India Company, which was granted a charter in 1621, established colonies and trade in North America and in the Caribbean. The success of these Dutch trading companies broke the dominance of European trade that Spain had enjoyed throughout the sixteenth century.

Question 57

Choice (C) is the correct answer. The Irish Potato Famine, which occurred from 1845 to 1849, spurred mass emigration of starving Irish families to Great Britain, the United States, Canada, and Australia. The famine resulted from the failure of the potato crop, a staple food for many Irish families. After a devastating potato fungus destroyed the potato crop, oppressive economic policies and incompetent farming methods created widespread hunger throughout Ireland. Hundreds of thousands of Irish died or emigrated as a direct result of the famine.

Question 58

Choice (D) is the correct answer. Maize and potatoes originated in South America and spread throughout the world as a result of European colonization. Potatoes, first grown in the Andes Mountains, were brought to Spain in the sixteenth century and eventually became a major European staple. Likewise maize, originated in ancient Mesoamerica and was brought to the Old World by Europeans.

Question 59

Choice (B) is the correct answer. In 1856, Tsar Alexander II of Russia signed the Treaty of Paris with the United Kingdom, France, and the Ottoman Empire to end the Crimean War. Following the war, Alexander II emancipated the serfs and instituted radical government reforms that reflected the progressive ideas of the educated classes. He hoped these measures would help to restore Russian power.

Question 60

Choice (D) is the correct answer. After gaining independence from the United Kingdom in 1947, India pursued a foreign policy of nonalignment. Prime Minister Jawaharlal Nehru first outlined the principles of nonalignment in 1954 as a guide to India's relationship with China. The principles were: respect for territorial integrity; mutual nonaggression; mutual noninterference in domestic affairs; equality and mutual benefit; and peaceful coexistence. These principles eventually became the foundation for the international organization, Nonaligned Movement, established in 1961.

Question 61

Choice (A) is the correct answer. In 1776, Scottish economist Adam Smith published his economic theory in *The Wealth of Nations*. The basic idea of his theory is that when producers compete to sell their goods to consumers in an unrestricted market, consumers will benefit by paying the cheapest sustainable prices. Consequently, governments should regulate trade and manufacturing as little as possible, allowing the natural forces of competition among producers to regulate the prices of products. This is known as laissez-faire economics.

Question 62

Choice (E) is the correct answer. Venezuela, Nigeria, and Iraq are all members of OPEC. Founded in 1960 by Iran, Iraq, Kuwait, Saudi Arabia, and Venezuela, OPEC is an international association created to protect the interests of oil-producing countries. The organization was founded in response to price cuts of crude oil forced on these countries by European and U.S. oil companies. Since then, OPEC has worked to regulate and increase the profits of oil-producing countries. OPEC now

has 13 members: Iran, Iraq, Kuwait, Saudi Arabia, Venezuela, Algeria, Indonesia, Libya, Qatar, United Arab Emirates, Nigeria, Ecuador, and Angola.

Question 63

Choice (E) is the correct answer. Eighteenth-century British navigator James Cook charted the seas around Australia and New Zealand during his Pacific expeditions. A superior navigator and cartographer, Cook was the first European to discover the east coast of Australia and the Hawaiian Islands and to circumnavigate New Zealand.

Question 64

Choice (A) is the correct answer. In the seventeenth century, the Tokugawa shogunate became increasingly hostile to the influence of Western culture on Japanese society. As a result of trade with European nations, Western cultural practices like Christianity were gaining ground in Japan. The Tokugawa enacted a number of anti-Western policies and eventually closed its trading seaports to all foreigners except China and the Dutch East India Company.

Question 65

Choice (C) is the correct answer. During the 1500s, the Spanish colonies in the Americas, especially in Peru, opened large silver mines. The abundance of silver taken to European and world markets from these mines contributed to a huge price inflation in the European economy. As a result of the abundant mines and the increase in Spain's power, Spain strengthened its control over its colonies in the Americas. During this period, Spain was able to rebuff European attacks (E), suppress Native American culture (B), and quell political uprisings (D).

Question 66

Choice (A) is the correct answer. The Aztec society relied primarily on agriculture for its subsistence. Most of their diet consisted of maize and beans. They did domesticate turkeys and dogs, but maintaining large animals as livestock was not a significant part of their society. The domestication of livestock was a significant part of Chinese (B), Persian (C), Tartar (D), and Roman (E) societies.

Question 67

Choice (D) is the correct answer. In the nineteenth century, the Ottoman Empire was called "the Sick Man of Europe" by Nicholas I of Russia. The Ottoman Empire had been a major European power since the fifteenth century. By the nineteenth century, however, it had lost much of its territory in the Balkans and was economically dominated by other European nations. Following the end of the First World War, the Ottoman Empire finally collapsed in 1922.

Question 68

Choice (B) is the correct answer. The eighteenth-century philosophy of Deism, which based theology on rationality rather than church authority, was strongly denounced by the Roman Catholic Church. Enlightenment thinkers like Voltaire and Thomas Paine proposed Deism as a rational approach to religion, arguing that God set the universe on its course governed by natural laws and then ceased to intervene in its affairs. Religious ideas like miracles, divine intervention, and petitionary prayer were seen as irrational and false. The Catholic Church denounced Deism as heretical.

Question 69

Choice (C) is the correct answer. The 1400s and 1500s saw the decline of power for European feudal families and the rise of strong central monarchies, sometimes called the "new monarchs." The development of gunpowder gave a significant advantage to armies who used firearms. The high costs of equipping troops with firearms were more easily met by a larger centralized government, ruled by a monarch who had access to large tax revenues. Thus, monarchs were successful in gaining and maintaining power at the expense of feudal lords.

Question 70

Choice (D) is the correct answer. In the early 1800s, many of Spain's colonies in the Americas successfully revolted and declared independence. The success of these revolts was, in large part, due to the fact that Spain was unable to dedicate enough troops and resources to maintain control over the colonies. Spain had drained its resources battling Napoleon's forces. In 1807, Napoleon had invaded Spain, triggering a long and draining war. By 1813, Napoleon's forces had been driven out of Spain. These efforts, however, had seriously weakened Spanish power.

Question 71

Choice (C) is the correct answer. During the sixteenth and seventeenth centuries, European powers colonized the East Indies (Southeast Asia) to obtain spices for trading. In 1513, the Portuguese were the first Europeans to establish trade in modern-day Indonesia, obtaining cloves from Ternate, one of the Spice Islands. The United Kingdom, France, and Spain also established spice trade in the East Indies, but it was the Netherlands, through the Dutch East India Company, that eventually gained the greatest economic and political power in the region.

Question 72

Choice (D) is the correct answer. Enlightenment thought was characterized by reliance on reason, rather than religious or traditional authority, in the pursuit of truth. During the period of time historians call the Enlightenment, or the Age of Reason (seventeenth and

eighteenth centuries), philosophers such as René Descartes, Jean-Jacques Rousseau, Voltaire, and John Locke applied reason and the scientific method to the study of many aspects of human life. By shifting the study of philosophy, education, law, and politics away from tradition and religion and toward the use of rational methods of observation and argumentation, Enlightenment philosophers were profoundly influential.

Question 73

Choice (B) is the correct answer. Giuseppe Mazzini, Count Camillo Benso di Cavour, and Giuseppe Garibaldi were all major contributors to the Italian unification (Il Risorgimento), the process of unifying the various countries on the Italian peninsula into one Italian state during the nineteenth century. All three men worked, in different capacities, for the modernization and unification of Italy.

Question 74

Choice (C) is the correct answer. According to tradition, around 530 B.C.E., at age 29, Siddhartha Gautama (later called "the Buddha" or "the Enlightened One") left his life as a prince to travel as a monk in search of a way to relieve human suffering. After six years of extreme self-deprivation, Siddhartha achieved "enlightenment" and discovered "The Middle Way" between indulgence and deprivation to escape suffering. Siddhartha began to teach his idea that through correct thought and action, one could get rid of one's cravings, the source of human suffering. His teachings eventually developed into the major world religion known as Buddhism.

Question 75

Choice (C) is the correct answer. The ancient Egyptian civilization flourished for years along the banks of the Nile River in northern Africa. The yearly flooding of the Nile watered and refertilized Egypt, allowing the land to sustain a large population. Without the yearly flooding, the region would remain too dry to grow large amounts of crops. Because it was so essential to the survival of the civilization, the yearly flooding of the Nile was prominent in Egyptian legend and society.

Question 76

Choice (E) is the correct answer. In the eighteenth century, technological advances (particularly in agriculture and transportation) and industrialization began to change the lives of people in England. One benefit of the technological advances was a drop in death rates, which in turn led to population growth. Industrialization solidified gender roles and strengthened, not destroyed, the traditional nuclear family (A). Although unhealthy conditions in overcrowded cities contributed to a rising infant mortality rate (D), technological advances kept the death rate down (B), allowing the population to increase (C).

Question 77

Choice (B) is the correct answer. President Gamal Abdel Nasser, second president of Egypt from 1956 to 1970, was extremely powerful and influential in stabilizing and modernizing Egypt. Nasser sought to influence as much of Egyptian society as possible. His attempts to raise the standard of living of Egyptians, however, were partially thwarted by a high birth rate in the lower classes. This cartoon depicts Nasser showing Egyptians that lowering the birth rate would increase the available resources for Egyptian economic development.

Question 78

Choice (B) is the correct answer. All of these Southeast Asian countries are correctly matched with the dominating colonial power except Burma. Burma, also known as Myanmar, was colonized by Great Britain, not Germany. Under British control for most of the nineteenth century, Burma gained its independence from Great Britain in 1948.

Question 79

Choice (D) is the correct answer. The Boxer Rebellion was a revolt of the Chinese against Western imperialists in northern China from 1899 to 1901. The term "Boxers" referred to the "Righteous Uprising Society," a group of Chinese who rebelled against the economic and political exploitation of German, British, French, Belgian, Japanese, Russian, Dutch, and U.S. forces. Although the Boxers were eventually supported by the Chinese Imperial army, the Western powers were able to suppress the uprising.

Question 80

Choice (E) is the correct answer. This picture of Christ crowning a twelfth-century king of Sicily reflects the Byzantine influence on Sicilian culture. Sicily had been part of the Byzantine Empire from 552 to 965 C.E. After a period under a religiously tolerant Arab rule, it was governed by the Normans during the eleventh and twelfth centuries. Byzantine Christianity was still prevalent in Sicilian culture at this time, as seen in this traditional Byzantine iconic depiction of Christ crowning the monarch.

Question 81

Choice (D) is the correct answer. The site of Great Zimbabwe in southern Africa was a major center of African civilization, reaching its peak in the fifteenth century. The powerful civilization traded extensively with Arabs and the Swahili city-states (A); mined and smelted gold (B), copper, and bronze (E); and expanded its population into much of the Zimbabwean Plateau (C); but it did not record its history in a written epic.

Question 82

Choice (D) is the correct answer. Jazz originated in United States in the late 1800s. It combined African rhythms, European harmonies, and U.S. instruments, and emphasized the improvisational interplay of the musicians. Impressionism (A) is a school of painting that originated in France during the late 1800s. Surrealist poetry (B) is a movement in literature founded in Paris, France, in the 1920s. Social realism (C) is an artistic and literary movement that flourished in several countries in the years between World Wars I and II. Atonal music (E) developed in Germany in the early 1900s.

Question 83

Choice (E) is the correct answer. The Russian Provisional Government was created in 1917 when the Russian Empire finally collapsed and Tsar Nicholas II abdicated the throne. The Provisional Government continued Russia's involvement in the First World War. The Russian people, weary of fighting, rapidly became disillusioned with the government. The people's discontent and the Provisional Government's weakness eventually led to the Bolshevik Revolution (or October Revolution) and the rise to power of Vladimir Lenin.

Question 84

Choice (A) is the correct answer. Founded in 1885 to advance the political aspirations of educated Indians, the Indian National Congress (INC) was the first Indian organization to challenge British rule. During India's struggle for independence in the 1940s, the INC grew to include a diverse representation of India's population, including both Hindus and Muslims. Although never an official member, Mahatma Gandhi was supported by and associated with the INC during his efforts to free India of British rule.

Question 85

Choice (E) is the correct answer. Francisco Franco took control of the Spanish Nationalist Army in 1936, and later took control of all of Spain at the end of the Spanish Civil War in 1939. He ruled Spain for 36 years until his death in 1975. Hitler ruled Germany for 12 years, from 1933 to 1945 (A). Stalin ruled the Soviet Union for 29 years, from 1924 to 1953 (B). Mussolini ruled Italy for 21 years, from 1922 to 1943 (C). Pilsudski ruled Poland for 13 years, as a formal head of state from 1918 to 1922 and as military dictator from 1926 to 1935.

Question 86

Choice (B) is the correct answer. The Byzantine Empire, also called the Eastern Roman Empire, began in the fourth century C.E. and flourished for over a thousand years until its final collapse in the fifteenth century. Reaching its peak from the ninth to the eleventh centuries, the empire's success came from a sound economic base fueled by high

levels of production and trade. The Byzantine Empire was ruled by a centralized nonconstitutional monarchy—choices (A) and (C)—whose succession of power was not often clear (E). The Byzantine Empire also saw the separation of its Eastern Orthodox Christian church from the Roman Catholic Church (D).

Question 87

Choice (A) is the correct answer. In 1919, the League of Nations was established at the Paris Peace Conference as a means of settling international disputes. The League received its first major test when Japan invaded the Chinese territory of Manchuria in 1931. The League of Nations eventually determined that Japan had acted unfairly and called for Japan to relinquish control of Manchuria. Japan withdrew their membership from the League and ignored the decree. Unable to garner military or diplomatic support from its members or the United States, the League of Nations failed in rebuffing the Japanese aggression.

Question 88

Choice (B) is the correct answer. During the 1980s, Islamic fundamentalism flourished in the Islamic Republic of Iran. In 1979, Ayatollah Ruhollah Khomeini successfully led the Iranian Revolution, overthrowing the constitutional monarchy and establishing an Islamic theocratic republic under his control. During his rule, which lasted until his death in 1989, Khomeini enforced the Sharia law that governed Iranians' entire lives according to Islamic fundamentalist ideas.

Question 89

Choice (D) is the correct answer. In the 1920s, Mao Zedong revolutionized Chinese Marxist thought by claiming that the Chinese peasantry needed to be mobilized for a communist revolution to succeed in China. Traditional Marxist doctrine focused on the exploitation of the urban working class and their eventual overthrow of their oppressors. Mao Zedong argued that because China was predominantly an agrarian society, the massive support needed for a revolution had to be found in the rural peasantry. Eventually, in 1949, the Chinese communist revolution succeeded and the People's Republic of China was established under the leadership of Mao Zedong.

Question 90

Choice (A) is the correct answer. During much of the third quarter of the twentieth century, the economies of China, North Korea, and North Vietnam were isolated from the world economy because of their adherence to Marxist economic policies. In these economies, economic decisions regarding production and trade are all centrally planned and governed by the state. Fully governed by their states, these economies were isolated from the competition among private companies in the international markets.

Question 91

Choice (A) is the correct answer. The division of Korea into North and South Korea was primarily the result of the political rivalry between the United States and the Soviet Union. Japan ruled Korea from 1910 until the end of the Second World War. At the close of the war, the United States and the Soviet Union agreed that Japanese soldiers north of the 38th parallel would surrender to the Soviets, and those south of the line would surrender to the United States. The two powers then proceeded to establish and back governments aligned with their political perspectives. North Korea developed a communist government, while South Korea eventually developed into a democracy.

Question 92

Choice (B) is the correct answer. During the U.S. occupation of Japan following the Second World War from 1945 to 1952, U.S. and Japanese authorities were supported by Japanese business leaders. The U.S. occupiers had the task of maintaining control while reconstructing Japan's infrastructure and economy. Many Japanese business leaders benefited from the production and trade policies established by the U.S. occupiers and, as a result, they were generally supportive.

Question 93

Choice (E) is the correct answer. Many historians use the peace settlement reached by the major European powers at the Congress of Vienna in 1815 to mark the end of the French Revolutionary era. The settlement redefined European boundaries after the Napoleonic Wars and reestablished prerevolution monarchies. The Congress coincided with the final defeat of French Revolutionary leader Napoleon Bonaparte at Waterloo.

Question 94

Choice (C) is the correct answer. The signing of the Helsinki Accords in 1975 by the United States, Canada, the Soviet Union, and most European countries concluded the Conference on Security and Cooperation in Europe held in Helsinki, Finland. The Conference and the Helsinki Accords largely focused on establishing mutual cooperation and respect for the basic freedoms and rights of all humans, including racial minorities.

Question 95

Choice (B) is the correct answer. Toward the end of the twentieth century, politicians and engineers began questioning the value of building big dams to produce hydroelectricity because of their effect on the people who live along the dammed rivers. Although the huge dams produce electricity and create jobs, they also alter the flow of the river, flooding land and displacing many families from their homes. Many political activists have protested on behalf of the communities most affected, arguing that the detrimental effects of the projects outweigh their benefits.

World History – Practice Test 4

Practice Helps

The test that follows is an actual, previously administered SAT Subject Test in World History. To get an idea of what it's like to take this test, practice under conditions that are much like those of an actual test administration.

- Set aside an hour when you can take the test uninterrupted.

- Sit at a desk or table with no other books or papers. Dictionaries, other books, or notes are not allowed in the test room.

- Tear out an answer sheet from the back of this book and fill it in just as you would on the day of the test. One answer sheet can be used for up to three Subject Tests.

- Read the instructions that precede the practice test. During the actual administration, you will be asked to read them before answering test questions.

- Use a clock or kitchen timer to time yourself.

- After you finish the practice test, read the sections "How to Score the SAT Subject Test in World History" and "How Did You Do on the Subject Test in World History?"

- The appearance of the answer sheet in this book may differ from the answer sheet you see on test day.

WORLD HISTORY TEST

The top portion of the page of the answer sheet that you will use to take the World History Test must be filled in exactly as illustration below. When your supervisor tells you to fill in the circle next to the name of the test you are about to take, mark your answer sheet as shown.

○ Literature	○ Mathematics Level 1	○ German	○ Chinese Listening	○ Japanese Listening
○ Biology E	○ Mathematics Level 2	○ Italian	○ French Listening	○ Korean Listening
○ Biology M	○ U.S. History	○ Latin	○ German Listening	○ Spanish Listening
○ Chemistry	● World History	○ Modern Hebrew		
○ Physics	○ French	○ Spanish		

Background Questions: ① ② ③ ④ ⑤ ⑥ ⑦ ⑧ ⑨

After filling in the circle next to the name of the test you are taking, locate the Background Questions box on your answer sheet (as shown above). This is where you will answer the following Background Questions on your answer sheet.

BACKGROUND QUESTIONS

Please answer the two questions below by filling in the appropriate circle in the Background Questions box on your answer sheet. <u>The information you provide is for statistical purposes only and will not affect your test score.</u>

Question I

How many semesters of world history, world cultures, or European history have you taken from grade 9 to the present? (If you are taking a course this semester, count it as a full semester.) Fill in only <u>one</u> circle of circles 1- 4.

- One semester or less   —Fill in circle 1.
- Two semesters   —Fill in circle 2.
- Three semesters   —Fill in circle 3.
- Four or more semesters   —Fill in circle 4.

Question II

For the courses in world history, world cultures, or European history you have taken, which of the following geographical areas did you study? Fill in <u>all</u> of the circles that apply.

- Africa   —Fill in circle 5.
- Asia   —Fill in circle 6.
- Europe   —Fill in circle 7.
- Latin America   —Fill in circle 8.
- Middle East   —Fill in circle 9.

When the supervisor gives the signal, turn the page and begin the World History Test. There are 100 numbered circles on the answer sheet and 95 questions in the World History Test. Therefore, use only circles 1 to 95 for recording your answers.

WORLD HISTORY TEST

Directions: Each of the questions or incomplete statements below is followed by five suggested answers or completions. Select the one that is best in each case and then fill in the corresponding circle on the answer sheet.

Note: The World History Test uses the chronological designations B.C.E. (before common era) and C.E. (common era). These labels correspond to B.C. (before Christ) and A.D. (anno Domini), which are used in some world history textbooks.

1. Current knowledge about the Paleolithic Age comes mainly from which of the following sources?

    (A) Building foundations
    (B) Inscriptions
    (C) Woven textiles
    (D) Stone tools
    (E) Ruined forts and abandoned mines

2. Which of the following was the primary basis for the Roman persecution of Christians in the second and third centuries?

    (A) Christianity was seen as a sect of Judaism.
    (B) Christian slaves often refused to serve their masters.
    (C) All sectarian religious movements were illegal under Roman law.
    (D) Christians refused to serve in the Roman army.
    (E) Christians refused to worship the Roman emperors.

3. Rome's most far-reaching contribution to the development of Western society was in the area of

    (A) philosophy
    (B) religion
    (C) literature
    (D) law
    (E) art

4. The result of the Edict of Toleration issued by Emperor Constantine was to

    (A) make Christianity the official religion of the Roman Empire
    (B) make the cult of Mithra the official religion of the Roman Empire
    (C) celebrate Constantine's initiation into the ancient mysteries of Eleusis
    (D) legalize the practice of Christianity within the Roman Empire
    (E) establish the supremacy of Rome over all other Christian bishoprics

5. Egyptian and Chinese civilizations before 1000 C.E. may both be used to support the argument that

    (A) very little social stratification existed in classical civilizations
    (B) civilizations thrive only when they are expanding through military conquest
    (C) agricultural economies based on maize and potato cultivation cannot sustain rapid population growth
    (D) large-scale irrigation is associated with the formation of centralized states
    (E) agricultural economies cannot generate sufficient surplus to fund large building projects

GO ON TO THE NEXT PAGE

6. The Great Wall of China was built to

(A) keep the Chinese people from having contact
   with foreigners
(B) defend China's northern borders
(C) bring peace among rival factions seeking to
   dominate China
(D) stimulate China's stagnant economy
(E) provide a barrier between China and Korea

7. At its peak, Mayan culture was characterized by
   all of the following EXCEPT

(A) a sophisticated mathematical knowledge
(B) a dual calendar system
(C) cities dominated by colossal pyramidal tombs
(D) priest-kings who presided over sacrifices
(E) the belief in a single supreme god

8. When historians use the term "the Byzantine
   Empire," they are referring to the

(A) Roman Empire between the reigns of
   Diocletian and Odoacer
(B) empire of Charlemagne
(C) Sassanid dynasty of Persia
(D) western portions of the Muslim world
(E) eastern Roman Empire after the fifth
   century C.E.

9. At its height, the Ottoman Empire bureaucracy
   was able to maintain internal peace primarily by

(A) allowing France and Russia to protect
   Christians in the Empire
(B) banning intermarriage between members of
   different religions
(C) giving Muslim clerics control of education
(D) encouraging separatist movements by Jews,
   Christians, and Muslims
(E) giving considerable freedom and autonomy
   to all religious communities

10. "A ruler, therefore, must not mind incurring
    the charge of cruelty for the purpose of keeping
    his subjects united and faithful; . . . he will be
    more merciful than those who, from excess of
    tenderness, allow disorders to arise . . . for these
    [disorders] as a rule injure the whole community,
    while the executions carried out by the ruler injure
    only individuals."

The passage above was written by

(A) Pico della Mirandola
(B) Niccolò Machiavelli
(C) Martin Luther
(D) Oliver Cromwell
(E) John Calvin

11. Completion of the Suez Canal in 1869 was
    important for which of the following reasons?

(A) It stabilized the control of the Egyptian
    government.
(B) It shortened the sea route between Europe
    and Africa.
(C) It shortened the sea route between Europe
    and Asia.
(D) It alleviated competition among European
    powers.
(E) It improved the economic status of the
    majority of Middle Eastern residents.

12. The country that acted to limit Germany's
    acquisition of African colonies in the late
    nineteenth century was

(A) Belgium
(B) Great Britain
(C) Italy
(D) Portugal
(E) Spain

GO ON TO THE NEXT PAGE

13. "India can never become a great manufacturing country, but by cultivating her connection with England she may become one of the greatest agricultural countries in the world."

    This observation made in Great Britain in 1937 reflects which of the following generalizations about the relationship between colonial powers and colonized nations?

    (A) Colonial powers directly subsidized the economies of the colonies.
    (B) Colonial powers allowed tariff-free exports from their colonies.
    (C) Colonies lacked the population required to become industrial centers.
    (D) Colonies could potentially attain the same status as the colonial powers.
    (E) Colonial powers used their colonies chiefly as sources of raw materials.

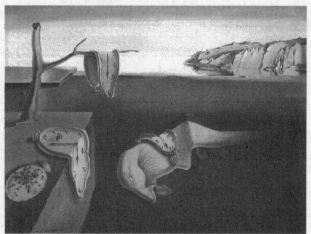

Collection, The Museum of Modern Art, New York. Given anonymously.

14. The painting above by Salvador Dalí is representative of which of the following artistic movements?

    (A) Romanticism
    (B) Art Nouveau
    (C) Impressionism
    (D) Bauhaus
    (E) Surrealism

15. A devout Muslim is expected to do all of the following EXCEPT

    (A) pray five times a day
    (B) give alms to the poor
    (C) fast from dawn to sundown during one month of the year
    (D) devote two years to missionary service
    (E) make a pilgrimage to Mecca once in a lifetime

16. Which of the following best describes matrilineal succession, as it was practiced in some African societies before 1500 ?

    (A) Women passed their wealth only to their daughters.
    (B) Women were responsible for controlling local governments.
    (C) Women were trained as warriors and had primary responsibility for defense.
    (D) Men were banned from owning property.
    (E) Inheritance was passed to the oldest male through the mother's side of the family.

17. A candidate for the Chinese imperial civil service had to pass competitive examinations testing knowledge of

    (A) foreign languages
    (B) Manchu etiquette
    (C) Confucian classics
    (D) agricultural technology
    (E) military tactics

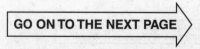 GO ON TO THE NEXT PAGE

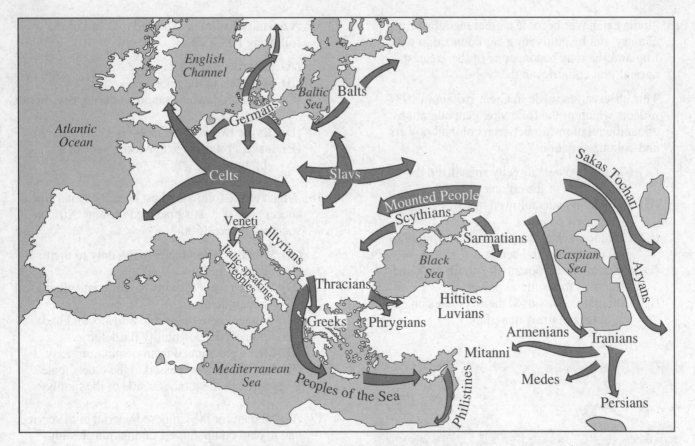

18. The map above illustrates

    (A) invasions by Mongols
    (B) the expansions of Indo-European peoples
    (C) major central European trade routes
    (D) invasions by Huns and Vandals
    (E) the spread of the Black Death

GO ON TO THE NEXT PAGE

19. Which of the following statements most accurately describes overland trade in Asia between 700 and 1100 C.E.?

   (A) Goods moved regularly over a large area.
   (B) Traders shared a common currency.
   (C) Most trade routes linked pilgrimage sites.
   (D) Traders spoke Arabic exclusively.
   (E) Trade with non-Islamic groups was prohibited.

20. Many aspects of Roman culture, including art, architecture, religion, and social and military organization, were derived directly from or influenced by the civilization of the

   (A) Etruscans
   (B) Carthaginians
   (C) Minoans
   (D) Berbers
   (E) Gauls

21. Which of the following primarily accounted for the wealth of the Minoan civilization?

   (A) Seaborne trade
   (B) War booty
   (C) Silk manufacturing
   (D) Coal mining
   (E) Fishing

22. Toussaint L'Ouverture led a successful rebellion against French colonists that resulted in the establishment of which of the following nations?

   (A) Morocco
   (B) Liberia
   (C) Argentina
   (D) Cuba
   (E) Haiti

23. Renaissance humanism is most closely associated with which of the following?

   (A) Religious crusades
   (B) Monasticism
   (C) Scholarly study of classical texts
   (D) Rejection of Platonic philosophy
   (E) Translation of the Bible into the vernacular

Werner Forman/Art Resource

24. The large stone sculpture shown above is characteristic of artwork in which of the following civilizations?

   (A) Nubian
   (B) Assyrian
   (C) Olmec
   (D) Harappan
   (E) Shang

25. Germany was divided after the Second World War primarily because

   (A) the German people could not reach consensus on the kind of government they wanted
   (B) ethnic and religious divisions within Germany deepened after the war
   (C) the Allies were competing for economic and political control of central Europe
   (D) the Allies believed that the economic cost of uniting Germany was prohibitive
   (E) some parts of Germany had suffered more damage than others

GO ON TO THE NEXT PAGE

26. "The Proletarians have nothing to lose but their chains. They have a world to win. Workers of the world, unite!"

The quotation above is taken from which of the following?

(A) *Reason in History*, Georg Wilhelm Friedrich Hegel
(B) *The Protestant Ethic and the Spirit of Capitalism*, Max Weber
(C) *The Communist Manifesto*, Karl Marx and Friedrich Engels
(D) *Utopia*, Thomas More
(E) *The Wealth of Nations*, Adam Smith

27. Following the First World War, which of the following countries formerly in the Ottoman Empire modernized and nationalized most closely along the Western model?

(A) Egypt
(B) Syria
(C) Turkey
(D) Iran
(E) Iraq

28. "The Great Royal Road was constructed to speed soldiers, supplies, and goods from one part of the empire to another. It was more than 1,500 miles long, extending from Susa, one of the capitals of the empire, to Sardis in Asia Minor. More than 100 way stations supplied travelers with lodging and state messengers with fresh horses."

The paragraph above refers to the ancient kingdom of

(A) Egypt
(B) Macedonia
(C) Persia
(D) Sumeria
(E) Judea

29. The British established informal rule over Egypt in the late nineteenth century primarily to

(A) supply much of the raw cotton for the Lancashire cotton industry
(B) compete with Germany in establishing a foothold in North Africa
(C) exploit the oil resources of Egypt
(D) establish a monopoly over Egyptian antiquities
(E) exercise control over the Suez Canal

30. The population of which of the following Middle Eastern countries currently includes a sizeable Kurdish minority?

(A) Iraq
(B) Egypt
(C) Lebanon
(D) Saudi Arabia
(E) Kuwait

31. The cultural and political development of Vietnam was most heavily influenced by which of the following countries?

(A) Korea
(B) Japan
(C) China
(D) Indonesia
(E) Mongolia

32. From earliest to latest, what is the order in which the following religions came into existence?

(A) Confucianism, Judaism, Christianity, Islam
(B) Islam, Confucianism, Judaism, Christianity
(C) Judaism, Confucianism, Christianity, Islam
(D) Judaism, Christianity, Islam, Confucianism
(E) Judaism, Confucianism, Islam, Christianity

33. The Sandinista Front for National Liberation dominated national politics in

(A) Guatemala during the 1950's
(B) Cuba during the 1960's
(C) Puerto Rico during the 1970's
(D) Nicaragua during the 1980's
(E) El Salvador during the 1980's

34. One of the main aims of the groups who financed the European voyages of exploration in the fifteenth and sixteenth centuries was to

(A) supply wealthy European households with non-European slaves
(B) demonstrate European naval superiority over Africa and Asia
(C) circumvent the Middle East to gain direct access to Asian goods
(D) seek new crops to boost the European food supply
(E) chart the extent of the Arab world

GO ON TO THE NEXT PAGE

35. Medieval Muslim merchants traveled more frequently to India than to Italy because

   (A) travel to India was easier and safer
   (B) papal bulls forbade Muslims from entering Christian harbors
   (C) Christian crusades effectively closed off the Mediterranean Sea to Muslims
   (D) there was a shortage of timber for ship-building along the southern Mediterranean coast
   (E) Indian spices yielded greater profits than did Italian products

36. In the fifteenth century, overseas expeditions involving dozens of ships and thousands of men were mounted by the

   (A) British
   (B) French
   (C) Maya
   (D) Japanese
   (E) Chinese

37. Saint Paul is known as the "second founder of Christianity" primarily because he

   (A) gathered the materials for the New Testament
   (B) became the leader of the apostles after Jesus' death
   (C) was a great missionary and theologian
   (D) founded the Vatican in Rome
   (E) began the great monastic movement

38. Which of the following colonies in the Americas imported the largest number of slaves between 1500 and 1800 ?

   (A) Argentina
   (B) Cuba
   (C) Mexico
   (D) Jamaica
   (E) Brazil

39. At the battle of Isandhlwana in 1879, the Zulu defeated armies from which of the following?

   (A) Belgium
   (B) Great Britain
   (C) Germany
   (D) France
   (E) Italy

40. During the eighteenth century, the partitioning of Poland among Austria, Prussia, and Russia resulted mainly from

   (A) Poland's lack of cultural unity
   (B) Poland's small land area and population
   (C) instability in the area as a result of constant civil wars
   (D) the oppressive policies of the Polish kings
   (E) Poland's weak central government

41. Persia became the focus of European imperialists in the late nineteenth century for all the following reasons EXCEPT:

   (A) Persia was adjacent to India.
   (B) Persia was the source of Islamic fundamentalism.
   (C) Persia shared a border with Russia.
   (D) Persia provided strategic access to the Arabian Sea.
   (E) Persia's ruling dynasty was too weak to resist foreign advances.

42. All of the following technologies had widespread and important effects on nineteenth-century life EXCEPT

   (A) railroads
   (B) automobiles
   (C) the telegraph
   (D) the power loom
   (E) the open-hearth furnace

43. Women gained the right to vote in most of western Europe and in the United States immediately after which of the following?

   (A) The French Revolution
   (B) The Seneca Falls Conference
   (C) The American Civil War
   (D) The First World War
   (E) The Second World War

GO ON TO THE NEXT PAGE

44. The Indian caste system evolved because of the

   (A) clashes between patriarchal and matriarchal social orders
   (B) conquest of northern India by Alexander the Great
   (C) popular uprisings in the Indus Valley civilization
   (D) desire by Aryan invaders to distinguish themselves from non-Aryan groups
   (E) attempts by central Asian invaders to convert the people to Islam

45. Which of the following statements best characterizes the feudal system of medieval western Europe?

   (A) The social structure was nonhierarchical.
   (B) Peasants were not allowed to own land.
   (C) Lords and vassals were bound together by family ties.
   (D) The power structure was decentralized.
   (E) Only men were allowed to own land.

46. Which of the following statements regarding women's lives in Western Europe in the early medieval period is accurate?

   (A) Law and custom restricted women to working only in the home.
   (B) Changes in church law in the thirteenth century allowed women greater religious authority.
   (C) Aristocratic women enjoyed greater power and prominence in periods of military activity when men were away fighting.
   (D) Women could serve as feudal lords, but not as feudal vassals.
   (E) Among men and women of humbler status, the division of labor between the sexes was very strict.

47. Between 1638 and the mid-nineteenth century, Japan prohibited contact with all Western traders EXCEPT those from

   (A) Spain
   (B) Portugal
   (C) the Netherlands
   (D) France
   (E) England

48. Which of the following religions became firmly consolidated in Persia under the Safavid dynasty (1502-1736) ?

   (A) Shi'ite Islam
   (B) Sunni Islam
   (C) Sikhism
   (D) Nestorian Christianity
   (E) Jainism

49. Robert Owen sought to show through his textiles factory in New Lanark, Scotland, that

   (A) Great Britain could compete effectively in world trade
   (B) a profitable industry could be run without using the latest technology
   (C) increased profits and improved conditions could go hand in hand
   (D) manufactured goods could be equal in quality to handmade goods
   (E) the most effective way to increase productivity was through a combination of discipline and a longer working day

50. Which of the following was a legacy of the Napoleonic expedition to Egypt, 1798-1799 ?

   (A) Revival of the Coptic Church in Egypt
   (B) Plans for building the Suez Canal and the Aswan Dam
   (C) Interest in Egyptian archaeology and discovery of the Rosetta Stone
   (D) Heightened interest by Europeans in exploring the interior of Africa
   (E) Restoration of Mamluk rule in all of Egypt

GO ON TO THE NEXT PAGE

51. The February Revolution in Russia in 1917 was sparked primarily by which of the following events?

    (A) The death of Grigory Rasputin
    (B) The Allied invasion of Russia at Vladivostock
    (C) A Cossack rebellion
    (D) Strikes and food riots in Petrograd
    (E) The killing of the tsar and his family

52. Following 1910, political leaders in Mexico promoted the image of the mestizo as the "true Mexican" as a means of

    (A) fostering national unity
    (B) increasing the economic power of the mestizo after the revolution
    (C) recognizing the increased power of the mestizo in the military
    (D) countering the growing influence of the Roman Catholic Church
    (E) acknowledging European economic influence

53. One of Lenin's most important original contributions to Marxist ideology was his argument that

    (A) parliamentary elections would soon lead to a Communist party victory
    (B) a socialist revolution would first occur in a highly industrialized state
    (C) a centralized party had to organize and lead a socialist revolution
    (D) the dictatorship of the proletariat was not a necessary step in achieving a communist society
    (E) a mass coalition of socialist and democratic parties would rule after the revolution

54. Which of the following sentences best captures the essence of Jean-Jacques Rousseau's *The Social Contract* ?

    (A) Government should be based on the general will of the society.
    (B) Divine-right monarchy is the best form of government.
    (C) Industrialization will eliminate social and economic inequalities.
    (D) Most of Europe's social ills can be traced to a lack of land for agricultural expansion.
    (E) National economic prosperity can be maintained through constant involvement in war.

55. The Greek thinker Galen's study of anatomy in the second century C.E. was not significantly improved on in Europe until the sixteenth-century publication of the work of

    (A) Leonardo da Vinci
    (B) Tycho Brahe
    (C) Isaac Newton
    (D) Anton van Leeuwenhoek
    (E) Andreas Vesalius

56. From the thirteenth through the fourteenth centuries, the African empire of Mali did which of the following?

    (A) Rejected Islamic teaching
    (B) Resisted Christian missionaries
    (C) Exported large amounts of sorghum
    (D) Encouraged inhabitants to migrate eastward
    (E) Established a center of learning in Timbuktu

GO ON TO THE NEXT PAGE

57. Which of the following ancient written languages is still used by some priests in religious studies and ceremonies?

    (A) Sumerian
    (B) Sanskrit
    (C) Etruscan
    (D) Hittite
    (E) Phoenician

58. In the 1960's the United States sent a large number of troops to support South Vietnam in its conflict with North Vietnam primarily because

    (A) the Soviet Union was sending troops to North Vietnam
    (B) such action would allow the United States to regain respect in Southeast Asia after losing the Korean War
    (C) the United Nations Security Council encouraged all nations to send troops to defend South Vietnam against a North Vietnamese invasion
    (D) the population of North Vietnam far exceeded that of South Vietnam and the United States sought to nullify this advantage
    (E) United States policymakers believed the fall of South Vietnam to communism would endanger other countries in Southeast Asia

59. Which of the following best describes the twelfth and thirteenth centuries in Europe?

    (A) A time of population expansion and urban growth
    (B) A time of recovery from plague and famine
    (C) A period of transition from an agricultural to an industrial society
    (D) A period of political turmoil resulting in economic stagnation
    (E) An era of prosperity due to an influx of silver and gold

60. In the tenth century, the Spanish cities of Córdoba and Seville were most renowned as centers of

    (A) popular support for the Crusades
    (B) Islamic architecture and scholarship
    (C) the study of plant hybridization
    (D) textile production
    (E) gold and silver production

61. The first Russian state developed around which of the following cities?

    (A) Kiev
    (B) Novosibirsk
    (C) Saint Petersburg
    (D) Moscow
    (E) Murmansk

62. A primary reason for the rapid drop in the economic growth rates of Venezuela and Mexico in the 1980's was

    (A) low birthrates and a shrinking labor pool
    (B) insurgencies that disrupted the democratic process
    (C) the curtailment of aid from the Soviet Union
    (D) the abrupt decline of world oil prices
    (E) a decline in literacy rates

GO ON TO THE NEXT PAGE

63. When Hernando de Soto traveled from the region now called Florida to the region west of the Mississippi River, he observed which of the following?

    (A) Domesticated horses
    (B) Iron hoes
    (C) Domesticated sheep and pigs
    (D) Populated areas linked by trade
    (E) Indians worshiping gold and silver objects

64. A common factor in the emergence of totalitarianism in Italy and Germany was

    (A) the strife of civil wars
    (B) rapid industrialization
    (C) a decline in nationalism
    (D) severe economic depression
    (E) the violent overthrow of existing governments

65. Friedrich Nietzsche and Sigmund Freud would most likely have agreed that

    (A) human nature is essentially good
    (B) civic virtue holds society together in difficult times
    (C) the nonrational is key to understanding the human condition
    (D) there are natural laws that govern human relationships
    (E) human reason is best used as a tool for social reform

66. Socialist political parties, once allied in a single international organization, split into socialist and communist wings immediately following the

    (A) publication of the *Communist Manifesto* in 1848
    (B) outbreak of the Franco-Prussian War in 1870
    (C) outbreak of the Bolshevik Revolution in 1917
    (D) signing of the Nazi-Soviet Pact in 1939
    (E) outbreak of the Chinese Revolution in 1949

67. Which of the following Southeast Asian countries was the first to achieve political independence after the Second World War?

    (A) Indonesia
    (B) Malaysia
    (C) Myanmar (Burma)
    (D) The Philippines
    (E) Vietnam

68. John Maynard Keynes believed that increased government intervention in the economy during a depression would lead to which of the following?

    (A) Dangerous dependence on government subsidies
    (B) Rapid and successful industrialization
    (C) Stronger labor unions
    (D) Increased employment and economic growth
    (E) Disruption of the natural forces regulating a healthy economy

GO ON TO THE NEXT PAGE

69. Which of the following events occurred most recently in the history of Poland?

   (A) The division of Poland among Russia, Prussia, and Austria
   (B) The creation of the Grand Duchy of Warsaw
   (C) The formation of the Solidarity Union
   (D) The occupation of Poland by Soviet forces
   (E) The defeat by Prussia and Russia of Polish forces under Tadeusz Kościuszko

70. Russia's eastward expansion, which began in the sixteenth century, was mainly possible because of its

   (A) navigable rivers
   (B) protected mountain ranges
   (C) abundance of warm-water ports
   (D) great uninterrupted plains
   (E) moderate fluctuations in seasonal temperatures

71. British support for a Jewish national homeland in Palestine, with the provision that the rights of existing non-Jewish communities in Palestine be safeguarded, was stated in the

   (A) Balfour Declaration
   (B) Beveridge Report
   (C) Camp David Accords
   (D) Locarno Pact
   (E) Atlantic Charter

72. The French *Encyclopédie*, a project to collect all human knowledge, was first published in 1751 under the editorship of

   (A) Diderot and d'Alembert
   (B) Montesquieu and Fénelon
   (C) Lavoisier and Rousseau
   (D) Condorcet and Turgot
   (E) d'Holbach and Condillac

73. Which of the following technological innovations contributed to the Hyksos' success in overthrowing the ruling Egyptian dynasty?

   (A) The horse-drawn chariot
   (B) Gunpowder and cannons
   (C) The lateen sail
   (D) The crossbow
   (E) Stirrups

74. Which of the following statements about European labor unions as they developed in the nineteenth and twentieth centuries is true?

   (A) They descended with relatively few modifications from the medieval guild system.
   (B) They developed mainly as the workers' response to industrialization.
   (C) They were applauded by the Roman Catholic church and by the Protestant clergy.
   (D) They were not supported by socialists.
   (E) They were designed principally to nominate candidates for public office.

75. The First World War had which of the following effects on the continent of Africa?

   (A) A number of former colonies gained their independence.
   (B) The British and the French acquired territory formerly controlled by Germany.
   (C) Russia received African colonies as part of the Paris Peace Conference.
   (D) The United States became a new mandate power in Africa.
   (E) China and Japan began to supply Africa with manufactured goods.

GO ON TO THE NEXT PAGE

"My wife is a woman of mind."

76. The purpose of the late nineteenth-century British cartoon above was to

(A) invite men to help their working wives with child care

(B) condemn intellectual women as unfit wives and mothers

(C) encourage women to use their education even though they had children

(D) criticize fathers who left the children's discipline to their wives

(E) suggest that fathers were just as good at looking after children as mothers were

GO ON TO THE NEXT PAGE

77. Which of the following was true of the European colonial penetration of Africa in the nineteenth century?

    (A) The preexisting patterns of regional political organization determined colonial boundaries.
    (B) Only the Bantu kingdoms south and west of Lake Tanganyika remained unconquered.
    (C) The German and Austrian governments were the first to make military conquests.
    (D) African social, economic, and religious organations were left intact.
    (E) Private ventures by Europeans were later recognized and supported by home governments.

78. In most areas of Europe during the medieval period, women were prohibited from

    (A) reading and writing
    (B) performing agricultural labor
    (C) inheriting land and goods
    (D) participating in business and trade
    (E) administering sacraments in church

79. "I believe in the doctrine of nonviolence as a weapon of the weak. I believe in the doctrine of nonviolence as a weapon of the strongest. I believe that a man is the strongest soldier for daring to die unarmed."

    The political philosophy stated above was espoused by many

    (A) Nationalist Chinese in their attempt to wrest control from the Communists
    (B) Indians in their attempt to gain independence from British rule
    (C) Jews in their attempt to gain a national homeland
    (D) Black South Africans in their struggle to end apartheid
    (E) Irish Republican Army members in their attempt to unify Ireland

80. The first Indian empire was founded by

    (A) Kanishka
    (B) Samudragupta
    (C) Chandragupta Maurya
    (D) Ashoka
    (E) Akbar

81. Which of the following was a goal of both Peter the Great of Russia and Joseph Stalin of the Soviet Union?

    (A) Achievement of economic equality for all citizens
    (B) Final conquest of Siberia
    (C) An isolationist foreign policy
    (D) Increased use of Western technology
    (E) Preservation of traditional village life

82. During the 1960's "neocolonialism" was the term used to describe

    (A) continued military control of parts of Africa by European powers
    (B) the influx of workers from developing countries into Western countries
    (C) the spread of revolutionary socialist doctrines in Africa and Latin America
    (D) continued economic domination by Western states of former colonial areas
    (E) Soviet control of Central Asian Muslim societies

83. "From every sentence deep, original, and sublime thoughts arise, and the whole is pervaded by a high and holy and earnest spirit. Indian air surrounds us, and original thoughts of kindred spirits."

    The statement above about an ancient Indian text is most representative of which of the following intellectual movements?

    (A) Materialism
    (B) Deism
    (C) Positivism
    (D) Romanticism
    (E) Utilitarianism

GO ON TO THE NEXT PAGE

84. Charles de Gaulle returned to power in 1958 following a national crisis in France over

(A) French colonial rule in Algeria
(B) France's military role in the North Atlantic Treaty Organization (NATO)
(C) France's continued role in the occupation of Germany
(D) the replacement of the French franc with a common European currency
(E) an attempted coup led by the Communist party

85. In response to European challenges in the nineteenth century, rulers in Morocco, Tunisia, Egypt, Persia, and the Ottoman Empire did which of the following?

(A) Embarked on a program of land reform that favored small farmers
(B) Encouraged the reform of Islamic doctrine and law
(C) Sought to unify themselves under a revived caliphate
(D) Expelled all foreigners and closed themselves off from the West
(E) Reformed their bureaucracies and armies

86. "From Magna Carta to the Declaration of Rights, it has been the uniform policy of our constitution to claim and assert our liberties as an *entailed inheritance* derived to us from our forefathers, and to be transmitted to our posterity; as an estate specially belonging to the people of this kingdom, without any reference whatever to any other more general or prior right."

The statement above was most likely made by which of the following?

(A) A French radical urging the crowd to storm the Bastille
(B) An American revolutionary urging the people to support the new Constitution as the law of the land
(C) A German philosopher who believed that freedom exists only within the human will, regardless of the laws
(D) An Indian leader arguing for the freeing of India from colonial domination by the British
(E) A British conservative who believed that freedom and human rights were part of a cultural inheritance

87. In Latin America, the term *caudillismo* refers to

(A) electoral reform
(B) land development
(C) economic independence
(D) social equality
(E) military dictatorship

88. Beginning in 1929, the value of Chile's exports fell by 80 percent, and the value of exports of other Latin American countries fell by at least half.

The economic disaster in Latin America referred to above was the result of

(A) internal political instability
(B) government confiscation of the means of production
(C) crop failures and other natural disasters
(D) the worldwide economic depression
(E) labor unrest in the factories and mines

89. The French Utopian socialists of the late eighteenth and the nineteenth centuries believed that

(A) revolution is essential to the formation of a socialist state
(B) all history is the history of class struggle
(C) capitalists are the key to the creation of socialism
(D) economic planning should not be the responsibility of the state
(E) property should be communally owned

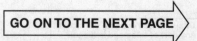

GO ON TO THE NEXT PAGE

90. Which of the following groups spearheaded new nationalist movements in Egypt and the Ottoman Empire in the late nineteenth century?

    (A) Junior army officers
    (B) Writers
    (C) Religious leaders
    (D) Women's rights activists
    (E) Industrialists

91. The Sino-Japanese and Russo-Japanese wars were similar in that both

    (A) retarded Japan's economic growth
    (B) resulted in huge indemnities for Japan
    (C) began with disputes over Korea
    (D) were opposed by the bulk of Japan's citizens
    (E) were resolved with the help of the President of the United States

92. During the seventh and eighth centuries, the Arabs conquered all of the following EXCEPT

    (A) Spain
    (B) Persia
    (C) Constantinople
    (D) Jerusalem
    (E) Damascus

93. The Indian subcontinent was partitioned into India and Pakistan in order to

    (A) reflect linguistic and ethnic differences
    (B) reestablish the political boundaries of the ancient Indian kingdoms
    (C) provide for Indian Muslims who had been dispossessed under British rule
    (D) make a concession to the rajahs, who sought autonomy in Pakistan
    (E) satisfy the Muslim League's demand for an independent Muslim state

94. During the Middle Ages, Northern European agriculture differed from Mediterranean agriculture because Northern Europe

    (A) was more mountainous
    (B) was wetter and colder for most of the year
    (C) was dryer and colder for most of the year
    (D) produced more grapes and wine
    (E) did not have both hunting and agricultural economies

95. Which of the following African countries is a member of the Organization of Petroleum Exporting Countries (OPEC) and a major supplier of oil on the world market?

    (A) Liberia
    (B) Nigeria
    (C) Mali
    (D) Ivory Coast
    (E) Senegal

STOP

If you finish before time is called, you may check your work on this test only.
Do not turn to any other section in the test.

How to Score the SAT Subject Test in World History

When you take an actual SAT Subject Test in World History, your answer sheet will be "read" by a scanning machine that will record your responses to each question. Then a computer will compare your answers with the correct answers and produce your raw score. You get one point for each correct answer. For each wrong answer, you lose one-quarter of a point. Questions you omit (and any for which you mark more than one answer) are not counted. This raw score is converted to a scaled score that is reported to you and to the colleges you specify.

Worksheet 1. Finding Your Raw Test Score

STEP 1: Table A on the following page lists the correct answers for all the questions on the Subject Test in World History that is reproduced in this book. It also serves as a worksheet for you to calculate your raw score.

- Compare your answers with those given in the table.

- Put a check in the column marked "Right" if your answer is correct.

- Put a check in the column marked "Wrong" if your answer is incorrect.

- Leave both columns blank if you omitted the question.

STEP 2: Count the number of right answers.

Enter the total here: _____

STEP 3: Count the number of wrong answers.

Enter the total here: _____

STEP 4: Multiply the number of wrong answers by .250.

Enter the product here: _____

STEP 5: Subtract the result obtained in Step 4 from the total you obtained in Step 2.

Enter the result here: _____

STEP 6: Round the number obtained in Step 5 to the nearest whole number.

Enter the result here: _____

The number you obtained in Step 6 is your raw score.

Answers to Practice Test 4 for World History

Table A
Answers to the SAT Subject Test in World History - Practice Test 4 and Percentage of Students Answering
Each Question Correctly

Question Number	Correct Answer	Right	Wrong	Percentage of Students Answering the Question Correctly*	Question Number	Correct Answer	Right	Wrong	Percentage of Students Answering the Question Correctly*
1	D			74	26	C			78
2	E			63	27	C			63
3	D			57	28	C			48
4	D			71	29	E			72
5	D			63	30	A			29
6	B			85	31	C			59
7	E			79	32	C			33
8	E			68	33	D			23
9	E			74	34	C			74
10	B			68	35	E			44
11	C			61	36	E			22
12	B			79	37	C			26
13	E			59	38	E			36
14	E			74	39	B			38
15	D			87	40	E			61
16	E			55	41	B			55
17	C			63	42	B			51
18	B			72	43	D			53
19	A			54	44	D			44
20	A			40	45	D			39
21	A			47	46	C			32
22	E			60	47	C			37
23	C			59	48	A			35
24	C			46	49	C			41
25	C			58	50	C			37

Table A continued on next page

Table A continued from previous page

Question Number	Correct Answer	Right	Wrong	Percentage of Students Answering the Question Correctly*
51	D			50
52	A			57
53	C			51
54	A			76
55	E			21
56	E			38
57	B			52
58	E			83
59	A			20
60	B			41
61	A			37
62	D			20
63	D			29
64	D			65
65	C			37
66	C			47
67	D			33
68	D			31
69	C			46
70	D			48
71	A			56
72	A			44
73	A			36
74	B			76
75	B			62

Question Number	Correct Answer	Right	Wrong	Percentage of Students Answering the Question Correctly*
76	B			73
77	E			33
78	E			30
79	B			68
80	C			30
81	D			62
82	D			49
83	D			27
84	A			31
85	E			33
86	E			49
87	E			26
88	D			70
89	E			45
90	A			16
91	C			31
92	C			31
93	E			55
94	B			48
95	B			39

* These percentages are based on an analysis of the answer sheets of a representative sample of 12,958 students who took the original administration of this test and whose mean score was 579. They may be used as an indication of the relative difficulty of a particular question.

Finding Your Scaled Score

When you take SAT Subject Tests, the scores sent to the colleges you specify are reported on the College Board scale, which ranges from 200 to 800. You can convert your practice test raw score to a scaled score by using Table B. To find your scaled score, locate your raw score in the left-hand column of Table B; the corresponding score in the right-hand column is your scaled score. For example, a raw score of 39 on this particular edition of the SAT Subject Test in World History corresponds to a scaled score of 580.

Raw scores are converted to scaled scores to ensure that a score earned on any one edition of a particular Subject Test is comparable to the same scaled score earned on any other edition of the same Subject Test. Because some editions of the tests may be slightly easier or more difficult than others, College Board scaled scores are adjusted so that they indicate the same level of performance regardless of the edition of the test taken and the ability of the group that takes it. Thus, for example, a score of 400 on one edition of a test taken at a particular administration indicates the same level of achievement as a score of 400 on a different edition of the test taken at a different administration.

When you take the SAT Subject Tests during a national administration, your scores are likely to differ somewhat from the scores you obtain on the tests in this book. People perform at different levels at different times for reasons unrelated to the tests themselves. The precision of any test is also limited because it represents only a sample of all the possible questions that could be asked.

Table B
Scaled Score Conversion Table
Subject Test in World History Test – Practice Test 4

Raw Score	Scaled Score	Raw Score	Scaled Score	Raw Score	Scaled Score
95	800	55	680	15	440
94	800	54	670	14	430
93	800	53	670	13	430
92	800	52	660	12	420
91	800	51	660	11	420
90	800	50	650	10	410
89	800	49	640	9	400
88	800	48	640	8	400
87	800	47	630	7	390
86	800	46	630	6	390
85	800	45	620	5	380
84	800	44	610	4	370
83	800	43	610	3	370
82	800	42	600	2	360
81	800	41	600	1	360
80	800	40	590	0	350
79	800	39	580	−1	340
78	800	38	580	−2	340
77	800	37	570	−3	330
76	800	36	570	−4	330
75	800	35	560	−5	320
74	790	34	550	−6	320
73	790	33	550	−7	310
72	780	32	540	−8	300
71	770	31	540	−9	300
70	770	30	530	−10	290
69	760	29	520	−11	290
68	760	28	520	−12	280
67	750	27	510	−13	270
66	740	26	510	−14	270
65	740	25	500	−15	260
64	730	24	490	−16	260
63	730	23	490	−17	250
62	720	22	480	−18	240
61	720	21	480	−19	240
60	710	20	470	−20	230
59	700	19	460	−21	230
58	700	18	460	−22	220
57	690	17	450	−23	210
56	690	16	450	−24	210

How Did You Do on the Subject Test in World History?

After you score your test and analyze your performance, think about the following questions:

Did you run out of time before reaching the end of the test?

If so, you may need to pace yourself better. For example, maybe you spent too much time on one or two hard questions. A better approach might be to skip the ones you can't answer right away and try answering all the remaining questions on the test. Then if there's time, go back to the questions you skipped.

Did you take a long time reading the directions?

You will save time when you take the test by learning the directions to the Subject Test in World History ahead of time. Each minute you spend reading directions during the test is a minute that you could use to answer questions.

How did you handle questions you were unsure of?

If you were able to eliminate one or more of the answer choices as wrong and guess from the remaining ones, your approach probably worked to your advantage. On the other hand, making haphazard guesses or omitting questions without trying to eliminate choices could cost you valuable points.

How difficult were the questions for you compared with other students who took the test?

Table A shows you how difficult the multiple-choice questions were for the group of students who took this test during its national administration. The right-hand column gives the percentage of students that answered each question correctly.

A question answered correctly by almost everyone in the group is obviously an easier question. For example, 85 percent of the students answered question 6 correctly. However, only 16 percent answered question 90 correctly.

Keep in mind that these percentages are based on just one group of students. They would probably be different with another group of students taking the test.

If you missed several easier questions, go back and try to find out why: Did the questions cover material you haven't yet reviewed? Did you misunderstand the directions?

Answer Explanations

For Practice Test 4

Question 1

Choice (D) is the correct answer. Few artifacts have survived from the
Paleolithic Age, which lasted from about 2.5 million years ago to about
10,000 years ago. Most of what we know about the Paleolithic Age
comes primarily from the study of stone tools. Building foundations
(A), inscriptions (B), woven textiles (C), and ruined forts and
abandoned mines (E) would also be evidence of a human presence,
but few of these types of remains dating from the Paleolithic Age have
been found.

Question 2

Choice (E) is the correct answer. Christians refused to worship
the Roman emperors. Christianity within the Roman Empire was
a predominantly urban religion that accepted and benefited from
many facets of the Roman civil order, but Christians drew the line at
accepting the divinity of the Roman emperor, which was required of
all Roman citizens, because this practice conflicted with Christians'
monotheistic belief. Many early Christians were persecuted and
martyred over this issue by the Roman authorities. Choice (A) is
incorrect because the Roman authorities had no particular interest
in the fact that Christianity had sprung from Judaism. Choice (B) is
incorrect because slave–master relationships were not a major point of
contention between Christians and the Roman authorities. Christians
accepted the institution of slavery in this period and did not encourage
slaves to revolt or disobey. Choice (C) is incorrect; a wide variety of
religions was tolerated by the Roman authorities, especially if their
practice did not conflict with Roman law. Choice (D) is incorrect
because Christians did serve in the Roman army throughout the
Empire.

Question 3

Choice (D) is the correct answer. Historians are in agreement that the
most important and enduring Roman contribution to future generations
was Roman law. Roman law and legal practice became the basis
of law in all of western Europe, with the exception of England, and
through colonial and commercial contacts it has spread worldwide.
Roman civilization had achievements in the fields of philosophy (A),
religion (B), literature (C), and art (E), but none of these have affected
the daily lives of more people, worldwide, than has Roman law.

Question 4

Choice (D) is the correct answer. Emperor Constantine's sudden decision in 313 C.E., at a conference held at Milan, to extend complete freedom of worship to Christians and to order the return of their confiscated property ended Christian persecution by the Roman authorities. Christians acquired a privileged juridical status that they would retain, in many Western lands, until the eighteenth and nineteenth centuries. Choice (A) is incorrect; this did not occur until 392 C.E., when the Roman Emperor, Theodosius the Great, forbade the practice of all religions except the form of Christianity recognized by the government. Choice (B) is incorrect; Mithra was originally a Persian god that was popular with members of the Roman army. Choice (C) is incorrect; the mysteries of Eleusis refer to ancient religious rites celebrated at Eleusis, near ancient Athens, in honor of Demeter. Choice (E) is incorrect; the position of the bishoprics of Rome in the Church was not dealt with in the Edict of Toleration.

Question 5

Choice (D) is the correct answer. One theory of why states first formed holds that in the late Neolithic period, the need to coordinate large-scale irrigation efforts in river valleys necessitated the creation of more centralized forms of government. Before 1000 C.E., both Egypt and China were early centralized states whose formation was associated with the beginning of large-scale irrigation. Choice (A) is incorrect; there was considerable social stratification in classical Egypt and classical China. Choice (B) is incorrect; expansion of ancient civilizations usually occurred during periods of peace, not during periods of conflict. Choice (C) is incorrect; rapid population expansion can be and has been sustained in civilizations based on cultivation of maize and potatoes, New World staple products. Choice (E) is incorrect; the economies of ancient Egypt and China were primarily agricultural and both generated food surpluses sufficient to support massive building projects.

Question 6

Choice (B) is the correct answer. The Great Wall of China was built primarily to defend China's northern borders against raids and incursions by nomadic peoples living in the steppe regions north of the Great Wall. Choice (A) is incorrect; the Chinese continued to have extensive trade contact with peoples beyond the Great Wall after its construction. Choice (C) is incorrect; the Great Wall was not built as a means of bringing peace among internal Chinese factions. Choice (D) is incorrect; the Great Wall was not built to stimulate the Chinese economy. Choice (E) is incorrect; the Great Wall did not form a barrier between China and Korea.

Question 7

Choice (E) is the correct answer. Mayan religion was not monotheistic; the Maya believed in many gods and goddesses. Choices (A), (B), (C), and (D) are all correct and cite important aspects of Mayan civilization.

Question 8

Choice (E) is the correct answer. The Byzantine Empire is the name used by modern historians to describe the primarily Greek-speaking eastern portion of the Roman Empire that survived after the Western Roman Empire collapsed in the fifth century. The Byzantine Empire was centered in Constantinople (formerly called Byzantium) and it lasted until the fall of that city to the Ottoman Turks in 1453. Choice (A) is incorrect; the Roman Empire is the designation generally used for the entire (eastern and western) Empire prior to the deposition of the last emperor in the west in 476 C.E. Choice (B) is incorrect; from 778 to 814 C.E., Charlemagne ruled over the Frankish Empire, which became the Holy Roman Empire in the year 800 C.E. Choice (C) is incorrect; the Sassanid dynasty ruled from 224 to 651 C.E. in ancient Iran. Choice (D) is incorrect; the official religion of the Byzantine Empire was Eastern Orthodox Christianity; it was later overwhelmed by the forces of Islam.

Question 9

Choice (E) is the correct answer. The Ottoman Empire, at its peak, allowed considerable autonomy to the various religious communities within the Empire, though Islam was the favored religion. Choice (A) is incorrect; it was only late in Ottoman history, in the nineteenth and early twentieth centuries, when the Ottoman government was considerably weakened, that it allowed European powers to act as protectors of Christian minorities in the Ottoman Empire. Choice (B) is incorrect; banning of marriages between Muslims and non-Muslims was not used by the Ottoman government as a means of maintaining internal peace. Choice (C) is incorrect; control of education by the Muslim clerics was not a method used by the Ottoman rulers to maintain internal peace. Choice (D) is incorrect; separatist movements were not tolerated by the Ottoman Empire at its height.

Question 10

Choice (B) is the correct answer. In his political essay, *The Prince* (written circa 1505), Machiavelli set down rules for princes or leaders of states to follow. This passage epitomizes Machiavelli's belief that a strong, ruthless ruler was often best for a state. Choice (A) is incorrect; Pico della Mirandola was primarily a Neoplatonist and a Renaissance humanist, not a political philosopher. Choice (C) is incorrect;

Martin Luther was a theologian concerned primarily with questions of individual salvation and would not have written this passage. Choice (D) is incorrect; Oliver Cromwell was a seventeenth-century English soldier and revolutionary; he did not write this passage. Choice (E) is incorrect; John Calvin was a Swiss reform theologian and did not share this philosophy of government.

Question 11

Choice (C) is the correct answer. The Suez Canal shortened the sea route between Europe and Asia. The canal linked the Mediterranean Sea and the Red Sea (and ultimately the Indian Ocean) and reduced the need for west–east shipping to go around the African continent. It changed military and commercial shipping patterns and made the Isthmus of Suez a major global strategic location. Choice (A) is incorrect because after the opening of the Suez Canal, the British gradually assumed financial and administrative control of the canal from the Egyptians. Choice (B) is incorrect; sea routes from Europe to some eastern African ports were shortened, but the primary importance of the canal was the shortening of commercial and military routes between Europe and South and East Asia. Choice (D) is incorrect; after 1869, military and colonial competition among the European powers intensified. Choice (E) is incorrect; the opening of the Suez Canal had very little, if any immediate, impact on the economic status of the majority of Middle Eastern people.

Question 12

Choice (B) is the correct answer. Great Britain tried to block some of Germany's attempts to establish a colonial empire in Africa. The other four countries, Belgium (A), Italy (C), Portugal (D), and Spain (E), all had colonies in Africa, but were not significant impediments to German colonial expansion in that area.

Question 13

Choice (E) is the correct answer. Colonial powers used their colonies chiefly as sources of raw materials. The quotation refers to the mercantilist vision Britain had for its colonies, such as India. According to the mercantilist scheme, the colonies would provide raw materials that would be processed into finished industrial goods in Great Britain. These goods would later be distributed and sold worldwide with most of the economic gain going to Great Britain. Choice (A) is incorrect; Great Britain and other colonial powers expected the colonial economies to pay for the costs of their own administration and provide a revenue stream for the mother country. Choice (B) is incorrect; nothing is said in the passage concerning tariffs. Choice (C) is incorrect; the passage does not cite lack of population as an impediment to a colony's industrial development. Choice (D) is incorrect; it directly contradicts the main point of the passage.

Question 14

Choice (E) is the correct answer. Salvador Dalí was a major member of the Surrealist school of painting, and the painting shown, *The Persistence of Memory*, is typical of the Surrealist style. Choices (A), (B), (C), and (D) are incorrect because this painting is not representative of any of these artistic movements.

Question 15

Choice (D) is the correct answer. Muslims are not required to devote two years to missionary service. Choices (A), (B), (C), and (E) all describe obligations of devout Muslims as described in the Qur'an and are, in fact, statements of four of the "Five Pillars" of Islamic faith.

Question 16

Choice (E) is the correct answer. Matrilineal succession, as it was practiced in some African societies prior to 1500, involved the passage of property and certain privileges and honors through the female line of descent, rather than through the male line. It is not to be confused with matriarchy, a form of government in which women wield the most political power. Choice (A) is incorrect; women did not pass their wealth only to their daughters. Choice (B) is incorrect; women did not control local governments. Choice (C) is incorrect; women did not have primary responsibility for defense. Choice (D) is incorrect; men were not banned from owning property in matrilineal African societies.

Question 17

Choice (C) is the correct answer. Chinese imperial civil service examinations required extensive knowledge of the Confucian classics, which dealt with issues of social and political order. Questions on foreign languages (A), Manchu etiquette (B), agricultural technology (D), and military tactics (E) were not generally found on these examinations.

Question 18

Choice (B) is the correct answer. The map shows the expansions of Indo-European peoples. The labels next to the arrows provide the names of the major groups speaking Indo-European languages and what is known of their expansion in the second and first millennia B.C.E. Choices (A), (C), (D), and (E) are incorrect.

Question 19

Choice (A) is the correct answer. During the period from 700 to 1100 C.E., goods moved regularly overland over defined Asian caravan routes. Choice (B) is incorrect; the traders did not have a common currency. Choice (C) is incorrect; pilgrimage sites were associated with stops along some, but not a majority, of the trade routes. Choice (D) is incorrect; Arabic was not the exclusive language of the merchants on these routes. Choice (E) is incorrect; trade was not limited to Islamic groups.

Question 20

Choice (A) is the correct answer. The Etruscans lived primarily in the area in the Italian peninsula between the Tiber and Arno rivers west and south of the Apennine Mountains (hence the modern name "Tuscany"). Their urban culture reached its height in the sixth century B.C.E. Many features of Etruscan culture were adopted by the Romans, their successors. Choices (B), (C), (D), and (E) are incorrect; these groups had little or no influence on Roman culture in its formative period.

Question 21

Choice (A) is the correct answer. Minoan civilization, which flourished in the Aegean region in the second millennium B.C.E., was remarkable for its great cities and palaces and its extensive seaborne trade throughout the eastern Mediterranean basin and beyond. Choices (B), (C), (D), and (E) are incorrect; none of these were major factors accounting for the wealth of the Minoans.

Question 22

Choice (E) is the correct answer. Toussaint L'Ouverture was responsible for the establishment of the independent country of Haiti. He had nothing to do with rebellions in Morocco (A), Liberia (B), Argentina (C), and Cuba (D).

Question 23

Choice (C) is the correct answer. Renaissance humanists devoted their time to recovering, studying, and applying classical Greek and Roman texts. Renaissance humanism is not closely associated with religious crusades (A), monasticism (B), the rejection of Platonic philosophy (D), or the translation of the Bible into the vernacular (E).

Question 24

Choice (C) is the correct answer. The stone sculpture depicted in the photograph is a famous example of Olmec artwork. The civilizations mentioned in choices (A), (B), (D), and (E) did not produce artwork in this style.

Question 25

Choice (C) is the correct answer. Germany was a central point of contention in the Cold War rivalry between the Soviet Union and the United States that developed after the Second World War. Germany was originally divided into occupation zones by the victorious Allied powers, but the continued split between East and West Germany was an expression of the confrontation between liberal capitalism and communism. Germany remained divided until 1989; its reunification marked the end of the Cold War. Choices (A), (B), (D), and (E) were not reasons why Germany was divided.

Question 26

Choice (C) is the correct answer. This is a quotation describing a central idea from *The Communist Manifesto*. The quotation is not from any of the works listed in choices (A), (B), (D), or (E).

Question 27

Choice (C) is the correct answer. Under the post-First World War leadership of Mustafa Kemal Atatürk, Turkey (the ethnically Turkish core region of the defunct Ottoman Empire) undertook a radical modernization program, following a Western model, which included secularization of the state and the adoption of the Roman alphabet. Egypt (A), Syria (B), and Iraq (E) were new countries that also emerged from the breakup of the Ottoman Empire, but all of them were under European dominance in the post-First World War period and did not undertake modernization programs of the same scope as Turkey's. Iran (D) was not a state that emerged from the breakup of the Ottoman Empire, and it did not undertake a major modernization program at this time.

Question 28

Choice (C) is the correct answer. The passage describes the course of the Persian Empire's Great Royal Road, which was constructed in the sixth century B.C.E. When completed, it stretched from the center of the Persian Empire across hundreds of miles of modern-day Iran, Iraq, Syria, and Turkey, terminating at Sardis, near the Aegean coast. The Great Royal Road was not located in Egypt (A), Macedonia (B), Sumeria (D), or Judea (E).

Question 29

Choice (E) is the correct answer. It was in order to control the Suez Canal and to keep it open for vital commerce between Europe and Asia that Great Britain established a protectorate over Egypt in 1882. Great Britain maintained this informal rule until after the Second World War. Choice (A) is incorrect; Egypt was already supplying much of the cotton for the British textile industry before Great Britain took control. Choice (B) is incorrect; Germany was not seriously seeking holdings in North Africa. Choice (C) is incorrect; no significant oil reserves had been discovered in Egypt by 1882. Choice (D) is incorrect; gaining access to antiquities was not sufficient motivation for Great Britain to take control of Egypt.

Question 30

Choice (A) is the correct answer. A large Kurdish population dwells in northern Iraq. There are also significant Kurdish populations in Iran, Turkey, and Syria, but there are no significant Kurdish minorities in Egypt (B), Lebanon (C), Saudi Arabia (D), or Kuwait (E).

Question 31

Choice (C) is the correct answer. For hundreds of years, Vietnamese culture and politics were heavily influenced by China and Chinese models. Korea (A), Japan (B), Indonesia (D), and Mongolia (E) did not serve as cultural or political models for Vietnam.

Question 32

Choice (C) is the correct answer. Judaism emerged in the second millennium B.C.E. Confucius wrote his texts in the sixth and fifth centuries B.C.E. Christianity appeared in the first century C.E. Islam appeared in the seventh century C.E. The four religions are in the proper chronological sequence in choice (C); the other four choices are incorrect.

Question 33

Choice (D) is the correct answer. The Sandinista Front for National Liberation played a key role in the overthrow of the Nicaraguan dictator, Anastasio Somoza, in 1979. The Front then ruled Nicaragua until its electoral defeat by an anti-Sandinista coalition in 1990. The Sandinista Front is not associated with Guatemala during the 1950s (A), Cuba during the 1960s (B), Puerto Rico during the 1970s (C), or El Salvador during the 1980s (E).

Question 34

Choice (C) is the correct answer. Prior to the European voyages of exploration, the main route for spices and other luxury goods traveling from India, the East Indies, and China to Europe was through Muslim-held lands in the Middle East, with Muslim merchants acting as middlemen. European merchants and their backers sought to circumvent the Middle East to gain direct access to East and South Asian goods and thereby increase their profits. Choice (A) does not describe a major motive; though some slaves were taken in the course of early African exploration, this was much less important motivation than choice (C), and the slaves were generally not intended for noble households. Choice (B) is incorrect; Europeans came to dominate in the field of naval technology during this period, but there was no conscious effort to show the superiority of European ships over African and Asian vessels. Choice (D) is incorrect; it describes an unplanned gain from the voyages rather than a primary factor in persuading European investors to fund European voyages of exploration. Choice (E) is incorrect; this was not a major aim of the voyages.

Question 35

Choice (E) is the correct answer. In their home markets, medieval Muslim merchants in the Levant (eastern Mediterranean coast) and Africa found a much larger and more lucrative market for Indian spices than for Italian luxury goods. Choice (A) is incorrect; travel to India was not easier or safer than travel to Italy. Choice (B) is incorrect; there was no papal restriction on Muslim traders entering Christian ports, though the pope did try to prevent Christian merchants from selling weapons to the Muslims. Choice (C) is incorrect; Christian crusaders were not able to close the Mediterranean Sea to Muslim vessels. Choice (D) is incorrect; this was not a factor in influencing whether Muslim merchants traveled to India rather than Italy to trade.

Question 36

Choice (E) is the correct answer. During the fifteenth century, the Chinese admiral Zheng He built huge ocean-going vessels and led large treasure fleets to Malaya, Ceylon, India, Burma, the Philippines, the Persian Gulf, the southwest coast of Arabia, and the east coast of Africa with the aim of establishing the prestige of the Ming Empire and getting tribute. No voyages of this magnitude were undertaken during this period by the British (A), the French (B), the Maya (C), or the Japanese (D).

Question 37

Choice (C) is the correct answer. Christianity was universalized and widely spread by Paul of Tarsus, a Jewish convert to Christianity who developed both an organization and a literature for the new Christian church. It was largely through Paul's efforts that Christianity spread beyond its initial community of Jewish converts. Choice (A) is incorrect; Paul did write some of the epistles, or letters, that were later compiled into the Christian New Testament, but he himself did not help put together the New Testament. Choice (B) is incorrect; Peter, not Paul, became the leader of the apostles after Jesus' death. Choice (D) is incorrect; Peter, not Paul, established Rome as the center of the Roman Catholic Church. Choice (E) is incorrect; Paul did not begin the monastic movement.

Question 38

Choice (E) is the correct answer. Brazil imported by far the largest number of slaves of any nation in the Western Hemisphere. Choice (A) is incorrect; Argentina imported very few slaves. Choice (B) is incorrect; Cuba imported African slaves, but fewer than Brazil. Choice (C) is incorrect; Mexico also imported slaves during this period, but fewer than Brazil. Choice (D) is incorrect; Jamaica had a large plantation economy, but it imported fewer slaves than Brazil.

Question 39

Choice (B) is the correct answer. During the 1870s, the British forces in South Africa engaged in a series of wars seeking domination of all the Zulu-controlled areas. They suffered a major defeat by the Zulu warriors at Isandhlwana, though they eventually defeated the Zulus. Armies of Belgium (A), Germany (C), France (D), and Italy (E) were not involved in this encounter.

Question 40

Choice (E) is the correct answer. During this period, Poland's government was dominated by the landed aristocracy. The individual members of the assembly of nobles, which was Poland's legislature, each had an absolute veto over any government action, and they frequently used it to block attempts to strengthen the king and the central government. As a result, the more centralized states of Prussia, Russia, and Austria were eventually able to conquer and divide Poland. Choice (A) is incorrect; Poland had a strong linguistic and cultural identity. Choice (B) is incorrect; Poland covered a vast land area and had a large population. Choice (C) is incorrect; chronic civil war was not a problem in Poland during this period. Choice (D) is incorrect; because of the decentralization of authority, the Polish kings did not have the power to be oppressive.

Question 41

Choice (B) is the correct answer. During the late nineteenth century, Islamic fundamentalism was not prevalent in Persia. Shi'ite (or Shi'a) fundamentalism became important there much later, in the 1960s and 1970s. Choices (A), (C), (D), and (E) all describe factors that contributed to Persia's becoming the object of intense European colonial power rivalries (particularly between Russia and Great Britain) during this period.

Question 42

Choice (B) is the correct answer. The automobile had its major impact in the twentieth century, not the nineteenth century. The other four technologies—railroads (A), the telegraph (C), the power loom (D), and the open-hearth furnace (E)—were technologies that had important effects on the world economy in the nineteenth century.

Question 43

Choice (D) is the correct answer. Suffrage was gained by women in the United States and much of western Europe after the First World War. The French Revolution (A) is too early, as are The Seneca Falls Conference (B), and the American Civil War (C). The Second World War (E) is too late; by this time, women in most countries of western Europe and in the United States had already won the vote.

Question 44

Choice (D) is the correct answer. Many scholars believe that the Aryans, who are believed to have conquered the Harappan civilization of the Indus Valley around 1500 B.C.E., were very conscious of differences between themselves and the Harappans. Because of their strong sense of superiority, the Aryans tried to preserve social distinction between themselves and the Harappans. These efforts eventually evolved into a system of four hereditary castes. Choices (A), (B), and (C) are incorrect; the evolution of the caste system had nothing to do with patriarchal/matriarchal struggles (A), the appearance of Alexander the Great in northern India (B), or popular uprisings in the Indus Valley (C). Choice (E) is incorrect; the basic rules of caste were laid down between 1200 and 600 B.C.E., well over a thousand years before the advent of Islam.

Question 45

Choice (D) is the correct answer. Feudalism was based on a decentralized system of hierarchical responsibilities. The primary linkage in feudal society was between lords and vassals; lords gave land to vassals in return for loyal service. Choice (A) is incorrect; the social structure was strongly hierarchical. Choice (B) is incorrect; peasants did sometimes own small plots of land. Choice (C) is incorrect; lords and vassals were at times related, but were not necessarily so. Choice (E) is incorrect; land ownership was not restricted to men.

Question 46

Choice (C) is the correct answer. In feudal Europe, aristocratic women often assumed much more responsibility and power when their spouses and male relatives were away at war. Choice (A) is incorrect; women were not legally barred from working outside the home. Choice (B) is incorrect; no such changes occurred in thirteenth-century church law. Choice (D) is incorrect; women could be either lords or vassals. Choice (E) is incorrect; there were probably fewer gender divisions regarding work among those of humbler status; for example, women often worked beside men doing heavy farm work.

Question 47

Choice (C) is the correct answer. Even when Japan was isolated from European trade and diplomacy under the Tokugawa Shoguns, one Dutch ship a year was allowed to come to Nagasaki and the Dutch were allowed to maintain a small trading post on an island in Nagasaki Harbor. Spain (A), Portugal (B), France (D), and England (E) had no regular contact with Japan during this period.

Question 48

Choice (A) is the correct answer. The Safavids who ruled Persia during this period were Shi'ite (or Shi'a) Muslims, who had a dispute with the Sunni Muslims concerning who was the proper successor to Muhammad as the leader of Islam. Choice (B) is incorrect; Sunnis stood in opposition to the Shi'ites and accepted the legitimacy of the Umayyad caliphs as the successors to Muhammad. Sikhism (C) and Jainism (E) both originated in South Asia and had few adherents in Persia at this time. Nestorian Christians (D) were found mostly in central Asia and western China; there were few in Persia at this time.

Question 49

Choice (C) is the correct answer. Owen believed that better-paid factory laborers working under humane conditions would be more productive than underpaid, exploited workers. Choice (A) is incorrect; Owen was comparing his mills to other mills in Great Britain, which was the world leader in industrialized textile production in the early nineteenth century. Choice (B) is incorrect; Owen was an advocate of utilizing the newest technology. Choice (D) is incorrect; Owen did not seek to show that manufactured goods equaled handmade goods in quality. Choice (E) is incorrect; Owen advocated more freedom for the workers and shorter working hours.

Question 50

Choice (C) is the correct answer. French scientists accompanying Napoleon's military expedition brought back new information about ancient Egypt, including the Rosetta stone, which researchers used to decipher Egyptian hieroglyphics. Napoleon's expedition did not lead to a revival of the Coptic Church in Egypt (A), plans for building the Suez Canal and the Aswan Dam (B), or the restoration of Mamluk rule (E) (in fact, Napoleon destroyed Mamluk rule in Egypt). Choice (D) is incorrect; extensive European exploration of the African interior was not undertaken until much later and was not a direct consequence of Napoleon's expedition.

Question 51

Choice (D) is the correct answer. Strikes and food riots in Petrograd were the primary cause for the February Revolution in Russia in 1917. Choice (A) is incorrect; the murder (in December 1916) of Rasputin, a self-proclaimed holy man and healer who wielded great influence over the tsar's family, actually removed a major source of discontent in Russia. Choice (C) is incorrect; no Cossack rebellion against the tsar's regime occurred. Choices (B) and (E) are incorrect; both events occurred after the February Revolution.

Question 52

Choice (A) is the correct answer. The mestizos, people of mixed Spanish and Indian ancestry, formed the majority of the Mexican population, and the leaders of the Mexican Revolution needed their support to successfully govern the nation. There was no plan by the revolution's leaders to economically empower the mestizos as a class (B), or to increase the mestizo presence in the military (C). Choice (D) is incorrect; the Roman Catholic Church had been degraded and its property seized by the revolutionary government. Choice (E) is incorrect; there was no desire by the political leaders to acknowledge European economic influence in Mexico.

Question 53

Choice (C) is the correct answer. Lenin asserted that in order for a socialist revolution to succeed, decision making must be concentrated within a small group of "professional revolutionaries." Choice (A) is incorrect; Lenin had no faith in parliamentary elections. Choice (B) is incorrect; this was a Marxist belief, which Lenin in effect set aside when he led a socialist revolution in Russia, a relatively undeveloped state. Choice (D) is incorrect; Lenin did believe, along with Marx, that the dictatorship of the proletariat was necessary to build a communist society; he differed with Marx as to the means by which the proletariat would gain power. Choice (E) is incorrect; Lenin did not believe in sharing power with nonsocialist groups.

Question 54

Choice (A) is the correct answer. Government should be based on the general will of the society. Rousseau felt that each of us places his person and authority under the supreme direction of the general will of society through a "social contract." Governments that ignored the general will were in violation of this social contract. Choice (B) is incorrect; Rousseau grew up under divine-right monarchy and despised it. Choice (C) is incorrect; Rousseau did not discuss the impact of industrialization in *The Social Contract*. Both choices (D) and (E) are incorrect; these ideas were not part of *The Social Contract*.

Question 55

Choice (E) is the correct answer. Andreas Vesalius published his *On the Fabric of the Human Body* in 1543. It was the first major advance on Galen's work in Europe. Choice (A) is incorrect; da Vinci's work, though it includes some studies of anatomy, was not highly influential in this field. Choice (B) is incorrect; Brahe was an astronomer. Choice (C) is incorrect; Newton's main accomplishments were in mathematics and physics. Choice (D) is incorrect; van Leeuwenhoek was the inventor of the microscope, not an important anatomist.

Question 56

Choice (E) is the correct answer. Under the rule of the Mali Empire, the city of Timbuktu became a center of learning and culture, including several colleges of Islamic scholars who taught theology, law, and other subjects. Choice (A) is incorrect; Mali's rulers were devout Muslims. Choice (B) is incorrect; there was no significant attempt by Christians to send missionaries to Mali during this period. Choice (C) is incorrect; although sorghum was an important crop in Mali, it was not exported in large quantities. Choice (D) is incorrect; Mali's rulers did not encourage emigration.

Question 57

Choice (B) is the correct answer. The language spoken by the Aryan tribes that invaded the Indus Valley prior to 1200 B.C.E. was a form of Sanskrit, which became the language used by Hindu priests. Sumerian (A), Etruscan (C), Hittite (D), and Phoenician (E) are ancient languages that are no longer used for religious rites.

Question 58

Choice (E) is the correct answer. United States policymakers believed in the "Domino Theory," fearing that if South Vietnam became communist, other Southeast Asian countries would soon also become communist. Choice (A) is incorrect; although the Soviet Union sent arms, economic aid, and military advisers to North Vietnam, it never committed troops. Choice (B) is incorrect; the Korean War was not seen as a United States defeat. Choice (C) is incorrect; the U.N. Security Council did not urge U.N. members to support the South Vietnamese government. Choice (D) is incorrect; the North Vietnamese population was not significantly larger than the population of South Vietnam.

Question 59

Choice (A) is the correct answer. Spurred initially by increased agricultural productivity, the population and the economy of Europe (particularly western Europe) expanded greatly during this period. Towns grew rapidly, fueled by local and long-distance trade. Romanesque and Gothic art and architecture developed, and many great works of Latin and vernacular literature were written. Choice (B) is incorrect; this is a description of the fourteenth and fifteenth centuries. Choice (C) is incorrect; this is a description of the late-eighteenth and the nineteenth centuries. Choice (D) is incorrect; this is a description of the seventeenth century. Choice (E) is incorrect; in the twelfth and thirteenth centuries, Europe experienced a net outflow of gold and silver; (E) is a description of the sixteenth century.

Question 60

Choice (B) is the correct answer. Beginning in the eighth century, Muslim forces conquered most of Spain and established flourishing urban centers of learning and artistic creativity, including Córdoba and Seville. During this period, Córdoba and Seville were not noted as centers of those things described in choices (A), (C), (D), and (E).

Question 61

Choice (A) is the correct answer. From the ninth to the twelfth century, Kiev was a center for trade and Orthodox Christianity and was the capital of the state known as Kievan Rus or Kievan Russia. The other Russian cities—Novosibirsk (B), Saint Petersburg (C), Moscow (D), and Murmansk (E)—developed later.

Question 62

Choice (D) is the correct answer. In the 1980s, both Venezuela and Mexico were highly dependent on revenue from petroleum exports and suffered because of the sharp decline in oil prices worldwide in the mid-1980s. Choices (A), (B), (C), and (E) are not primary reasons for the decline of these countries' economic growth rates.

Question 63

Choice (D) is the correct answer. From 1539 to 1542, Hernando de Soto led the first European expedition through what is now the southeastern United States. At the time, the region had flourishing Native American cultures with population centers linked by regular trade routes. Choices (A), (B), and (C) are incorrect; the Native Americans acquired the use of horses, sheep, pigs, and iron from the Europeans after de Soto's expedition. Choice (E) is incorrect; it is not an accurate description of Native American religious practices.

Question 64

Choice (D) is the correct answer. Totalitarian governments in Germany and Italy arose in large part because of discontent caused by the economic hardships and social upheavals of the postwar period. Choice (A) is incorrect; both the Nazis and the Fascists gained power through a combination of violence and electoral politics; neither Germany nor Italy was involved in full-scale civil wars. Choice (B) is incorrect; neither country experienced particularly rapid industrialization during this period. Choice (C) is incorrect; both Nazism and Fascism were aggressive nationalist movements. Choice (E) is incorrect; neither the Nazis nor the Fascists took over through exclusively violent means; both had considerable popular support and won large proportions of the popular vote in parliamentary elections.

Question 65

Choice (C) is the correct answer. In contrast to the Enlightenment tradition that stressed man's rational nature, both Nietzsche and Freud stressed the importance of nonrational factors, such as instinctive drives and early childhood conditioning, in determining human behavior, both individually and in groups. Choice (A) is incorrect; it is not a statement that would have had much meaning for either thinker. Choice (B) is incorrect; both would probably have disagreed with the statement. Choice (D) is incorrect; although Freud might have agreed with this, Nietzsche tended to see human relationships as grounded in contingent historical circumstances. Choice (E) is incorrect; although Freud had some hope of improving people's lives through a better understanding of the unconscious influences on their behavior, Nietzsche was not interested in social reform.

Question 66

Choice (C) is the correct answer. With the outbreak of the Bolshevik Revolution in 1917, Lenin split from the international democratic socialist movement and formed a totalitarian communist movement under the leadership of the Supreme Soviet in order to achieve his objective of socialist revolution in Russia. Socialism had a united international organization in both 1848 (A) and 1870 (B); the split had already occurred by 1939 (D) and 1949 (E).

Question 67

Choice (D) is the correct answer. The Philippines was granted independence from the United States in 1946, immediately after the Second World War. Independence for Indonesia (A), Malaysia (B), Myanmar (Burma) (C), and Vietnam (E) came later.

Question 68

Choice (D) is the correct answer. Keynes believed that in times of economic recession, governments could stimulate the economy by deficit spending on goods and services. Choice (A) is incorrect; it expresses a belief almost diametrically opposed to Keynes' ideas. Choice (B) is incorrect; Keynes was not concerned with the process of industrialization. Choice (C) is incorrect; he was not particularly interested in strengthening labor unions. Choice (E), like choice (A), expresses a belief almost diametrically opposed to Keynes' ideas.

Question 69

Choice (C) is the correct answer. The Solidarity Union was formed in Poland in 1980 and ultimately helped bring down the communist government. The other events listed occurred earlier in Polish history. The partitions mentioned in choice (A) happened in the late 1700s. Choice (B) happened in 1807. Choice (D) happened in 1939 and again in 1944. Choice (E) happened in 1794.

Question 70

Choice (D) is the correct answer. The flat terrain of European Russia and Siberia presented few natural barriers to the political expansion of the Russian state. Choice (A) is incorrect; Russia's navigable rivers tend to flow north and south and were not particularly helpful for its eastward growth. Choice (B) is incorrect; there were few significant mountain barriers to Russia's eastward expansion. Choice (C) is incorrect; Russia had few warm-water ports. Choice (E) is incorrect; most of Russia does in fact experience extreme seasonal temperature fluctuations.

Question 71

Choice (A) is the correct answer. In 1917, the British government, seeking Jewish support for the war effort against the Central Powers, issued the Balfour Declaration, which promised British support for a Jewish homeland in Palestine (at the time controlled by the Ottoman Empire, which was at war with Great Britain). The Declaration also stated that non-Jewish communities in Palestine should be protected. Choices (B), (C), (D), and (E) refer to diplomatic documents dealing with other issues.

Question 72

Choice (A) is the correct answer. The *Encyclopédie* (complete English title: *Encyclopedia, or the Classified Dictionary of Sciences, Arts, and Trades*) was probably the greatest effort to systematically present Enlightenment thought and technical knowledge. Denis Diderot (1713–1784) and Jean-Baptiste le Rond d'Alembert (1717–1783) were the editors of the first series of volumes, which began to be published in 1751. Choices (B), (C), (D), and (E) name pairs of distinguished French writers and thinkers, but they were not the editors of the *Encyclopédie*.

Question 73

Choice (A) is the correct answer. In the eighteenth century B.C.E., the Hyksos, possibly a Semitic people, settled in northern Egypt as subjects of the pharaohs. In about 1630 B.C.E., they rebelled and conquered much of Egypt with the aid of swift, horse-drawn chariots. Their rule lasted about 100 years. The Hyksos did not originate or make use of gunpowder and cannons (B), the lateen sail (C), the crossbow (D), or stirrups (E).

Question 74

Choice (B) is the correct answer. Trade unions first developed mainly by workers in response to low pay, unsafe working conditions, and chronic job insecurity during the early period of industrialization. Choice (A) is incorrect; modern unions were quite different from medieval guilds, which tended to be local associations of skilled artisans or merchants. Choice (C) is incorrect; for much of this period, unions were regarded with suspicion and even hostility by most members of both the Catholic and Protestant clergy. Choice (D) is incorrect; socialists were major supporters of unions. Choice (E) is incorrect; unions were designed to improve pay and working conditions. Involvement in politics was a means to that end, not an end in itself.

Question 75

Choice (B) is the correct answer. At the end of the war, the British and the French acquired African territories formally controlled by Germany and administered them under League of Nations mandates. Choice (A) is incorrect; no territories were granted independence. Choice (C) is incorrect; Russia was not represented at the Paris Peace Conference and received no African territories. Choice (D) is incorrect; the United States was not a member of the League of Nations and was not involved in the mandate system. Choice (E) is incorrect; China and Japan did not begin to supply manufactured goods to Africa until after the Second World War, when these areas gained political independence.

Question 76

Choice (B) is the correct answer. The purpose of this cartoon was to condemn intellectual women as unfit wives and mothers by showing a chaotic home in which the intellectual wife (seated at the desk to the left) neglects what was regarded by many people at the time as her "proper" duties of child care and household management. Choices (A), (C), (D), and (E) are not plausible readings of this late-nineteenth-century cartoon.

Question 77

Choice (E) is the correct answer. Many of the colonization efforts in the interior of Africa began as private ventures by European businessmen, explorers, or missionaries who were later recognized and supported by home governments. Choice (A) is incorrect; European explorers and administrators frequently ignored existing political and ethnic divisions in Africa. Choice (B) is incorrect; all of the Bantu kingdoms were conquered by Europeans. Choice (C) is incorrect; Germany was a latecomer in the race for African territory and Austria made no efforts to acquire African territory. Choice (D) is incorrect; generally the process of European colonization was highly destructive of indigenous African social, economic, and religious organizations.

Question 78

Choice (E) is the correct answer. Women in the medieval Roman Catholic Church were barred from administering sacraments. This continues to be true today. Choices (A), (B), (C), and (D) were all options open to women in medieval Europe.

Question 79

Choice (B) is the correct answer. This is a direct and well-known quote from Mohandas Gandhi, the most important leader in the Indian independence movement. Gandhi and his followers practiced a form of nonviolent resistance to British rule in India that proved highly effective. None of the other groups listed in choices (A), (C), (D), or (E) were exclusively devoted to nonviolence in the furtherance of their cause.

Question 80

Choice (C) is the correct answer. Chandragupta Maurya (ruled circa 321–297 B.C.E.), starting from the kingdom of Magadha in the Indus valley, conquered much of northern India and established India's first great empire, the Mauryan Empire. Kanishka (A), Samudragupta (B), Ashoka (D), and Akbar (E) are important Indian rulers but not founders of the first Indian empire.

Question 81

Choice (D) is the correct answer. It is the only statement that is true of both men. Peter the Great (ruled 1689–1725) worked with missionary zeal to introduce into Russia many new ideas and technologies from the more technologically advanced countries of western Europe. Communist leader Joseph Stalin (ruled 1924–1953) also pressed for the introduction of new technology and industrial processes into what was then the Soviet Union. Choice (A) is incorrect; Peter the Great was not a proponent of economic equality. Stalin paid lip service to this ideal but, in practice, considerable economic disparities existed within the Soviet state. Choice (B) is incorrect; Peter the Great sponsored Russian expansion in Siberia, but the region had been long incorporated into Russia when Stalin came to power. Choice (C) is incorrect; Peter the Great welcomed contact with other countries, and Stalin was isolationist only during part of his rule. Choice (E) is incorrect; neither Peter the Great nor Stalin had much interest in the preservation of traditional village life; both were more interested in economic development. Stalin, in particular, undertook a brutal campaign to eliminate the class of wealthy peasants (kulaks) who dominated most Russian villages.

Question 82

Choice (D) is the correct answer. Many of the newly politically independent African and Asian states continued to depend on their former colonizers as their main source of capital, high-tech goods, and markets for their exports of raw materials. Resentment over this continuation of essentially the same economic relationships that existed under colonization led to the creation of the term "neocolonialism." Choice (A) is incorrect; although European powers did intervene militarily in many African nations that had been granted independence, this was not generally described as "neocolonialism." Choice (B) is incorrect; when this occurred it too was not described as "neocolonialism." Choice (C) is incorrect; although this was happening in the 1960s, it was generally seen as the antidote to "neocolonialism" rather than an expression of it. Choice (E) is incorrect; the central Asian republics were not openly expressing neocolonial feelings toward the Russians in the 1960s.

Question 83

Choice (D) is the correct answer. Romanticism was an artistic and intellectual movement that emerged in Europe in the late-eighteenth and early-nineteenth centuries in reaction to the rationalism of the Enlightenment. Romanticism as an artistic approach stressed the importance of intuition, imagination, and irrationalism, an exaltation of the exceptional and creative; and a fascination with the mysterious and inaccessible. This passage is highly typical of a European Romantic's approach to an ancient Indian text. The thoughts expressed in the passage are not representative of materialism (A), deism (B), positivism (C), or utilitarianism (E).

Question 84

Choice (A) is the correct answer. The war to retain French control of Algeria against an Arab independence movement caused deep divisions in French society. Over a million Europeans lived in the French colony of Algeria and, by 1956, 400,000 French troops were fighting there. The war and its brutalities caused deep divisions in French society and, in 1958, Charles de Gaulle was called out of retirement to lead the country during this crisis. He granted Algeria independence in 1962. Choices (B), (C), (D), and (E) are not reasons why de Gaulle took power in 1958.

Question 85

Choice (E) is the correct answer. Nineteenth-century leaders in Morocco, Tunisia, Egypt, Persia, and the Ottoman Empire responded to the threat of European colonial takeovers by undertaking extensive reforms of their bureaucracies and armies following European models. Choice (A) is incorrect; there was no land reform favoring small farmers during this period. Choice (B) is incorrect; Islamic doctrines and law remained unchanged. Choice (C) is incorrect; there was no attempt to revive the caliphate in this area. Choice (D) is incorrect; these countries did not have the option of imitating Japan by expelling foreigners and ending contact with the West.

Question 86

Choice (E) is the correct answer. Both documents mentioned (the Magna Carta and the Declaration of Rights) in the quote are British and the statement reflects the philosophy expounded by Edmund Burke, a politically conservative British statesman. Choice (A) is incorrect; a French radical at the Bastille would not have cited the Magna Carta. Choice (B) is incorrect; an American revolutionary urging the people to support the Constitution would have been more likely to refer to natural rights rather than to rights based in the historic "inheritance" of English or British documents. Choice (C) is incorrect; the author of the passage has a high respect for law and legal limits. Choice (D) is incorrect; some Indian leaders did cite foundational English or British documents to make the case that Indians were entitled to more equitable treatment as citizens of the British Empire, but Indian leaders arguing for independence from Great Britain would have been more likely to use arguments based on national self-determination and natural rights.

Question 87

Choice (E) is the correct answer. The term *caudillo* refers to a military strongman, many of whom ruled Latin American nations after they gained their independence. *Caudillismo* is the general term for this type of rule. Choices (A), (B), (C), and (D) are incorrect.

Question 88

Choice (D) is the correct answer. Chile and other countries that depended heavily on the export of raw materials to industrial markets overseas were devastated by the Great Depression that swept the world beginning in 1929. Choices (A), (B), (C), and (E) are incorrect because they do not describe the actual cause of the economic problems mentioned.

Question 89

Choice (E) is the correct answer. French Utopian socialism was a reaction to the extremes of wealth and poverty created by private property and the Industrial Revolution and to the widespread misery of millions of industrial workers. Utopian socialists believed that the evils of industrialization could be eased by setting up communities in which all the workers communally owned their factories and other major property. Choice (A) is incorrect; Utopian socialists sought to create their new egalitarian society by peaceful means, not revolution. Choice (B) is incorrect; Utopian socialists did not generally share this belief, which is more typical of Marxist communists. Choice (C) is incorrect; Utopian socialists felt that capitalists were the source of many of the problems of industrialization, not the solution. Choice (D) is incorrect; Utopian socialists believed the state and the communes should take responsibility for economic planning; they did not favor a laissez-faire approach to the economy.

Question 90

Choice (A) is the correct answer. Junior army officers, many of whom had been either trained in western Europe or had been trained by officers who were familiar with nationalist European writers, led nationalist movements in Egypt and the Ottoman Empire. In the Ottoman Empire, one such group was the Young Turks, who tried to modernize the Ottoman military and stressed Turkish nationalism. In Egypt, the most important such leader was Ahmad Urabi, a junior officer who led a nationalist revolt against the Turkish elite that ruled Egypt at the time. Writers (B), religious leaders (C), women's rights activists (D), and industrialists (E) were aware of European nationalism, but none of them took the leadership positions assumed by the junior army officers in these countries.

Question 91

Choice (C) is the correct answer. The Sino-Japanese War (1894–95) developed out of rivalry for control of Korea. In 1875, Japan forced Korea to assert independence from China, its longtime overlord, and to open itself to foreign trade. Subsequently, Japan and China came to blows over who had the right to intervene in a Korean civil war in 1894. Similarly, the Russo-Japanese War (1904–05) was partly caused by disputes over spheres of influence in Korea. As part of the 1905 peace settlement of the Russo-Japanese War, Russia was forced to recognize Japanese interests in Korea and this paved the way for Japan's annexation of Korea in 1910. Choice (A) is incorrect; both wars stimulated the Japanese economic expansion. Choice (B) is incorrect; there were no indemnities for Japan. Choice (D) is incorrect; Japanese public opinion favored both wars. Choice (E) is incorrect; only the Russo-Japanese War was resolved by United States President Theodore Roosevelt.

Question 92

Choice (C) is the correct answer. Constantinople did not fall to Islamic Ottoman forces until 1453. Islamic armies in the seventh and eighth centuries conquered Spain (A), Persia (B), Jerusalem (D), and Damascus (E).

Question 93

Choice (E) is the correct answer. In 1947, the Muslim League, fearful that Muslims would suffer as a minority in the newly independent India, demanded partition and the creation of a separate Muslim state. Choice (A) is incorrect; the divisions were not primarily ethnic or linguistic. Choice (B) is incorrect; the borders drawn did not reflect ancient boundaries. Choice (C) is incorrect; Muslims had not generally been dispossessed under British rule. Choice (D) is incorrect; there were no rajahs who sought autonomy in Pakistan.

Question 94

Choice (B) is the correct answer. In the Middle Ages (and today as well), northern Europe's climate was colder and wetter than the climate of the Mediterranean region. This climatic difference meant that different crops and different agricultural techniques were found in each region. Choice (A) is incorrect; northern Europe was not more mountainous than the Mediterranean region. Choice (C) is incorrect; northern Europe's climate was not dryer, it was wetter. Choice (D) is incorrect; northern Europe did not produce more grapes and wine; it was the Mediterranean region that produced most of the wine. Choice (E) is incorrect; northern Europe did have both hunting and agricultural economies.

Question 95

Choice (B) is the correct answer. Nigeria is the largest oil-producing nation in sub-Saharan Africa and a member of the Organization of Petroleum Exporting Countries (OPEC). Nigeria supplies a significant proportion of world oil production. Liberia (A), Mali (C), Ivory Coast (D), and Senegal (E) are not members of OPEC and are not significant oil producers.

CollegeBoard

SAT Subject Tests™

COMPLETE MARK ●   **EXAMPLES OF INCOMPLETE MARKS** Ⓐ ⊗ ⊖ Ⓛ / ✓ ◉

You must use a No. 2 pencil and marks must be complete. Do not use a mechanical pencil. It is very important that you fill in the entire circle darkly and completely. If you change your response, erase as completely as possible. Incomplete marks or erasures may affect your score.

1 | **Your Name:**
(Print)

Last _____ First _____ M.I. _____

I agree to the conditions on the front and back of the SAT Subject Tests™ book. I also agree with the SAT Test Security and Fairness policies and understand that any violation of these policies will result in score cancellation and may result in reporting of certain violations to law enforcement.

Signature: _____   Today's Date: ___ / ___ / ___
MM DD YY

Home Address: _____
(Print) Number and Street   City   State/Country Zip Code

Phone: (___) _____   **Test Center:** _____
(Print)   City   State/Country

---

2 | **YOUR NAME**

Last Name (First 6 Letters) First Name (First 4 Letters) Mid. Init.

3 | **DATE OF BIRTH**

MONTH | DAY | YEAR

○ Jan
○ Feb
○ Mar
○ Apr
○ May
○ Jun
○ Jul
○ Aug
○ Sep
○ Oct
○ Nov
○ Dec

4 | **REGISTRATION NUMBER**
(Copy from Admission Ticket.)

Important: Fill in items 8 and 9 exactly as shown on the back of test book.

7 | **TEST BOOK SERIAL NUMBER**
(Copy from front of test book.)

8 | **BOOK CODE**
(Copy and grid as on back of test book.)

9 | **BOOK ID**
(Copy from back of test book.)

PLEASE MAKE SURE to fill in these fields completely and correctly. If they are not correct, we won't be able to score your test(s)!

5 | **ZIP CODE**

6 | **TEST CENTER**
(Supplied by Test Center Supervisor.)

FOR OFFICIAL USE ONLY
0 1 2 3 4 5 6
0 1 2 3 4 5 6
0 1 2 3 4 5 6

103648-77191 • NS1114C1085 • Printed in U.S.A.

© 2015 The College Board. College Board, SAT, and the acorn logo are registered trademarks of the College Board. SAT Subject Tests is a trademark owned by the College Board.

194415-001   1 2 3 4 5 A B C D E   Printed in the USA   ISD11312

783175

PLEASE DO NOT WRITE IN THIS AREA

SERIAL #

○ Literature
○ Biology E
○ Biology M
○ Chemistry
○ Physics

○ Mathematics Level 1
○ Mathematics Level 2
○ U.S. History
○ World History
○ French

○ German
○ Italian
○ Latin
○ Modern Hebrew
○ Spanish

○ Chinese Listening
○ French Listening
○ German Listening

○ Japanese Listening
○ Korean Listening
○ Spanish Listening

Background Questions: ① ② ③ ④ ⑤ ⑥ ⑦ ⑧ ⑨

1 Ⓐ Ⓑ Ⓒ Ⓓ Ⓔ   26 Ⓐ Ⓑ Ⓒ Ⓓ Ⓔ   51 Ⓐ Ⓑ Ⓒ Ⓓ Ⓔ   76 Ⓐ Ⓑ Ⓒ Ⓓ Ⓔ
2 Ⓐ Ⓑ Ⓒ Ⓓ Ⓔ   27 Ⓐ Ⓑ Ⓒ Ⓓ Ⓔ   52 Ⓐ Ⓑ Ⓒ Ⓓ Ⓔ   77 Ⓐ Ⓑ Ⓒ Ⓓ Ⓔ
3 Ⓐ Ⓑ Ⓒ Ⓓ Ⓔ   28 Ⓐ Ⓑ Ⓒ Ⓓ Ⓔ   53 Ⓐ Ⓑ Ⓒ Ⓓ Ⓔ   78 Ⓐ Ⓑ Ⓒ Ⓓ Ⓔ
4 Ⓐ Ⓑ Ⓒ Ⓓ Ⓔ   29 Ⓐ Ⓑ Ⓒ Ⓓ Ⓔ   54 Ⓐ Ⓑ Ⓒ Ⓓ Ⓔ   79 Ⓐ Ⓑ Ⓒ Ⓓ Ⓔ
5 Ⓐ Ⓑ Ⓒ Ⓓ Ⓔ   30 Ⓐ Ⓑ Ⓒ Ⓓ Ⓔ   55 Ⓐ Ⓑ Ⓒ Ⓓ Ⓔ   80 Ⓐ Ⓑ Ⓒ Ⓓ Ⓔ
6 Ⓐ Ⓑ Ⓒ Ⓓ Ⓔ   31 Ⓐ Ⓑ Ⓒ Ⓓ Ⓔ   56 Ⓐ Ⓑ Ⓒ Ⓓ Ⓔ   81 Ⓐ Ⓑ Ⓒ Ⓓ Ⓔ
7 Ⓐ Ⓑ Ⓒ Ⓓ Ⓔ   32 Ⓐ Ⓑ Ⓒ Ⓓ Ⓔ   57 Ⓐ Ⓑ Ⓒ Ⓓ Ⓔ   82 Ⓐ Ⓑ Ⓒ Ⓓ Ⓔ
8 Ⓐ Ⓑ Ⓒ Ⓓ Ⓔ   33 Ⓐ Ⓑ Ⓒ Ⓓ Ⓔ   58 Ⓐ Ⓑ Ⓒ Ⓓ Ⓔ   83 Ⓐ Ⓑ Ⓒ Ⓓ Ⓔ
9 Ⓐ Ⓑ Ⓒ Ⓓ Ⓔ   34 Ⓐ Ⓑ Ⓒ Ⓓ Ⓔ   59 Ⓐ Ⓑ Ⓒ Ⓓ Ⓔ   84 Ⓐ Ⓑ Ⓒ Ⓓ Ⓔ
10 Ⓐ Ⓑ Ⓒ Ⓓ Ⓔ   35 Ⓐ Ⓑ Ⓒ Ⓓ Ⓔ   60 Ⓐ Ⓑ Ⓒ Ⓓ Ⓔ   85 Ⓐ Ⓑ Ⓒ Ⓓ Ⓔ
11 Ⓐ Ⓑ Ⓒ Ⓓ Ⓔ   36 Ⓐ Ⓑ Ⓒ Ⓓ Ⓔ   61 Ⓐ Ⓑ Ⓒ Ⓓ Ⓔ   86 Ⓐ Ⓑ Ⓒ Ⓓ Ⓔ
12 Ⓐ Ⓑ Ⓒ Ⓓ Ⓔ   37 Ⓐ Ⓑ Ⓒ Ⓓ Ⓔ   62 Ⓐ Ⓑ Ⓒ Ⓓ Ⓔ   87 Ⓐ Ⓑ Ⓒ Ⓓ Ⓔ
13 Ⓐ Ⓑ Ⓒ Ⓓ Ⓔ   38 Ⓐ Ⓑ Ⓒ Ⓓ Ⓔ   63 Ⓐ Ⓑ Ⓒ Ⓓ Ⓔ   88 Ⓐ Ⓑ Ⓒ Ⓓ Ⓔ
14 Ⓐ Ⓑ Ⓒ Ⓓ Ⓔ   39 Ⓐ Ⓑ Ⓒ Ⓓ Ⓔ   64 Ⓐ Ⓑ Ⓒ Ⓓ Ⓔ   89 Ⓐ Ⓑ Ⓒ Ⓓ Ⓔ
15 Ⓐ Ⓑ Ⓒ Ⓓ Ⓔ   40 Ⓐ Ⓑ Ⓒ Ⓓ Ⓔ   65 Ⓐ Ⓑ Ⓒ Ⓓ Ⓔ   90 Ⓐ Ⓑ Ⓒ Ⓓ Ⓔ
16 Ⓐ Ⓑ Ⓒ Ⓓ Ⓔ   41 Ⓐ Ⓑ Ⓒ Ⓓ Ⓔ   66 Ⓐ Ⓑ Ⓒ Ⓓ Ⓔ   91 Ⓐ Ⓑ Ⓒ Ⓓ Ⓔ
17 Ⓐ Ⓑ Ⓒ Ⓓ Ⓔ   42 Ⓐ Ⓑ Ⓒ Ⓓ Ⓔ   67 Ⓐ Ⓑ Ⓒ Ⓓ Ⓔ   92 Ⓐ Ⓑ Ⓒ Ⓓ Ⓔ
18 Ⓐ Ⓑ Ⓒ Ⓓ Ⓔ   43 Ⓐ Ⓑ Ⓒ Ⓓ Ⓔ   68 Ⓐ Ⓑ Ⓒ Ⓓ Ⓔ   93 Ⓐ Ⓑ Ⓒ Ⓓ Ⓔ
19 Ⓐ Ⓑ Ⓒ Ⓓ Ⓔ   44 Ⓐ Ⓑ Ⓒ Ⓓ Ⓔ   69 Ⓐ Ⓑ Ⓒ Ⓓ Ⓔ   94 Ⓐ Ⓑ Ⓒ Ⓓ Ⓔ
20 Ⓐ Ⓑ Ⓒ Ⓓ Ⓔ   45 Ⓐ Ⓑ Ⓒ Ⓓ Ⓔ   70 Ⓐ Ⓑ Ⓒ Ⓓ Ⓔ   95 Ⓐ Ⓑ Ⓒ Ⓓ Ⓔ
21 Ⓐ Ⓑ Ⓒ Ⓓ Ⓔ   46 Ⓐ Ⓑ Ⓒ Ⓓ Ⓔ   71 Ⓐ Ⓑ Ⓒ Ⓓ Ⓔ   96 Ⓐ Ⓑ Ⓒ Ⓓ Ⓔ
22 Ⓐ Ⓑ Ⓒ Ⓓ Ⓔ   47 Ⓐ Ⓑ Ⓒ Ⓓ Ⓔ   72 Ⓐ Ⓑ Ⓒ Ⓓ Ⓔ   97 Ⓐ Ⓑ Ⓒ Ⓓ Ⓔ
23 Ⓐ Ⓑ Ⓒ Ⓓ Ⓔ   48 Ⓐ Ⓑ Ⓒ Ⓓ Ⓔ   73 Ⓐ Ⓑ Ⓒ Ⓓ Ⓔ   98 Ⓐ Ⓑ Ⓒ Ⓓ Ⓔ
24 Ⓐ Ⓑ Ⓒ Ⓓ Ⓔ   49 Ⓐ Ⓑ Ⓒ Ⓓ Ⓔ   74 Ⓐ Ⓑ Ⓒ Ⓓ Ⓔ   99 Ⓐ Ⓑ Ⓒ Ⓓ Ⓔ
25 Ⓐ Ⓑ Ⓒ Ⓓ Ⓔ   50 Ⓐ Ⓑ Ⓒ Ⓓ Ⓔ   75 Ⓐ Ⓑ Ⓒ Ⓓ Ⓔ   100 Ⓐ Ⓑ Ⓒ Ⓓ Ⓔ

PLEASE MAKE SURE to fill in these fields completely and correctly. If they are not correct, we won't be able to score your test(s)!

7 TEST BOOK SERIAL NUMBER (Copy from front of test book.)

8 BOOK CODE (Copy and grid as on back of test book.)

9 BOOK ID (Copy from back of test book.)

Quality Assurance Mark ●

Chemistry *Fill in circle CE only if II is correct explanation of I.

	I	II	CE*		I	II	CE*
101	Ⓣ Ⓕ	Ⓣ Ⓕ	○	109	Ⓣ Ⓕ	Ⓣ Ⓕ	○
102	Ⓣ Ⓕ	Ⓣ Ⓕ	○	110	Ⓣ Ⓕ	Ⓣ Ⓕ	○
103	Ⓣ Ⓕ	Ⓣ Ⓕ	○	111	Ⓣ Ⓕ	Ⓣ Ⓕ	○
104	Ⓣ Ⓕ	Ⓣ Ⓕ	○	112	Ⓣ Ⓕ	Ⓣ Ⓕ	○
105	Ⓣ Ⓕ	Ⓣ Ⓕ	○	113	Ⓣ Ⓕ	Ⓣ Ⓕ	○
106	Ⓣ Ⓕ	Ⓣ Ⓕ	○	114	Ⓣ Ⓕ	Ⓣ Ⓕ	○
107	Ⓣ Ⓕ	Ⓣ Ⓕ	○	115	Ⓣ Ⓕ	Ⓣ Ⓕ	○
108	Ⓣ Ⓕ	Ⓣ Ⓕ	○				

○ Literature
○ Biology E
○ Biology M
○ Chemistry
○ Physics

○ Mathematics Level 1
○ Mathematics Level 2
○ U.S. History
○ World History
○ French

○ German
○ Italian
○ Latin
○ Modern Hebrew
○ Spanish

○ Chinese Listening
○ French Listening
○ German Listening

○ Japanese Listening
○ Korean Listening
○ Spanish Listening

Background Questions: ① ② ③ ④ ⑤ ⑥ ⑦ ⑧ ⑨

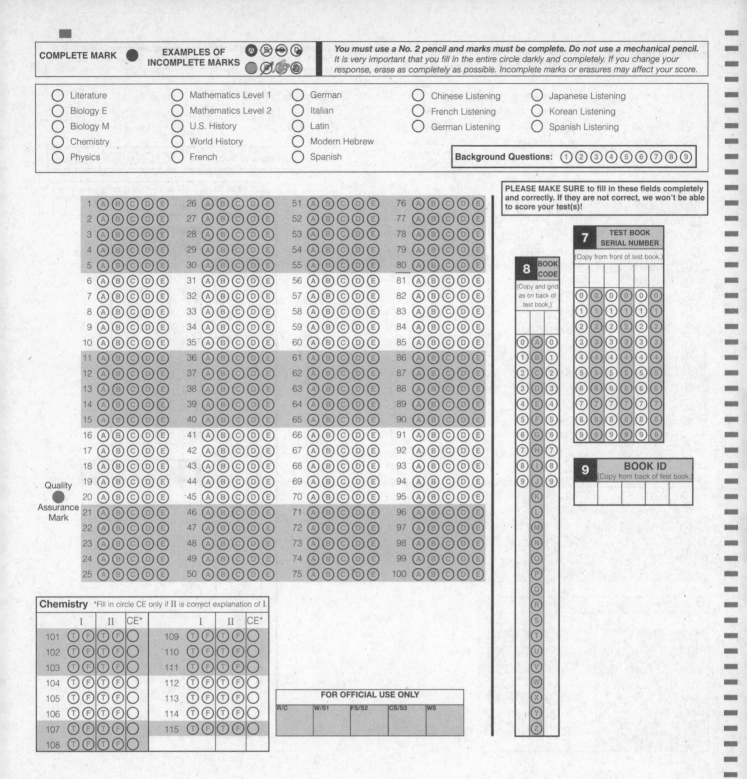

PLEASE MAKE SURE to fill in these fields completely and correctly. If they are not correct, we won't be able to score your test(s)!

7 TEST BOOK SERIAL NUMBER (Copy from front of test book.)

8 BOOK CODE (Copy and grid as on back of test book.)

9 BOOK ID (Copy from back of test book.)

Quality Assurance Mark ●

Chemistry *Fill in circle CE only if II is correct explanation of I.

	I	II	CE*		I	II	CE*
101	T F	T F	○	109	T F	T F	○
102	T F	T F	○	110	T F	T F	○
103	T F	T F	○	111	T F	T F	○
104	T F	T F	○	112	T F	T F	○
105	T F	T F	○	113	T F	T F	○
106	T F	T F	○	114	T F	T F	○
107	T F	T F	○	115	T F	T F	○
108	T F	T F	○				

FOR OFFICIAL USE ONLY				
R/C	W/S1	FS/S2	CS/S3	WS

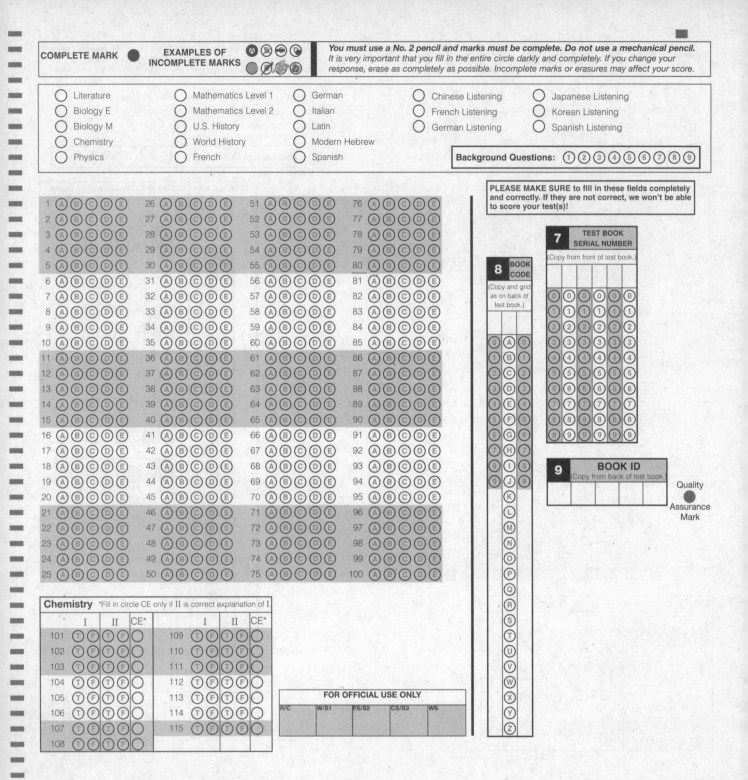

COMPLETE MARK ●   EXAMPLES OF INCOMPLETE MARKS

You must use a No. 2 pencil and marks must be complete. Do not use a mechanical pencil. *It is very important that you fill in the entire circle darkly and completely. If you change your response, erase as completely as possible. Incomplete marks or erasures may affect your score.*

○ Literature
○ Biology E
○ Biology M
○ Chemistry
○ Physics

○ Mathematics Level 1
○ Mathematics Level 2
○ U.S. History
○ World History
○ French

○ German
○ Italian
○ Latin
○ Modern Hebrew
○ Spanish

○ Chinese Listening
○ French Listening
○ German Listening

○ Japanese Listening
○ Korean Listening
○ Spanish Listening

Background Questions: ① ② ③ ④ ⑤ ⑥ ⑦ ⑧ ⑨

PLEASE MAKE SURE to fill in these fields completely and correctly. If they are not correct, we won't be able to score your test(s)!

7 TEST BOOK SERIAL NUMBER
(Copy from front of test book.)

8 BOOK CODE
(Copy and grid as on back of test book.)

9 BOOK ID
(Copy from back of test book.)

Quality Assurance Mark

Chemistry *Fill in circle CE only if II is correct explanation of I.

	I	II	CE*		I	II	CE*
101	T F	T F	○	109	T F	T F	○
102	T F	T F	○	110	T F	T F	○
103	T F	T F	○	111	T F	T F	○
104	T F	T F	○	112	T F	T F	○
105	T F	T F	○	113	T F	T F	○
106	T F	T F	○	114	T F	T F	○
107	T F	T F	○	115	T F	T F	○
108	T F	T F	○				

FOR OFFICIAL USE ONLY				
R/C	W/S1	FS/S2	CS/S3	WS

Page 4

PLEASE DO NOT WRITE IN THIS AREA

SERIAL #

CollegeBoard

SAT Subject Tests™

| COMPLETE MARK ● | EXAMPLES OF INCOMPLETE MARKS Ⓐ ⊗ ⊖ Ⓛ ◑ ⊘ ⊘ ⊛ | **You must use a No. 2 pencil and marks must be complete. Do not use a mechanical pencil.** It is very important that you fill in the entire circle darkly and completely. If you change your response, erase as completely as possible. Incomplete marks or erasures may affect your score. |

1 Your Name:
(Print)

Last _____ First _____ M.I. ____

I agree to the conditions on the front and back of the SAT Subject Tests™ book. I also agree with the SAT Test Security and Fairness policies and understand that any violation of these policies will result in score cancellation and may result in reporting of certain violations to law enforcement.

Signature: _____ Today's Date: ___/___/___
MM   DD   YY

Home Address: _____
(Print)   Number and Street   City   State/Country   Zip Code

Phone: (   )   Test Center: _____
(Print)   City   State/Country

2 YOUR NAME
Last Name (First 6 Letters)   First Name (First 4 Letters)   Mid. Init.

3 DATE OF BIRTH
MONTH   DAY   YEAR
Jan, Feb, Mar, Apr, May, Jun, Jul, Aug, Sep, Oct, Nov, Dec

4 REGISTRATION NUMBER
(Copy from Admission Ticket.)

5 ZIP CODE

6 TEST CENTER
(Supplied by Test Center Supervisor.)

Important: Fill in items 8 and 9 exactly as shown on the back of test book.

7 TEST BOOK SERIAL NUMBER
(Copy from front of test book.)

8 BOOK CODE
(Copy and grid as on back of test book.)

9 BOOK ID
(Copy from back of test book.)

PLEASE MAKE SURE to fill in these fields completely and correctly. If they are not correct, we won't be able to score your test(s)!

FOR OFFICIAL USE ONLY
0 1 2 3 4 5 6
0 1 2 3 4 5 6
0 1 2 3 4 5 6

103648-77191 • NS1114C1085 • Printed in U.S.A.

© 2015 The College Board. College Board, SAT, and the acorn logo are registered trademarks of the College Board. SAT Subject Tests is a trademark owned by the College Board.

194415-001   1 2 3 4 5 A B C D E   Printed in the USA   ISD11312

783175

PLEASE DO NOT WRITE IN THIS AREA

SERIAL #

○ Literature
○ Biology E
○ Biology M
○ Chemistry
○ Physics

○ Mathematics Level 1
○ Mathematics Level 2
○ U.S. History
○ World History
○ French

○ German
○ Italian
○ Latin
○ Modern Hebrew
○ Spanish

○ Chinese Listening
○ French Listening
○ German Listening

○ Japanese Listening
○ Korean Listening
○ Spanish Listening

Background Questions: ① ② ③ ④ ⑤ ⑥ ⑦ ⑧ ⑨

1–100 answer grid (A B C D E for each)

PLEASE MAKE SURE to fill in these fields completely and correctly. If they are not correct, we won't be able to score your test(s)!

7 TEST BOOK SERIAL NUMBER (Copy from front of test book.)
0 1 2 3 4 5 6 7 8 9

8 BOOK CODE (Copy and grid as on back of test book.)
0 A 0
1 B 1
2 C 2
3 D 3
4 E 4
5 F 5
6 G 6
7 H 7
8 I 8
9 J 9
K L M N O P Q R S T U V W X Y Z

9 BOOK ID (Copy from back of test book.)

Quality Assurance Mark ●

Chemistry *Fill in circle CE only if II is correct explanation of I.

	I	II	CE*		I	II	CE*
101	T F	T F	○	109	T F	T F	○
102	T F	T F	○	110	T F	T F	○
103	T F	T F	○	111	T F	T F	○
104	T F	T F	○	112	T F	T F	○
105	T F	T F	○	113	T F	T F	○
106	T F	T F	○	114	T F	T F	○
107	T F	T F	○	115	T F	T F	○
108	T F	T F	○				

FOR OFFICIAL USE ONLY

R/C	W/S1	FS/S2	CS/S3	WS

CERTIFICATION STATEMENT   Copy the statement below and sign your name as you would an official document.

I hereby agree to the conditions set forth online at sat.collegeboard.org and in any paper registration materials given to me and certify that I am the person whose name, address and signature appear on this answer sheet.

_____

_____

_____

_____

Signature _____   Date _____

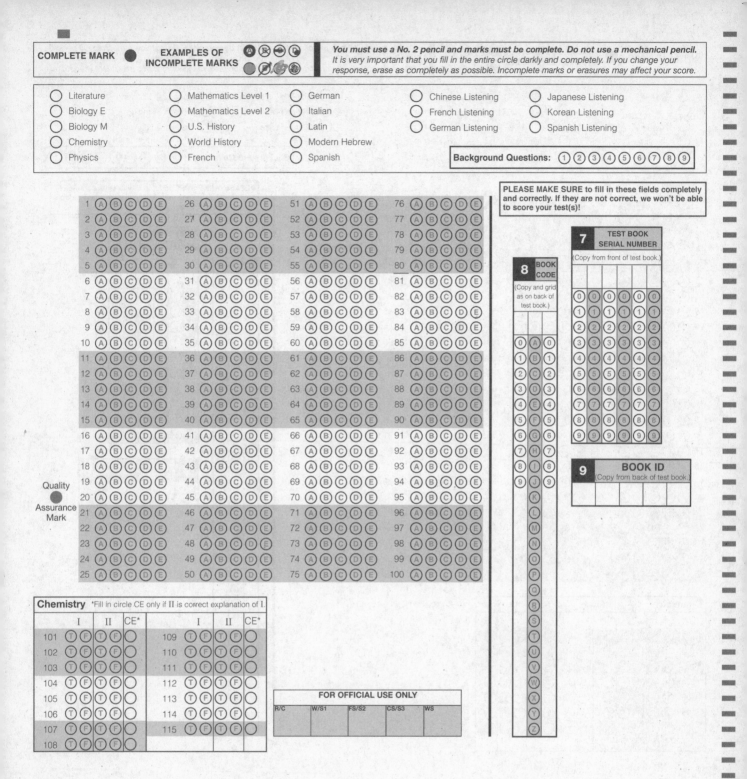

○ Literature ○ Mathematics Level 1 ○ German ○ Chinese Listening ○ Japanese Listening
○ Biology E ○ Mathematics Level 2 ○ Italian ○ French Listening ○ Korean Listening
○ Biology M ○ U.S. History ○ Latin ○ German Listening ○ Spanish Listening
○ Chemistry ○ World History ○ Modern Hebrew
○ Physics ○ French ○ Spanish

Background Questions: ① ② ③ ④ ⑤ ⑥ ⑦ ⑧ ⑨

PLEASE MAKE SURE to fill in these fields completely and correctly. If they are not correct, we won't be able to score your test(s)!

Questions 1–100: each with answer choices A B C D E

7 TEST BOOK SERIAL NUMBER (Copy from front of test book.)

8 BOOK CODE (Copy and grid as on back of test book.)

9 BOOK ID (Copy from back of test book.)

Quality Assurance Mark

Chemistry *Fill in circle CE only if II is correct explanation of I.

	I	II	CE*		I	II	CE*
101	T F	T F	○	109	T F	T F	○
102	T F	T F	○	110	T F	T F	○
103	T F	T F	○	111	T F	T F	○
104	T F	T F	○	112	T F	T F	○
105	T F	T F	○	113	T F	T F	○
106	T F	T F	○	114	T F	T F	○
107	T F	T F	○	115	T F	T F	○
108	T F	T F	○				

FOR OFFICIAL USE ONLY

R/C	W/S1	FS/S2	CS/S3	WS

Page 4

SERIAL #

CollegeBoard

SAT Subject Tests™

You must use a No. 2 pencil and marks must be complete. Do not use a mechanical pencil. It is very important that you fill in the entire circle darkly and completely. If you change your response, erase as completely as possible. Incomplete marks or erasures may affect your score.

1 **Your Name:**
(Print)

Last   First   M.I.

I agree to the conditions on the front and back of the SAT Subject Tests™ book. I also agree with the SAT Test Security and Fairness policies and understand that any violation of these policies will result in score cancellation and may result in reporting of certain violations to law enforcement.

Signature: _____   Today's Date: ___/___/___
                                                                              MM   DD   YY

Home Address: _____
(Print)   Number and Street   City   State/Country   Zip Code

Phone: ( )_____   Test Center: _____
                               (Print)   City   State/Country

2 **YOUR NAME**

Last Name (First 6 Letters)   First Name (First 4 Letters)   Mid. Init.

3 **DATE OF BIRTH**

MONTH	DAY	YEAR
Jan Feb Mar Apr May Jun Jul Aug Sep Oct Nov Dec		

4 **REGISTRATION NUMBER**
(Copy from Admission Ticket.)

5 **ZIP CODE**

6 **TEST CENTER**
(Supplied by Test Center Supervisor.)

Important: Fill in items 8 and 9 exactly as shown on the back of test book.

7 **TEST BOOK SERIAL NUMBER**
(Copy from front of test book.)

8 **BOOK CODE**
(Copy and grid as on back of test book.)

9 **BOOK ID**
(Copy from back of test book.)

PLEASE MAKE SURE to fill in these fields completely and correctly. If they are not correct, we won't be able to score your test(s)!

FOR OFFICIAL USE ONLY

PLEASE DO NOT WRITE IN THIS AREA

SERIAL #

COMPLETE MARK ● EXAMPLES OF INCOMPLETE MARKS

You must use a No. 2 pencil and marks must be complete. Do not use a mechanical pencil. *It is very important that you fill in the entire circle darkly and completely. If you change your response, erase as completely as possible. Incomplete marks or erasures may affect your score.*

○ Literature	○ Mathematics Level 1	○ German	○ Chinese Listening	○ Japanese Listening
○ Biology E	○ Mathematics Level 2	○ Italian	○ French Listening	○ Korean Listening
○ Biology M	○ U.S. History	○ Latin	○ German Listening	○ Spanish Listening
○ Chemistry	○ World History	○ Modern Hebrew		
○ Physics	○ French	○ Spanish		

Background Questions: ① ② ③ ④ ⑤ ⑥ ⑦ ⑧ ⑨

1 Ⓐ Ⓑ Ⓒ Ⓓ Ⓔ	26 Ⓐ Ⓑ Ⓒ Ⓓ Ⓔ	51 Ⓐ Ⓑ Ⓒ Ⓓ Ⓔ	76 Ⓐ Ⓑ Ⓒ Ⓓ Ⓔ
2 Ⓐ Ⓑ Ⓒ Ⓓ Ⓔ	27 Ⓐ Ⓑ Ⓒ Ⓓ Ⓔ	52 Ⓐ Ⓑ Ⓒ Ⓓ Ⓔ	77 Ⓐ Ⓑ Ⓒ Ⓓ Ⓔ
3 Ⓐ Ⓑ Ⓒ Ⓓ Ⓔ	28 Ⓐ Ⓑ Ⓒ Ⓓ Ⓔ	53 Ⓐ Ⓑ Ⓒ Ⓓ Ⓔ	78 Ⓐ Ⓑ Ⓒ Ⓓ Ⓔ
4 Ⓐ Ⓑ Ⓒ Ⓓ Ⓔ	29 Ⓐ Ⓑ Ⓒ Ⓓ Ⓔ	54 Ⓐ Ⓑ Ⓒ Ⓓ Ⓔ	79 Ⓐ Ⓑ Ⓒ Ⓓ Ⓔ
5 Ⓐ Ⓑ Ⓒ Ⓓ Ⓔ	30 Ⓐ Ⓑ Ⓒ Ⓓ Ⓔ	55 Ⓐ Ⓑ Ⓒ Ⓓ Ⓔ	80 Ⓐ Ⓑ Ⓒ Ⓓ Ⓔ
6 Ⓐ Ⓑ Ⓒ Ⓓ Ⓔ	31 Ⓐ Ⓑ Ⓒ Ⓓ Ⓔ	56 Ⓐ Ⓑ Ⓒ Ⓓ Ⓔ	81 Ⓐ Ⓑ Ⓒ Ⓓ Ⓔ
7 Ⓐ Ⓑ Ⓒ Ⓓ Ⓔ	32 Ⓐ Ⓑ Ⓒ Ⓓ Ⓔ	57 Ⓐ Ⓑ Ⓒ Ⓓ Ⓔ	82 Ⓐ Ⓑ Ⓒ Ⓓ Ⓔ
8 Ⓐ Ⓑ Ⓒ Ⓓ Ⓔ	33 Ⓐ Ⓑ Ⓒ Ⓓ Ⓔ	58 Ⓐ Ⓑ Ⓒ Ⓓ Ⓔ	83 Ⓐ Ⓑ Ⓒ Ⓓ Ⓔ
9 Ⓐ Ⓑ Ⓒ Ⓓ Ⓔ	34 Ⓐ Ⓑ Ⓒ Ⓓ Ⓔ	59 Ⓐ Ⓑ Ⓒ Ⓓ Ⓔ	84 Ⓐ Ⓑ Ⓒ Ⓓ Ⓔ
10 Ⓐ Ⓑ Ⓒ Ⓓ Ⓔ	35 Ⓐ Ⓑ Ⓒ Ⓓ Ⓔ	60 Ⓐ Ⓑ Ⓒ Ⓓ Ⓔ	85 Ⓐ Ⓑ Ⓒ Ⓓ Ⓔ
11 Ⓐ Ⓑ Ⓒ Ⓓ Ⓔ	36 Ⓐ Ⓑ Ⓒ Ⓓ Ⓔ	61 Ⓐ Ⓑ Ⓒ Ⓓ Ⓔ	86 Ⓐ Ⓑ Ⓒ Ⓓ Ⓔ
12 Ⓐ Ⓑ Ⓒ Ⓓ Ⓔ	37 Ⓐ Ⓑ Ⓒ Ⓓ Ⓔ	62 Ⓐ Ⓑ Ⓒ Ⓓ Ⓔ	87 Ⓐ Ⓑ Ⓒ Ⓓ Ⓔ
13 Ⓐ Ⓑ Ⓒ Ⓓ Ⓔ	38 Ⓐ Ⓑ Ⓒ Ⓓ Ⓔ	63 Ⓐ Ⓑ Ⓒ Ⓓ Ⓔ	88 Ⓐ Ⓑ Ⓒ Ⓓ Ⓔ
14 Ⓐ Ⓑ Ⓒ Ⓓ Ⓔ	39 Ⓐ Ⓑ Ⓒ Ⓓ Ⓔ	64 Ⓐ Ⓑ Ⓒ Ⓓ Ⓔ	89 Ⓐ Ⓑ Ⓒ Ⓓ Ⓔ
15 Ⓐ Ⓑ Ⓒ Ⓓ Ⓔ	40 Ⓐ Ⓑ Ⓒ Ⓓ Ⓔ	65 Ⓐ Ⓑ Ⓒ Ⓓ Ⓔ	90 Ⓐ Ⓑ Ⓒ Ⓓ Ⓔ
16 Ⓐ Ⓑ Ⓒ Ⓓ Ⓔ	41 Ⓐ Ⓑ Ⓒ Ⓓ Ⓔ	66 Ⓐ Ⓑ Ⓒ Ⓓ Ⓔ	91 Ⓐ Ⓑ Ⓒ Ⓓ Ⓔ
17 Ⓐ Ⓑ Ⓒ Ⓓ Ⓔ	42 Ⓐ Ⓑ Ⓒ Ⓓ Ⓔ	67 Ⓐ Ⓑ Ⓒ Ⓓ Ⓔ	92 Ⓐ Ⓑ Ⓒ Ⓓ Ⓔ
18 Ⓐ Ⓑ Ⓒ Ⓓ Ⓔ	43 Ⓐ Ⓑ Ⓒ Ⓓ Ⓔ	68 Ⓐ Ⓑ Ⓒ Ⓓ Ⓔ	93 Ⓐ Ⓑ Ⓒ Ⓓ Ⓔ
19 Ⓐ Ⓑ Ⓒ Ⓓ Ⓔ	44 Ⓐ Ⓑ Ⓒ Ⓓ Ⓔ	69 Ⓐ Ⓑ Ⓒ Ⓓ Ⓔ	94 Ⓐ Ⓑ Ⓒ Ⓓ Ⓔ
20 Ⓐ Ⓑ Ⓒ Ⓓ Ⓔ	45 Ⓐ Ⓑ Ⓒ Ⓓ Ⓔ	70 Ⓐ Ⓑ Ⓒ Ⓓ Ⓔ	95 Ⓐ Ⓑ Ⓒ Ⓓ Ⓔ
21 Ⓐ Ⓑ Ⓒ Ⓓ Ⓔ	46 Ⓐ Ⓑ Ⓒ Ⓓ Ⓔ	71 Ⓐ Ⓑ Ⓒ Ⓓ Ⓔ	96 Ⓐ Ⓑ Ⓒ Ⓓ Ⓔ
22 Ⓐ Ⓑ Ⓒ Ⓓ Ⓔ	47 Ⓐ Ⓑ Ⓒ Ⓓ Ⓔ	72 Ⓐ Ⓑ Ⓒ Ⓓ Ⓔ	97 Ⓐ Ⓑ Ⓒ Ⓓ Ⓔ
23 Ⓐ Ⓑ Ⓒ Ⓓ Ⓔ	48 Ⓐ Ⓑ Ⓒ Ⓓ Ⓔ	73 Ⓐ Ⓑ Ⓒ Ⓓ Ⓔ	98 Ⓐ Ⓑ Ⓒ Ⓓ Ⓔ
24 Ⓐ Ⓑ Ⓒ Ⓓ Ⓔ	49 Ⓐ Ⓑ Ⓒ Ⓓ Ⓔ	74 Ⓐ Ⓑ Ⓒ Ⓓ Ⓔ	99 Ⓐ Ⓑ Ⓒ Ⓓ Ⓔ
25 Ⓐ Ⓑ Ⓒ Ⓓ Ⓔ	50 Ⓐ Ⓑ Ⓒ Ⓓ Ⓔ	75 Ⓐ Ⓑ Ⓒ Ⓓ Ⓔ	100 Ⓐ Ⓑ Ⓒ Ⓓ Ⓔ

Chemistry *Fill in circle CE only if II is correct explanation of I.

	I	II	CE*		I	II	CE*
101	Ⓣ Ⓕ	Ⓣ Ⓕ	○	109	Ⓣ Ⓕ	Ⓣ Ⓕ	○
102	Ⓣ Ⓕ	Ⓣ Ⓕ	○	110	Ⓣ Ⓕ	Ⓣ Ⓕ	○
103	Ⓣ Ⓕ	Ⓣ Ⓕ	○	111	Ⓣ Ⓕ	Ⓣ Ⓕ	○
104	Ⓣ Ⓕ	Ⓣ Ⓕ	○	112	Ⓣ Ⓕ	Ⓣ Ⓕ	○
105	Ⓣ Ⓕ	Ⓣ Ⓕ	○	113	Ⓣ Ⓕ	Ⓣ Ⓕ	○
106	Ⓣ Ⓕ	Ⓣ Ⓕ	○	114	Ⓣ Ⓕ	Ⓣ Ⓕ	○
107	Ⓣ Ⓕ	Ⓣ Ⓕ	○	115	Ⓣ Ⓕ	Ⓣ Ⓕ	○
108	Ⓣ Ⓕ	Ⓣ Ⓕ	○				

PLEASE MAKE SURE to fill in these fields completely and correctly. If they are not correct, we won't be able to score your test(s)!

7 TEST BOOK SERIAL NUMBER

(Copy from front of test book.)

0	0	0	0	0	0
1	1	1	1	1	1
2	2	2	2	2	2
3	3	3	3	3	3
4	4	4	4	4	4
5	5	5	5	5	5
6	6	6	6	6	6
7	7	7	7	7	7
8	8	8	8	8	8
9	9	9	9	9	9

8 BOOK CODE

(Copy and grid as on back of test book.)

0	A	0
1	B	1
2	C	2
3	D	3
4	E	4
5	F	5
6	G	6
7	H	7
8	I	8
9	J	9
	K	
	L	
	M	
	N	
	O	
	P	
	Q	
	R	
	S	
	T	
	U	
	V	
	W	
	X	
	Y	
	Z	

9 BOOK ID

(Copy from back of test book.)

Quality Assurance Mark

FOR OFFICIAL USE ONLY

R/C	W/S1	FS/S2	CS/S3	WS

CERTIFICATION STATEMENT

Copy the statement below and sign your name as you would an official document.

I hereby agree to the conditions set forth online at sat.collegeboard.org and in any paper registration materials given to me and certify that I am the person whose name, address and signature appear on this answer sheet.

Signature ____________________ Date ____________________

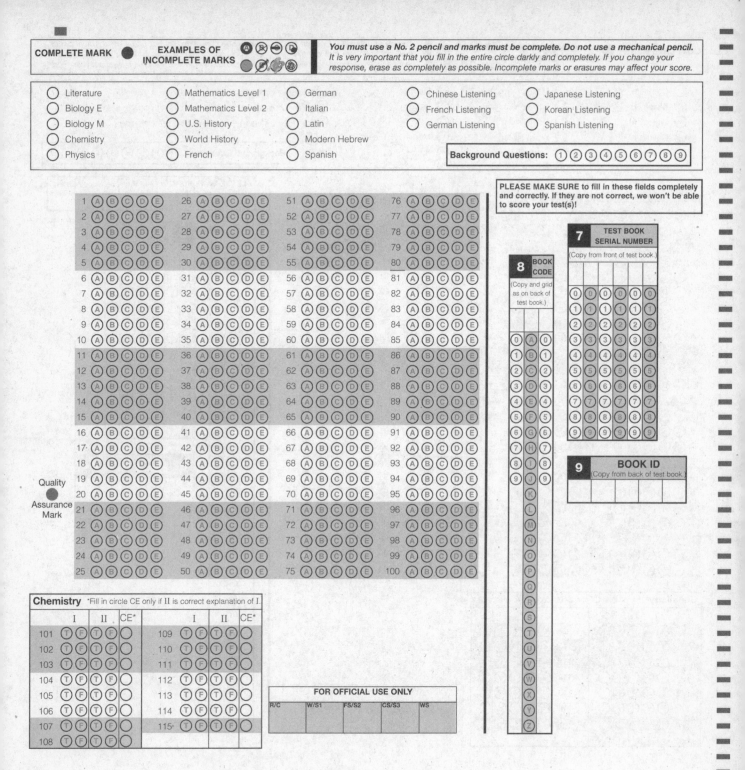

COMPLETE MARK ● EXAMPLES OF INCOMPLETE MARKS

You must use a No. 2 pencil and marks must be complete. Do not use a mechanical pencil. It is very important that you fill in the entire circle darkly and completely. If you change your response, erase as completely as possible. Incomplete marks or erasures may affect your score.

- Literature
- Biology E
- Biology M
- Chemistry
- Physics
- Mathematics Level 1
- Mathematics Level 2
- U.S. History
- World History
- French
- German
- Italian
- Latin
- Modern Hebrew
- Spanish
- Chinese Listening
- French Listening
- German Listening
- Japanese Listening
- Korean Listening
- Spanish Listening

Background Questions: ① ② ③ ④ ⑤ ⑥ ⑦ ⑧ ⑨

PLEASE MAKE SURE to fill in these fields completely and correctly. If they are not correct, we won't be able to score your test(s)!

Quality Assurance Mark

Chemistry *Fill in circle CE only if II is correct explanation of I.

FOR OFFICIAL USE ONLY

R/C	W/S1	FS/S2	CS/S3	WS

7 TEST BOOK SERIAL NUMBER (Copy from front of test book.)

8 BOOK CODE (Copy and grid as on back of test book.)

9 BOOK ID (Copy from back of test book.)

Page 3

COMPLETE MARK ●	EXAMPLES OF INCOMPLETE MARKS	You must use a No. 2 pencil and marks must be complete. Do not use a mechanical pencil. It is very important that you fill in the entire circle darkly and completely. If you change your response, erase as completely as possible. Incomplete marks or erasures may affect your score.

○ Literature
○ Biology E
○ Biology M
○ Chemistry
○ Physics

○ Mathematics Level 1
○ Mathematics Level 2
○ U.S. History
○ World History
○ French

○ German
○ Italian
○ Latin
○ Modern Hebrew
○ Spanish

○ Chinese Listening
○ French Listening
○ German Listening

○ Japanese Listening
○ Korean Listening
○ Spanish Listening

Background Questions: ① ② ③ ④ ⑤ ⑥ ⑦ ⑧ ⑨

PLEASE MAKE SURE to fill in these fields completely and correctly. If they are not correct, we won't be able to score your test(s)!

1–100: A B C D E answer bubbles (columns 1–25, 26–50, 51–75, 76–100)

8 BOOK CODE (Copy and grid as on back of test book.)

7 TEST BOOK SERIAL NUMBER (Copy from front of test book.)

9 BOOK ID (Copy from back of test book.)

Quality Assurance Mark ●

Chemistry *Fill in circle CE only if II is correct explanation of I.

	I	II	CE*		I	II	CE*
101	T F	T F	○	109	T F	T F	○
102	T F	T F	○	110	T F	T F	○
103	T F	T F	○	111	T F	T F	○
104	T F	T F	○	112	T F	T F	○
105	T F	T F	○	113	T F	T F	○
106	T F	T F	○	114	T F	T F	○
107	T F	T F	○	115	T F	T F	○
108	T F	T F	○				

FOR OFFICIAL USE ONLY				
R/C	W/S1	FS/S2	CS/S3	WS

Page 4

PLEASE DO NOT WRITE IN THIS AREA

SERIAL #

1 Your Name:
(Print)

Last   First   M.I.

I agree to the conditions on the front and back of the SAT Subject Tests™ book. I also agree with the SAT Test Security and Fairness policies and understand that any violation of these policies will result in score cancellation and may result in reporting of certain violations to law enforcement.

Signature: _____   Today's Date: ___ / ___ / ___
                                                                                          MM   DD   YY

Home Address: _____
(Print)   Number and Street   City   State/Country   Zip Code

Phone: ( )_____   Test Center: _____
                                          (Print)   City   State/Country

2 YOUR NAME

Last Name (First 6 Letters)   First Name (First 4 Letters)   Mid. Init.

3 DATE OF BIRTH

MONTH   DAY   YEAR

Jan Feb Mar Apr May Jun Jul Aug Sep Oct Nov Dec

4 REGISTRATION NUMBER

(Copy from Admission Ticket.)

Important: Fill in items 8 and 9 exactly as shown on the back of test book.

7 TEST BOOK SERIAL NUMBER

(Copy from front of test book.)

8 BOOK CODE

(Copy and grid as on back of test book.)

9 BOOK ID

(Copy from back of test book.)

PLEASE MAKE SURE to fill in these fields completely and correctly. If they are not correct, we won't be able to score your test(s)!

5 ZIP CODE

6 TEST CENTER

(Supplied by Test Center Supervisor.)

FOR OFFICIAL USE ONLY

0 1 2 3 4 5 6
0 1 2 3 4 5 6
0 1 2 3 4 5 6

103648-77191 • NS1114C1085 • Printed in U.S.A.

194415-001   1 2 3 4 5 A B C D E   Printed in the USA   ISD11312

783175

PLEASE DO NOT WRITE IN THIS AREA

SERIAL #

You must use a No. 2 pencil and marks must be complete. Do not use a mechanical pencil. It is very important that you fill in the entire circle darkly and completely. If you change your response, erase as completely as possible. Incomplete marks or erasures may affect your score.

- ○ Literature
- ○ Biology E
- ○ Biology M
- ○ Chemistry
- ○ Physics
- ○ Mathematics Level 1
- ○ Mathematics Level 2
- ○ U.S. History
- ○ World History
- ○ French
- ○ German
- ○ Italian
- ○ Latin
- ○ Modern Hebrew
- ○ Spanish
- ○ Chinese Listening
- ○ French Listening
- ○ German Listening
- ○ Japanese Listening
- ○ Korean Listening
- ○ Spanish Listening

Background Questions: ① ② ③ ④ ⑤ ⑥ ⑦ ⑧ ⑨

Questions 1–100: each with answer choices A B C D E

PLEASE MAKE SURE to fill in these fields completely and correctly. If they are not correct, we won't be able to score your test(s)!

7 TEST BOOK SERIAL NUMBER (Copy from front of test book.)

8 BOOK CODE (Copy and grid as on back of test book.)

Letters A–Z grid column

9 BOOK ID (Copy from back of test book.)

Quality Assurance Mark ●

Chemistry *Fill in circle CE only if II is correct explanation of I.

	I	II	CE*		I	II	CE*
101	T F	T F	○	109	T F	T F	○
102	T F	T F	○	110	T F	T F	○
103	T F	T F	○	111	T F	T F	○
104	T F	T F	○	112	T F	T F	○
105	T F	T F	○	113	T F	T F	○
106	T F	T F	○	114	T F	T F	○
107	T F	T F	○	115	T F	T F	○
108	T F	T F	○				

FOR OFFICIAL USE ONLY				
R/C	W/S1	FS/S2	CS/S3	WS

CERTIFICATION STATEMENT
Copy the statement below and sign your name as you would an official document.

I hereby agree to the conditions set forth online at sat.collegeboard.org and in any paper registration materials given to me and certify that I am the person whose name, address and signature appear on this answer sheet.

Signature _____ Date _____

COMPLETE MARK ● EXAMPLES OF INCOMPLETE MARKS Ⓐ Ⓧ ⊖ Ⓓ / Ⓒ Ⓘ

You must use a No. 2 pencil and marks must be complete. Do not use a mechanical pencil. It is very important that you fill in the entire circle darkly and completely. If you change your response, erase as completely as possible. Incomplete marks or erasures may affect your score.

○ Literature
○ Biology E
○ Biology M
○ Chemistry
○ Physics

○ Mathematics Level 1
○ Mathematics Level 2
○ U.S. History
○ World History
○ French

○ German
○ Italian
○ Latin
○ Modern Hebrew
○ Spanish

○ Chinese Listening
○ French Listening
○ German Listening

○ Japanese Listening
○ Korean Listening
○ Spanish Listening

Background Questions: ① ② ③ ④ ⑤ ⑥ ⑦ ⑧ ⑨

PLEASE MAKE SURE to fill in these fields completely and correctly. If they are not correct, we won't be able to score your test(s)!

Questions 1–100, each with answer choices A B C D E.

Quality Assurance Mark ●

7 TEST BOOK SERIAL NUMBER (Copy from front of test book.)
Digits 0–9

8 BOOK CODE (Copy and grid as on back of test book.)
0 A 0
1 B 1
2 C 2
3 D 3
4 E 4
5 F 5
6 G 6
7 H 7
8 I 8
9 J 9
K L M N O P Q R S T U V W X Y Z

9 BOOK ID (Copy from back of test book.)

Chemistry *Fill in circle CE only if II is correct explanation of I.

	I	II	CE*		I	II	CE*
101	T F	T F	○	109	T F	T F	○
102	T F	T F	○	110	T F	T F	○
103	T F	T F	○	111	T F	T F	○
104	T F	T F	○	112	T F	T F	○
105	T F	T F	○	113	T F	T F	○
106	T F	T F	○	114	T F	T F	○
107	T F	T F	○	115	T F	T F	○
108	T F	T F	○				

FOR OFFICIAL USE ONLY

R/C	W/S1	FS/S2	CS/S3	WS

Page 3

| COMPLETE MARK ● | EXAMPLES OF INCOMPLETE MARKS | You must use a No. 2 pencil and marks must be complete. Do not use a mechanical pencil. It is very important that you fill in the entire circle darkly and completely. If you change your response, erase as completely as possible. Incomplete marks or erasures may affect your score. |

- ○ Literature
- ○ Biology E
- ○ Biology M
- ○ Chemistry
- ○ Physics
- ○ Mathematics Level 1
- ○ Mathematics Level 2
- ○ U.S. History
- ○ World History
- ○ French
- ○ German
- ○ Italian
- ○ Latin
- ○ Modern Hebrew
- ○ Spanish
- ○ Chinese Listening
- ○ French Listening
- ○ German Listening
- ○ Japanese Listening
- ○ Korean Listening
- ○ Spanish Listening

Background Questions: ① ② ③ ④ ⑤ ⑥ ⑦ ⑧ ⑨

Questions 1–100: (A) (B) (C) (D) (E)

PLEASE MAKE SURE to fill in these fields completely and correctly. If they are not correct, we won't be able to score your test(s)!

8 BOOK CODE (Copy and grid as on back of test book.)

7 TEST BOOK SERIAL NUMBER (Copy from front of test book.)

9 BOOK ID (Copy from back of test book.)

Quality Assurance Mark

Chemistry *Fill in circle CE only if II is correct explanation of I.

	I	II	CE*		I	II	CE*
101	T F	T F	○	109	T F	T F	○
102	T F	T F	○	110	T F	T F	○
103	T F	T F	○	111	T F	T F	○
104	T F	T F	○	112	T F	T F	○
105	T F	T F	○	113	T F	T F	○
106	T F	T F	○	114	T F	T F	○
107	T F	T F	○	115	T F	T F	○
108	T F	T F	○				

FOR OFFICIAL USE ONLY				
R/C	W/S1	FS/S2	CS/S3	WS

Page 4